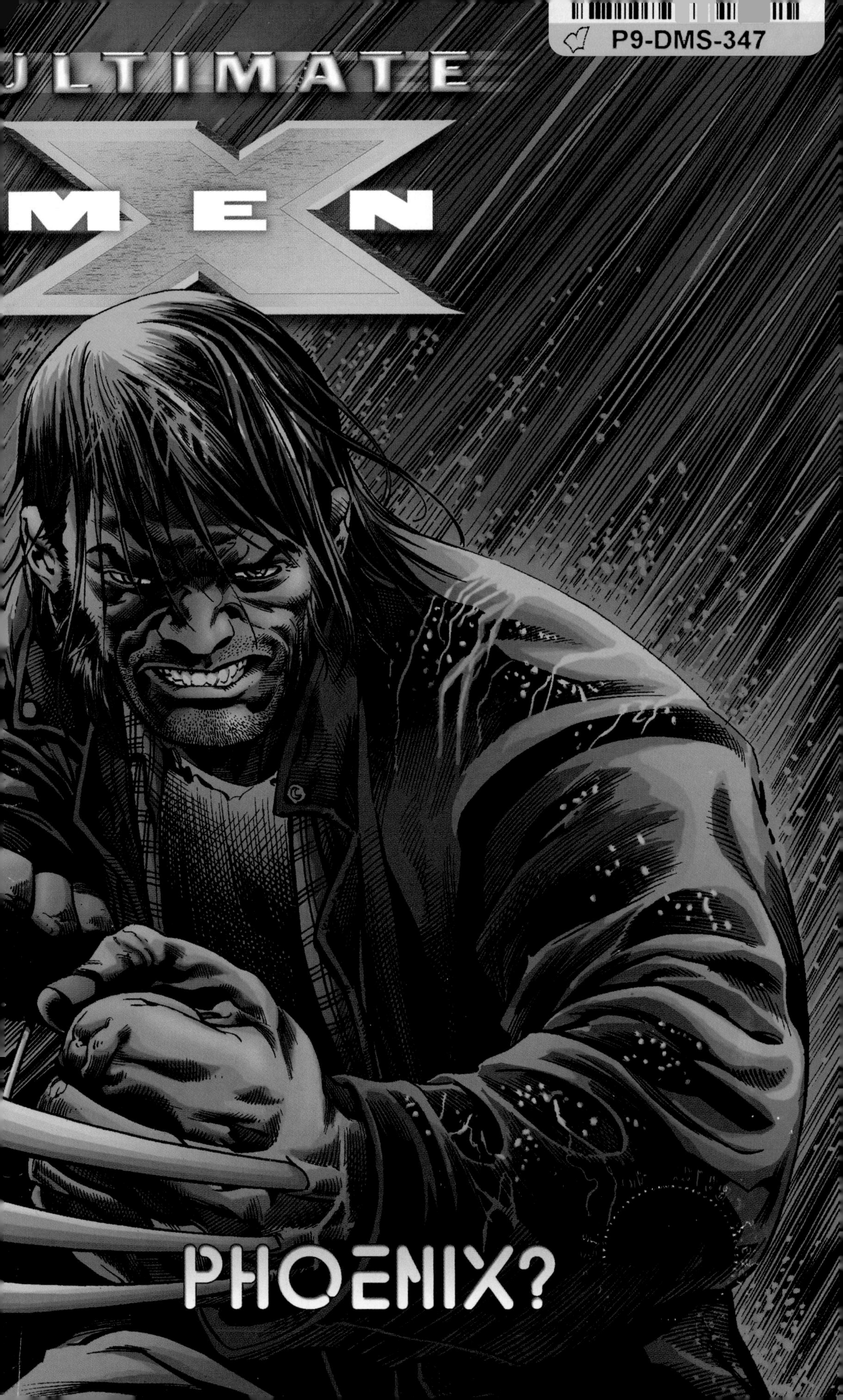
ULTIMATE
X-MEN
PHOENIX?

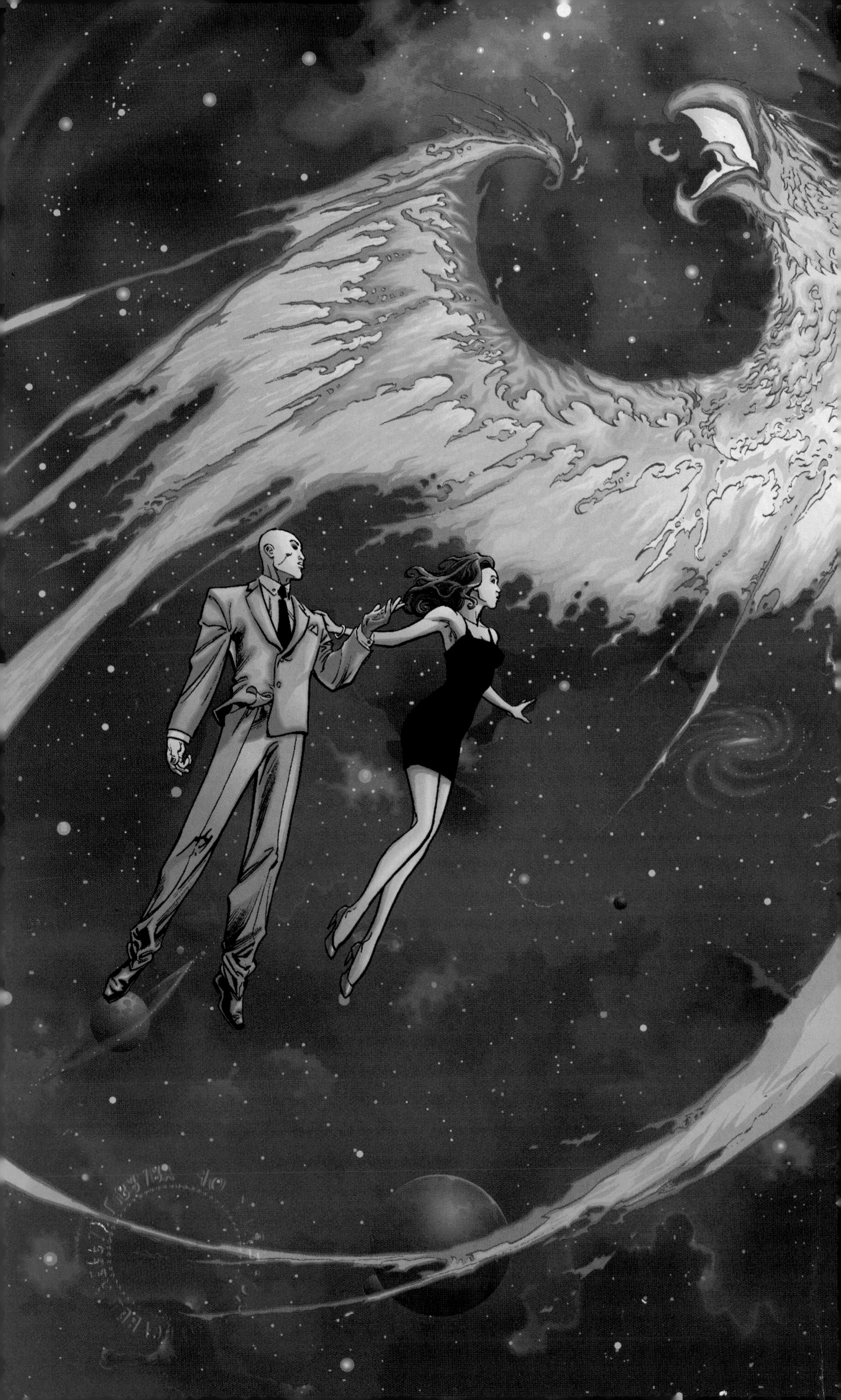

PHOENIX?

Writer
Robert Kirkman
Pencilers
Tom Raney & Ben Oliver

Inkers
Scott Hanna & Jonathan Glapion
with **Jay Leisten**
Colors
Gina Going-Raney & Jason Keith
Letters
**VC's Chris Eliopoulos,
Randy Gentile, Rus Wooton &
Joe Caramagna**

Assistant Editor
Nicole Boose
Associate Editor
John Barber
Editor
Ralph Macchio

Collection Editor
Jennifer Grünwald
Assistant Editor
Michael Short
Associate Editor
Mark D. Beazley
Senior Editor, Special Projects
Jeff Youngquist
Vice President of Sales
David Gabriel
Production
Jerron Quality Color
Vice President of Creative
Tom Marvelli

Editor in Chief
Joe Quesada
Publisher
Dan Buckley

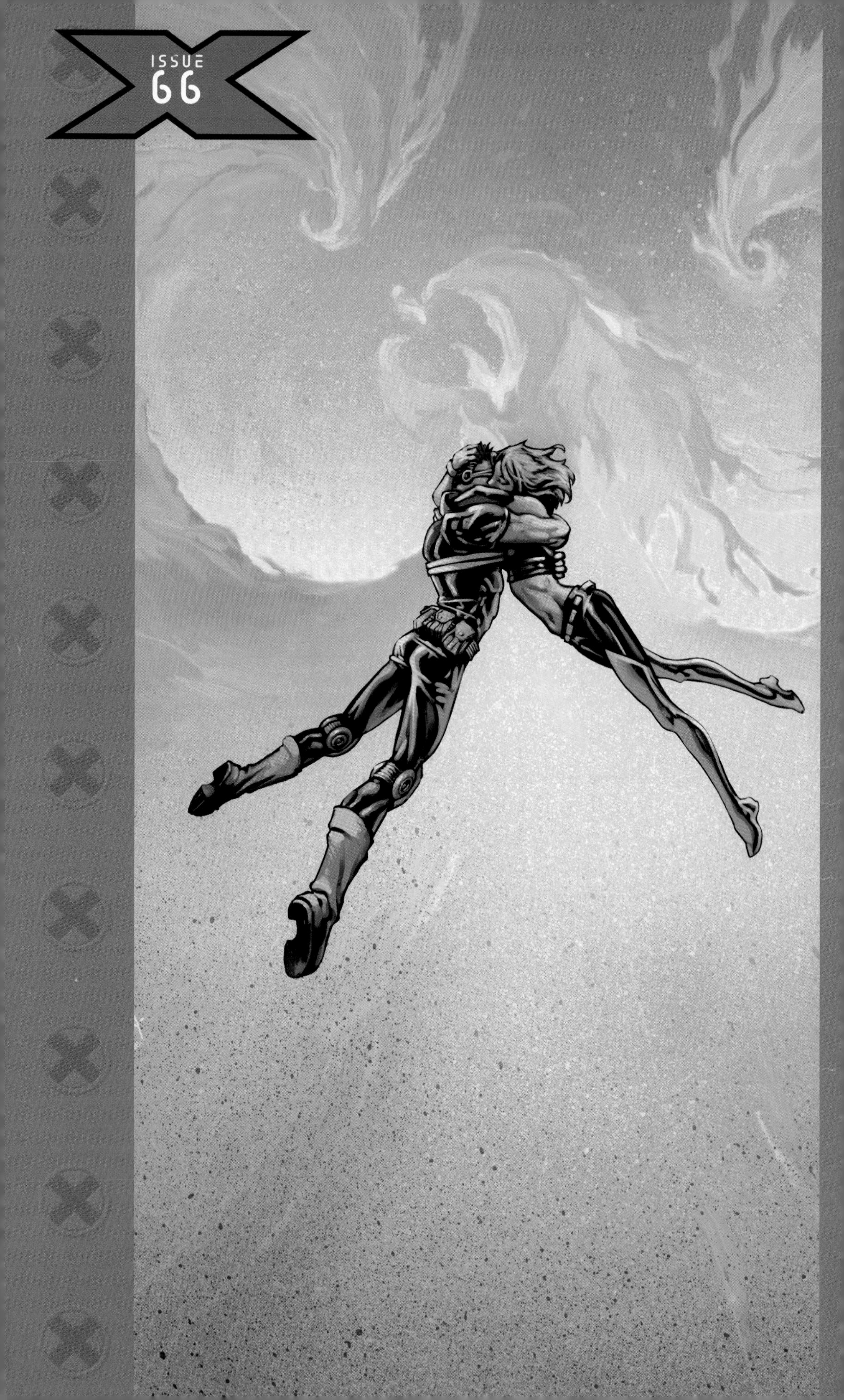
ISSUE
66

REVIOUSLY IN ULTIMATE X-MEN:

n with strange and amazing abilities, the X-Men are young mutant heroes, sworn to protect a world that rs and hates them. Recently they've been through a lot—ever since the death of their team member Beast they've fought a long succession of foes, with little time for anything else.

Now they're taking the night off.

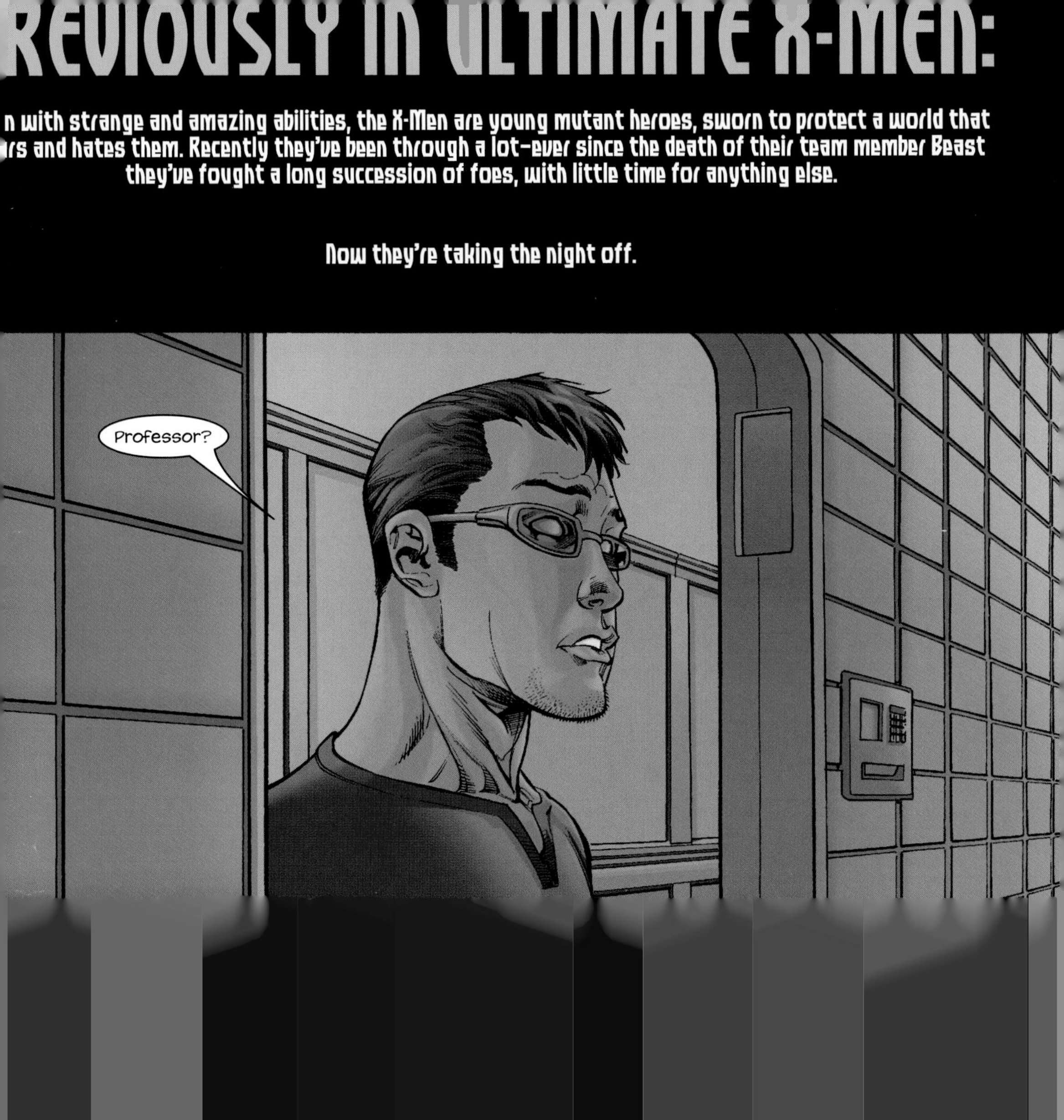
Professor?

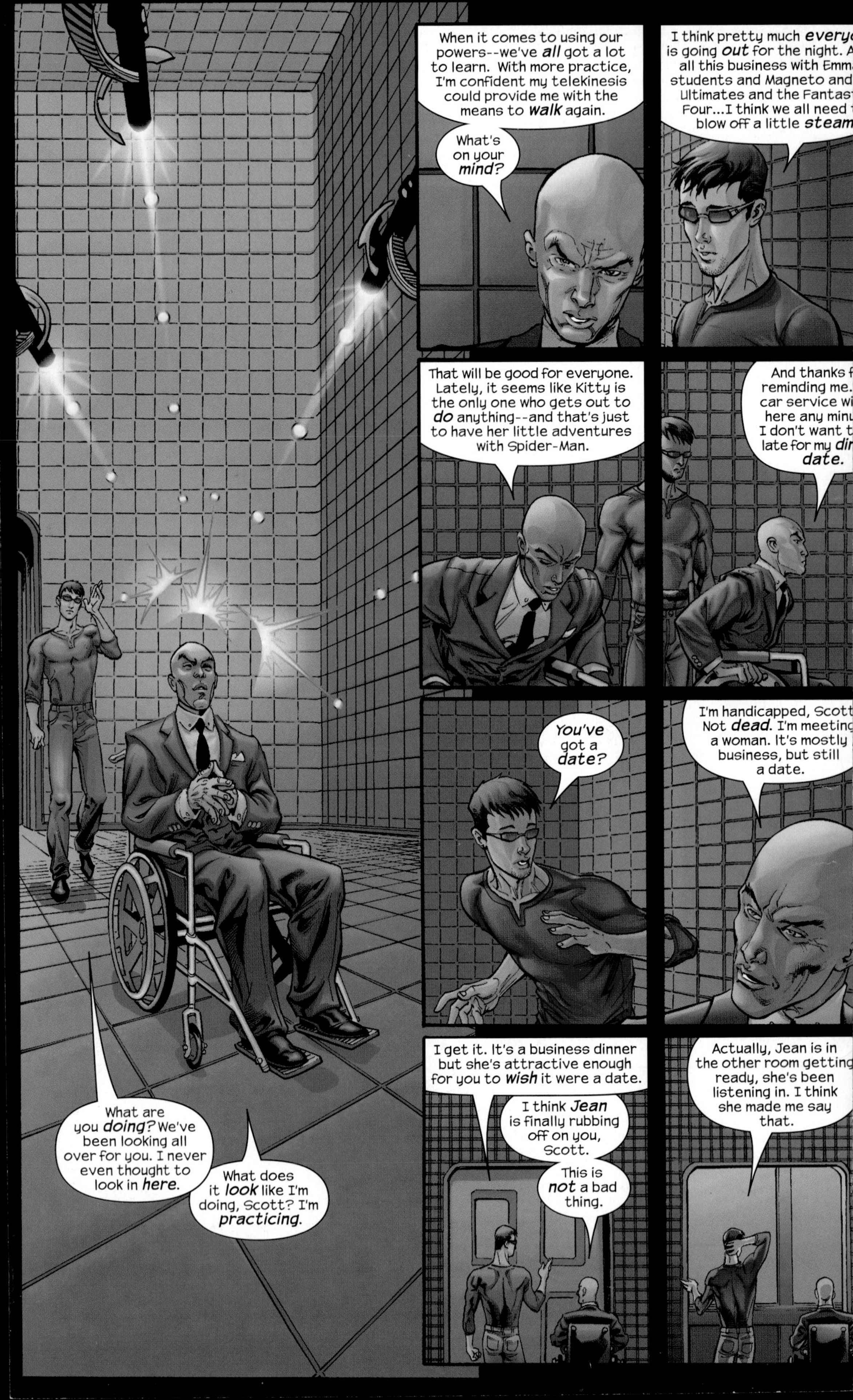

What are you doing? We've been looking all over for you. I never even thought to look in here.
What does it look like I'm doing, Scott? I'm practicing.
When it comes to using our powers--we've all got a lot to learn. With more practice, I'm confident my telekinesis could provide me with the means to walk again.
What's on your mind?
I think pretty much everyo
is going out for the night. A
all this business with Emma
students and Magneto and
Ultimates and the Fantas
Four...I think we all need t
blow off a little steam
That will be good for everyone. Lately, it seems like Kitty is the only one who gets out to do anything--and that's just to have her little adventures with Spider-Man.
And thanks f
reminding me.
car service wi
here any minu
I don't want t
late for my di
date.
You've got a date?
I'm handicapped, Scott
Not dead. I'm meeting
a woman. It's mostly
business, but still
a date.
I get it. It's a business dinner but she's attractive enough for you to wish it were a date.
I think Jean is finally rubbing off on you, Scott.
This is not a bad thing.
Actually, Jean is in the other room getting ready, she's been listening in. I think she made me say that.

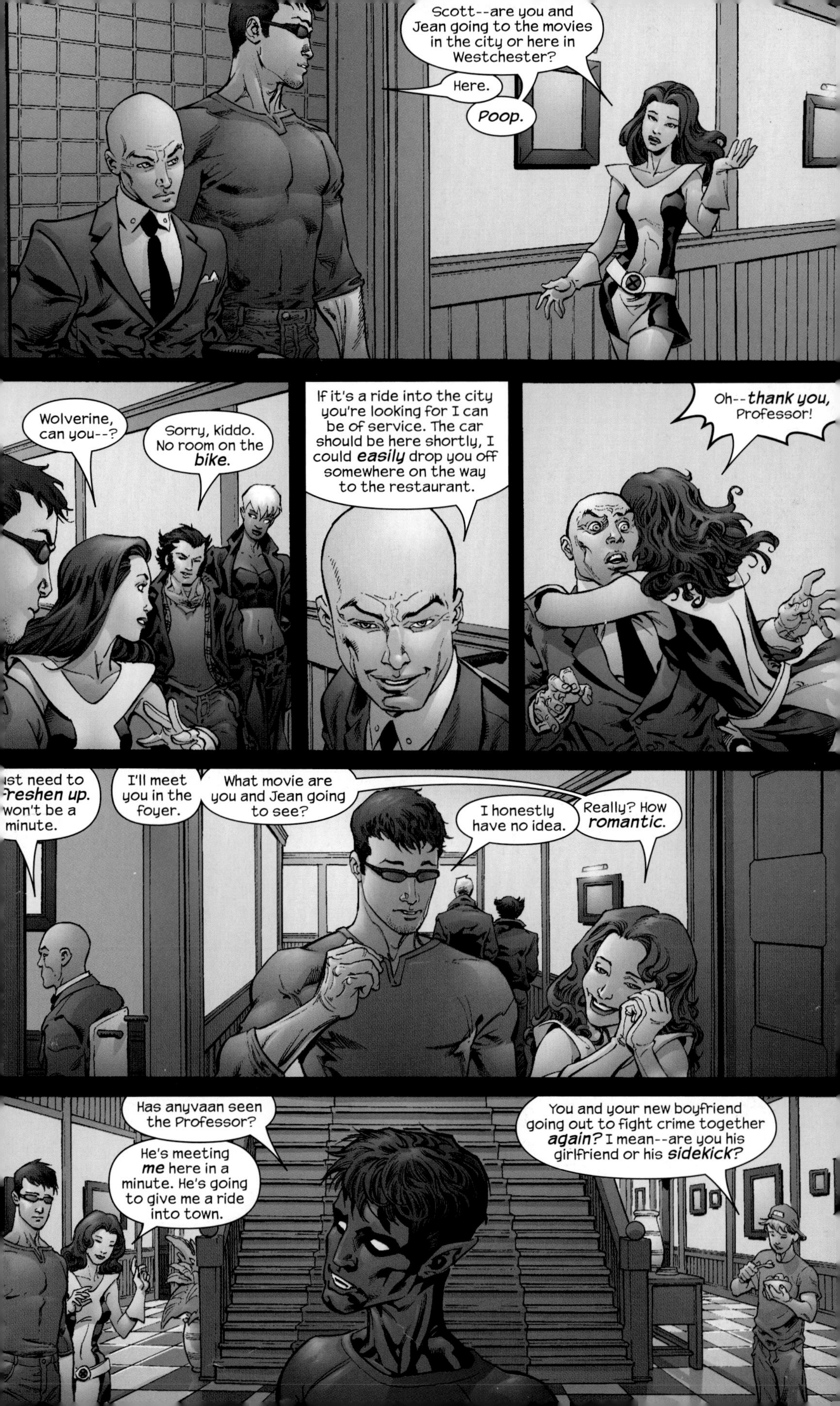

Scott--are you and Jean going to the movies in the city or here in Westchester?
Here.
Poop.
Wolverine, can you--?
Sorry, kiddo. No room on the bike.
If it's a ride into the city you're looking for I can be of service. The car should be here shortly, I could easily drop you off somewhere on the way to the restaurant.
Oh--thank you, Professor!
ust need to freshen up. won't be a minute.
I'll meet you in the foyer.
What movie are you and Jean going to see?
I honestly have no idea.
Really? How romantic.
Has anyvaan seen the Professor?
He's meeting me here in a minute. He's going to give me a ride into town.
You and your new boyfriend going out to fight crime together again? I mean--are you his girlfriend or his sidekick?

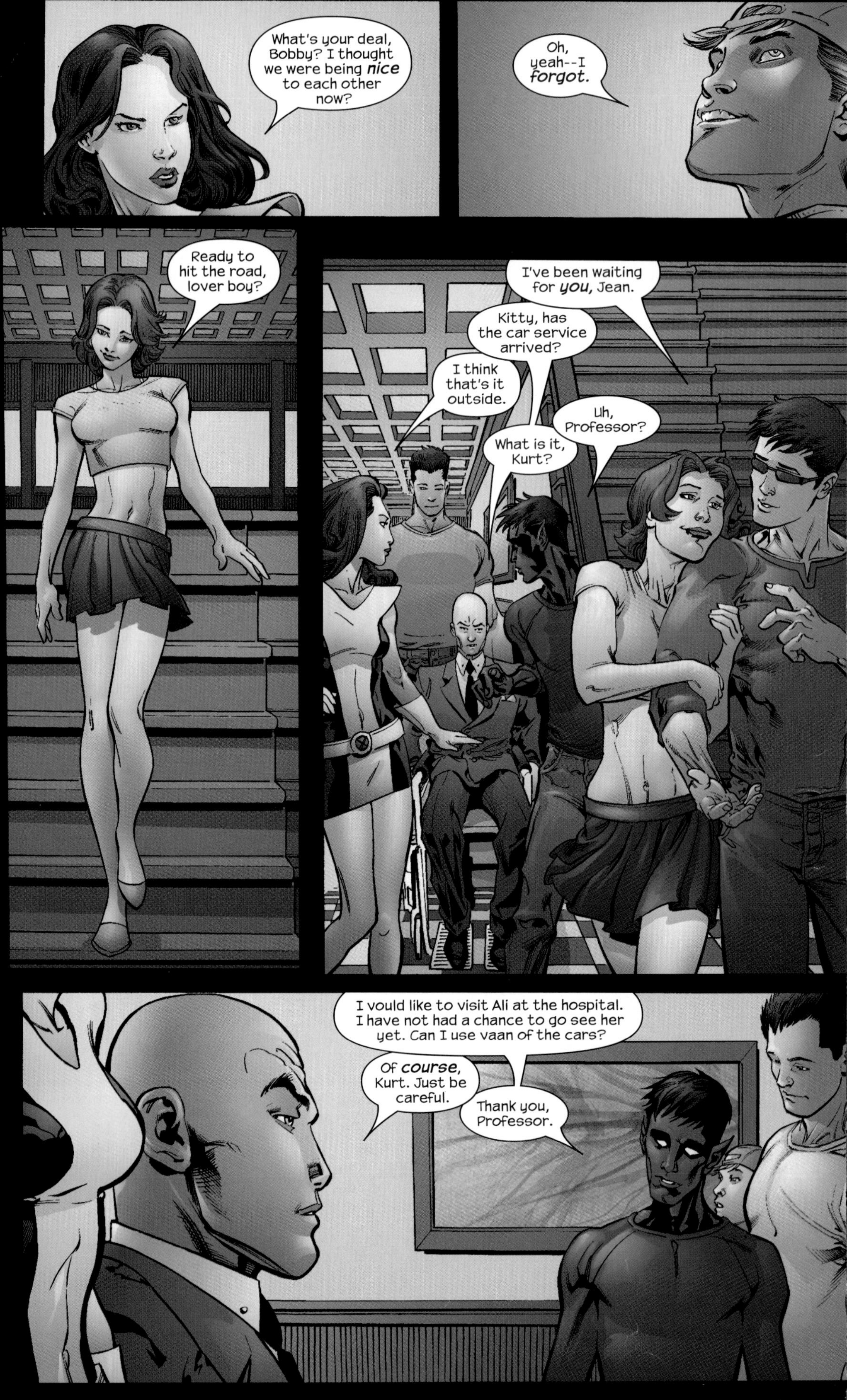

What's your deal, Bobby? I thought we were being *nice* to each other now?
Oh, yeah--I *forgot.*
Ready to hit the road, lover boy?
I've been waiting for *you,* Jean.
Kitty, has the car service arrived?
I think that's it outside.
Uh, Professor?
What is it, Kurt?
I vould like to visit Ali at the hospital. I have not had a chance to go see her yet. Can I use vaan of the cars?
Of *course,* Kurt. Just be careful.
Thank you, Professor.

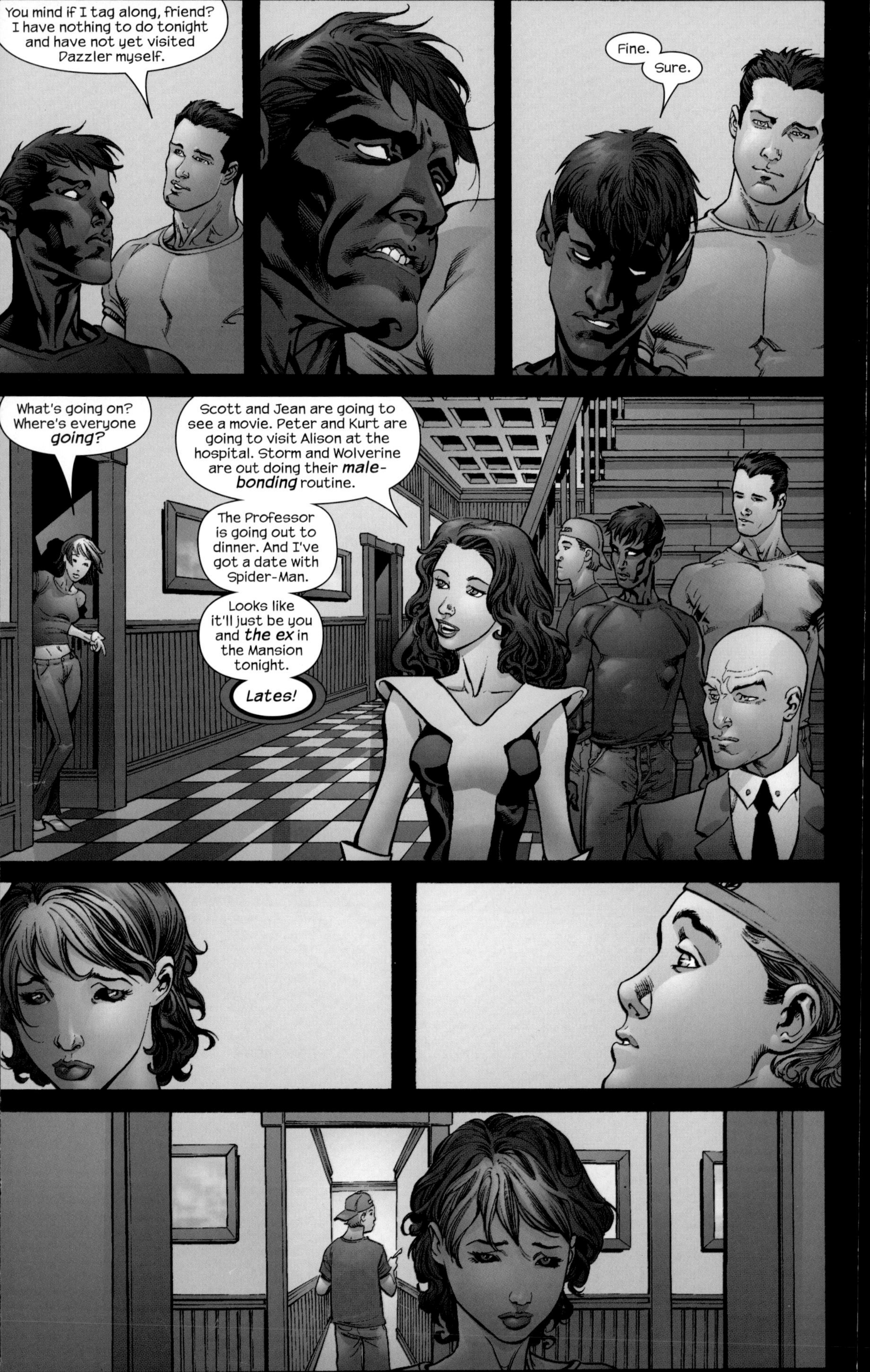
You mind if I tag along, friend? I have nothing to do tonight and have not yet visited Dazzler myself.
Fine.
Sure.
What's going on? Where's everyone *going*?
Scott and Jean are going to see a movie. Peter and Kurt are going to visit Alison at the hospital. Storm and Wolverine are out doing their *male-bonding* routine.
The Professor is going out to dinner. And I've got a date with Spider-Man.
Looks like it'll just be you and *the ex* in the Mansion tonight.
Lates!

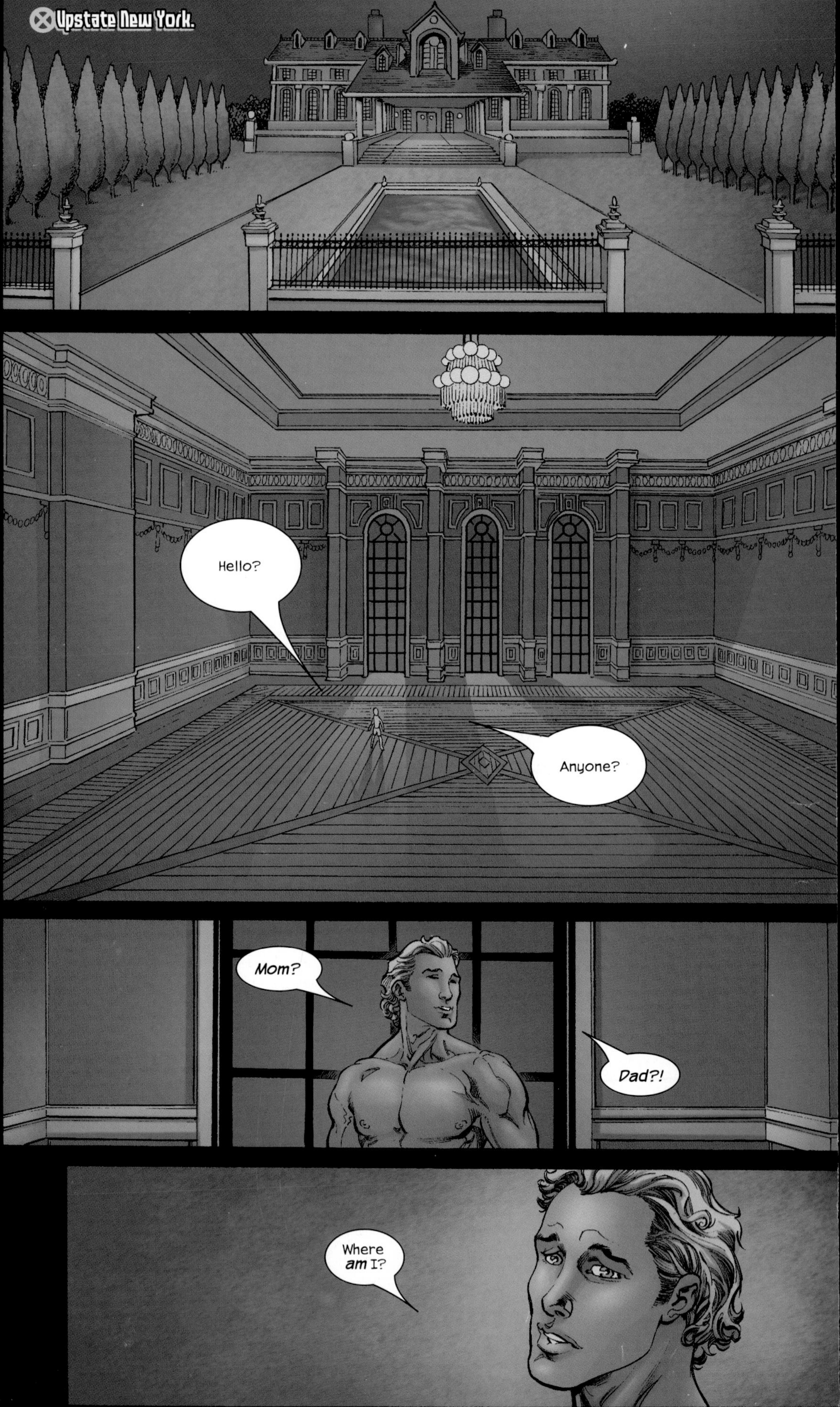
Upstate New York.
Hello?
Anyone?
Mom?
Dad?!
Where am I?

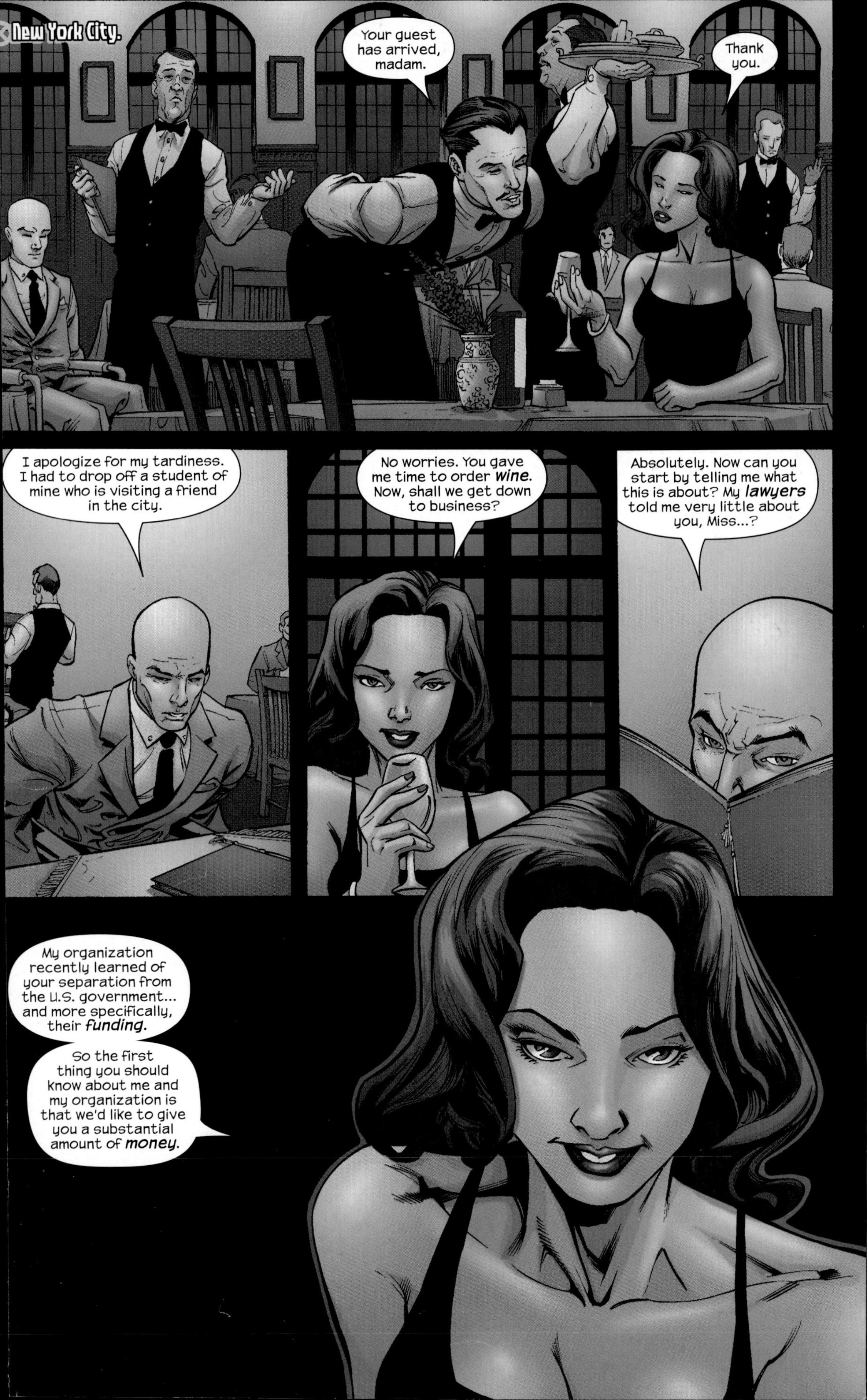
New York City.
Your guest has arrived, madam.
Thank you.
I apologize for my tardiness. I had to drop off a student of mine who is visiting a friend in the city.
No worries. You gave me time to order *wine*. Now, shall we get down to business?
Absolutely. Now can you start by telling me what this is about? My *lawyers* told me very little about you, Miss...?
My organization recently learned of your separation from the U.S. government... and more specifically, their *funding*.
So the first thing you should know about me and my organization is that we'd like to give you a substantial amount of *money*.

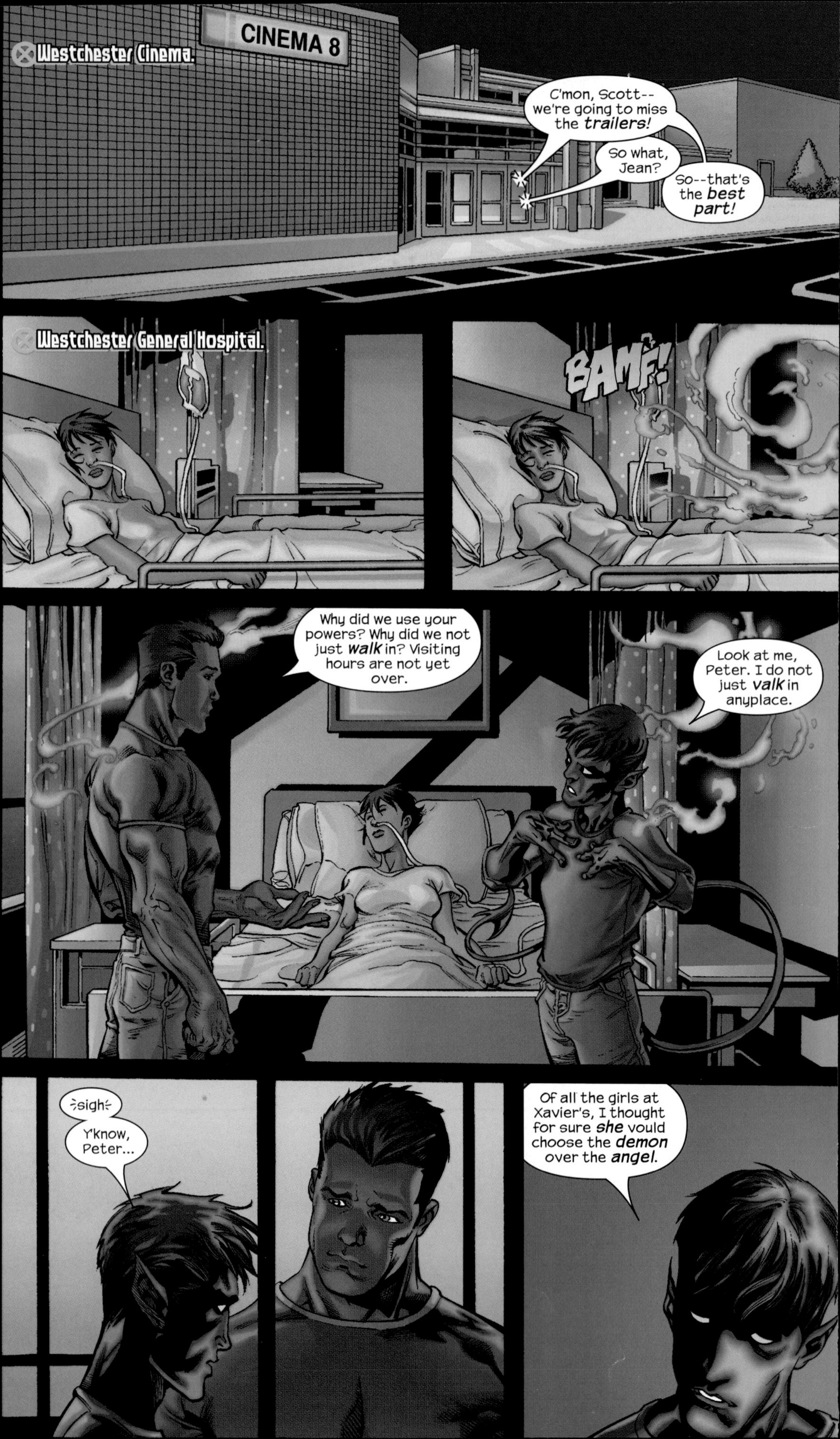
Westchester Cinema.
CINEMA 8
C'mon, Scott-- we're going to miss the trailers!
So what, Jean?
So--that's the best part!
Westchester General Hospital.
BAMF!
Why did we use your powers? Why did we not just walk in? Visiting hours are not yet over.
Look at me, Peter. I do not just valk in anyplace.
sigh
Y'know, Peter...
Of all the girls at Xavier's, I thought for sure she vould choose the demon over the angel.

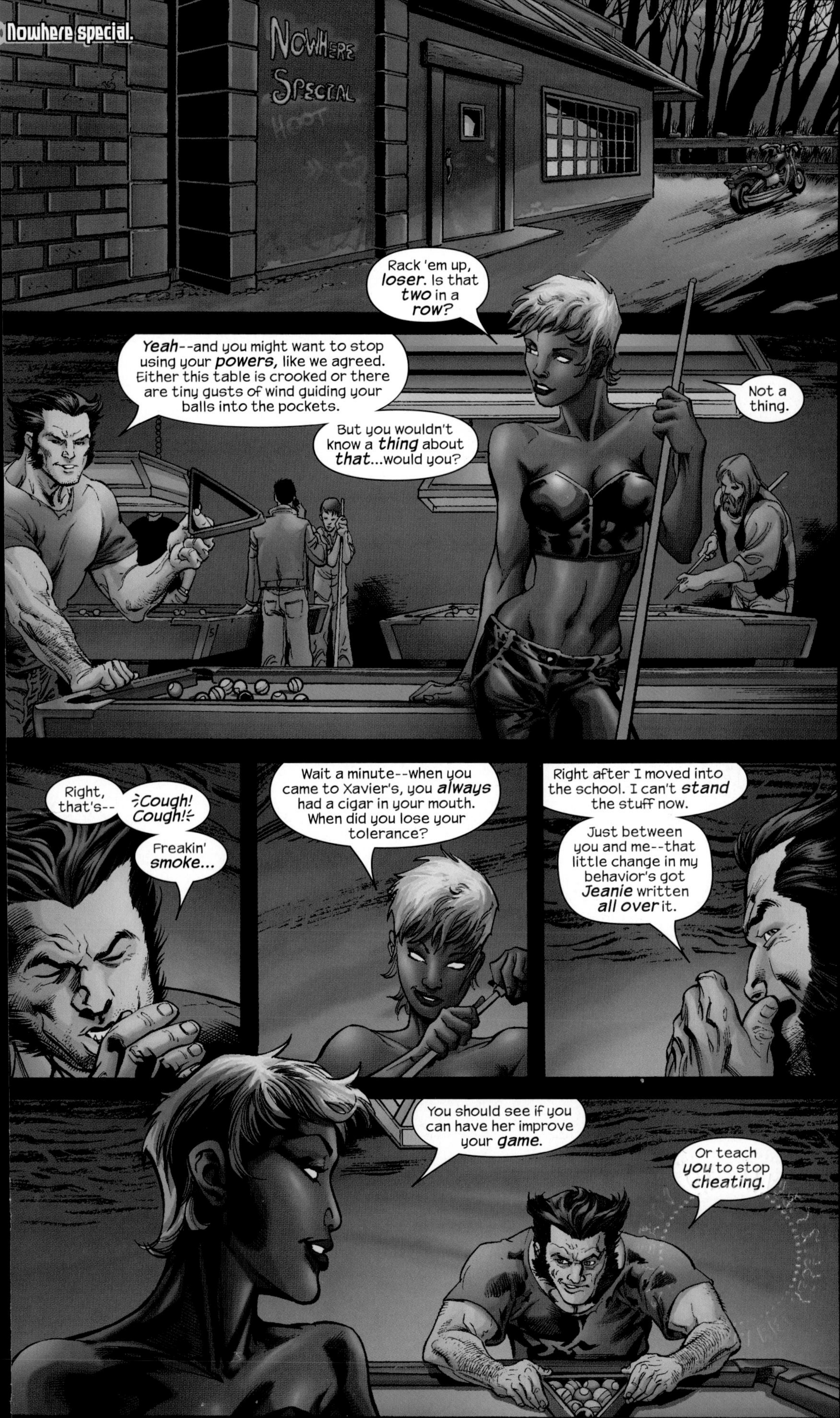
Nowhere special.
NOWHERE SPECIAL
Rack 'em up, loser. Is that two in a row?
Yeah--and you might want to stop using your powers, like we agreed. Either this table is crooked or there are tiny gusts of wind guiding your balls into the pockets.
Not a thing.
But you wouldn't know a thing about that...would you?
Right, that's--
Cough! Cough!
Freakin' smoke...
Wait a minute--when you came to Xavier's, you always had a cigar in your mouth. When did you lose your tolerance?
Right after I moved into the school. I can't stand the stuff now.
Just between you and me--that little change in my behavior's got Jeanie written all over it.
You should see if you can have her improve your game.
Or teach you to stop cheating.

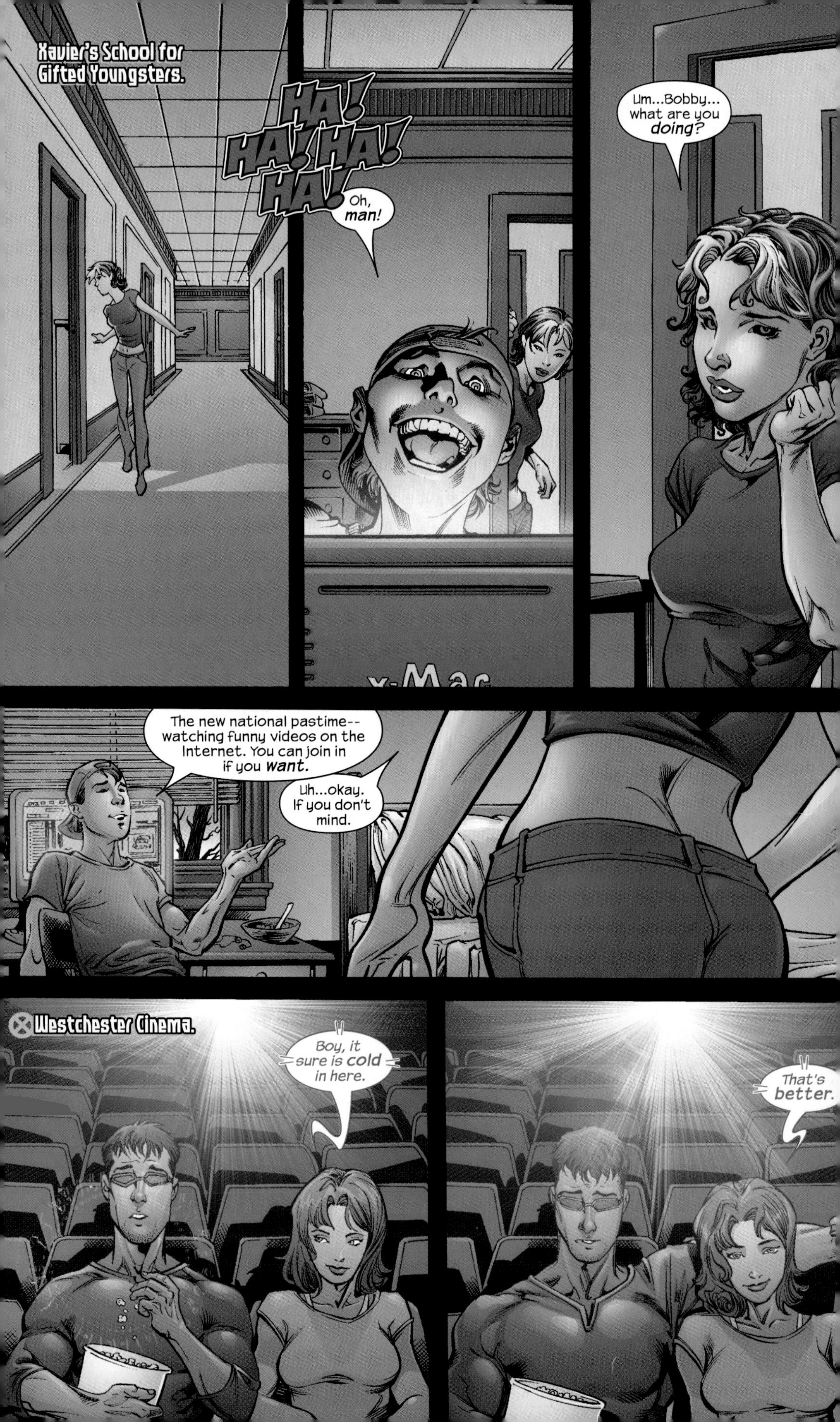
Xavier's School for Gifted Youngsters.
HA! HA! HA! HA!
Oh, *man!*
Um...Bobby... what are you *doing*?
X-Mac
The new national pastime-- watching funny videos on the Internet. You can join in if you **want.**
Uh...okay. If you don't mind.
Westchester Cinema.
Boy, it sure is **cold** in here.
That's **better.**

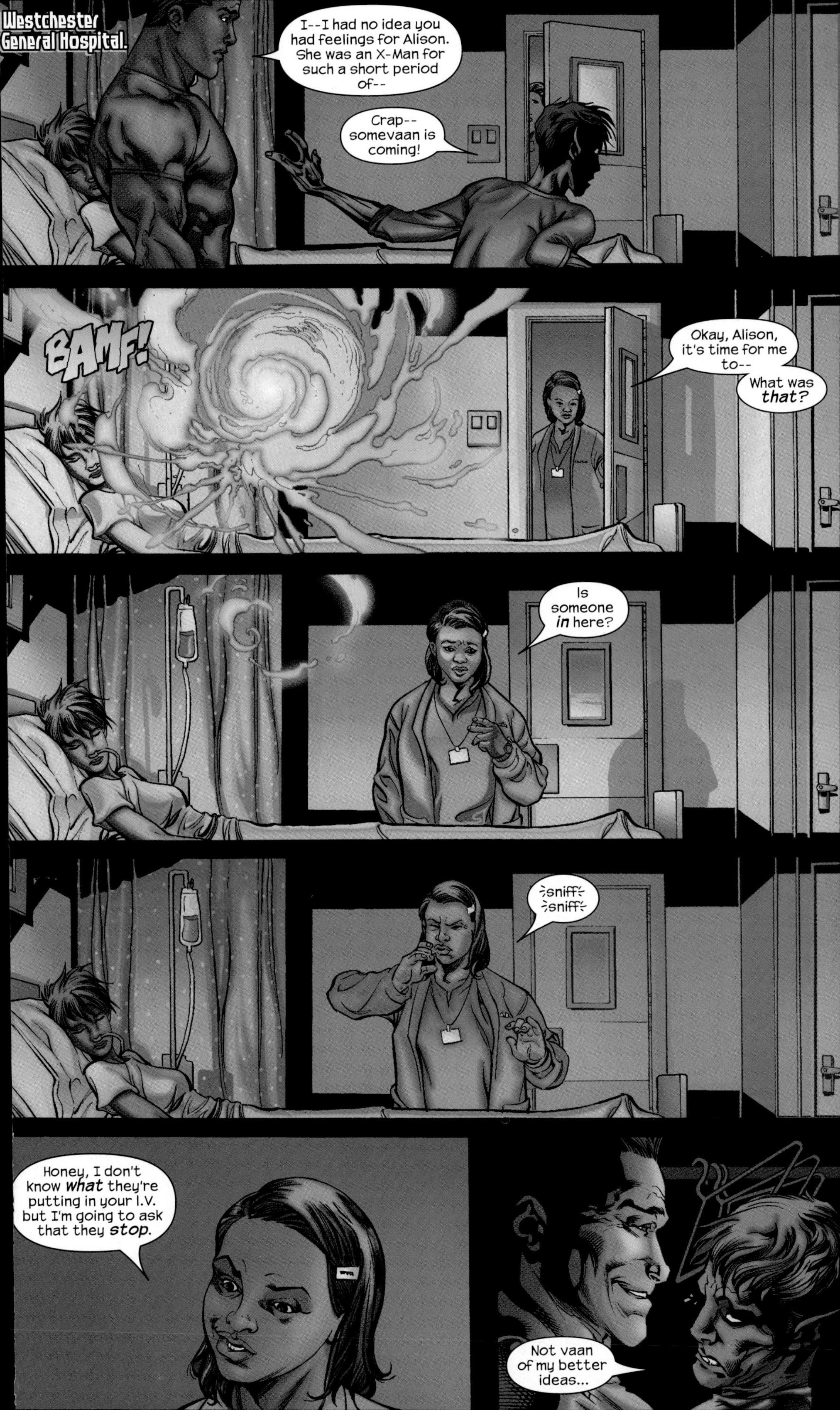
Westchester General Hospital.
I--I had no idea you had feelings for Alison. She was an X-Man for such a short period of--
Crap-- somevaan is coming!
BAMF!
Okay, Alison, it's time for me to--
What was *that?*
Is someone *in* here?
sniff sniff
Honey, I don't know *what* they're putting in your I.V. but I'm going to ask that they *stop*.
Not vaan of my better ideas...

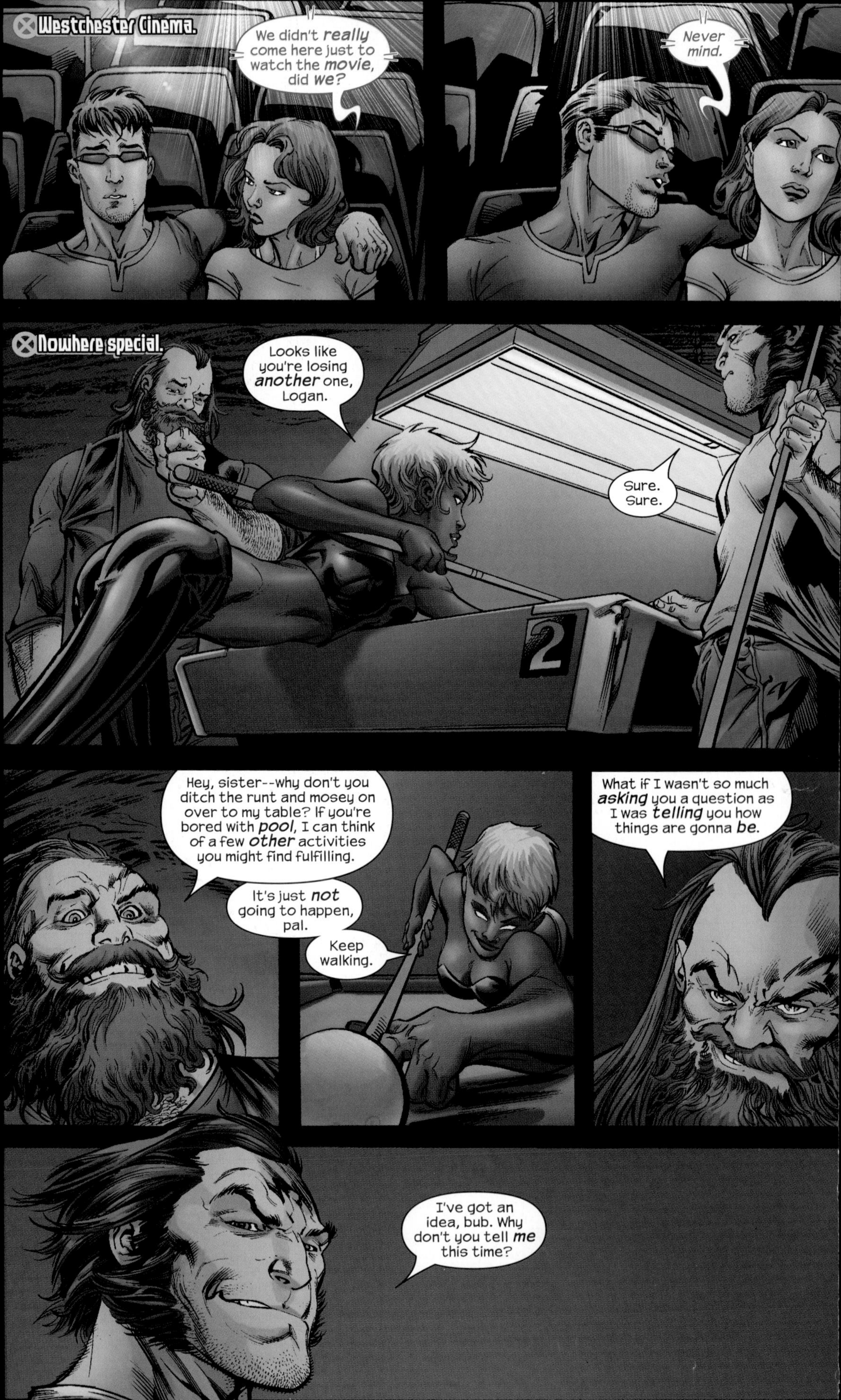
Westchester Cinema.
We didn't really come here just to watch the movie, did we?
Never mind.
Nowhere special.
Looks like you're losing another one, Logan.
Sure. Sure.
Hey, sister--why don't you ditch the runt and mosey on over to my table? If you're bored with pool, I can think of a few other activities you might find fulfilling.
It's just not going to happen, pal.
Keep walking.
What if I wasn't so much asking you a question as I was telling you how things are gonna be.
I've got an idea, bub. Why don't you tell me this time?

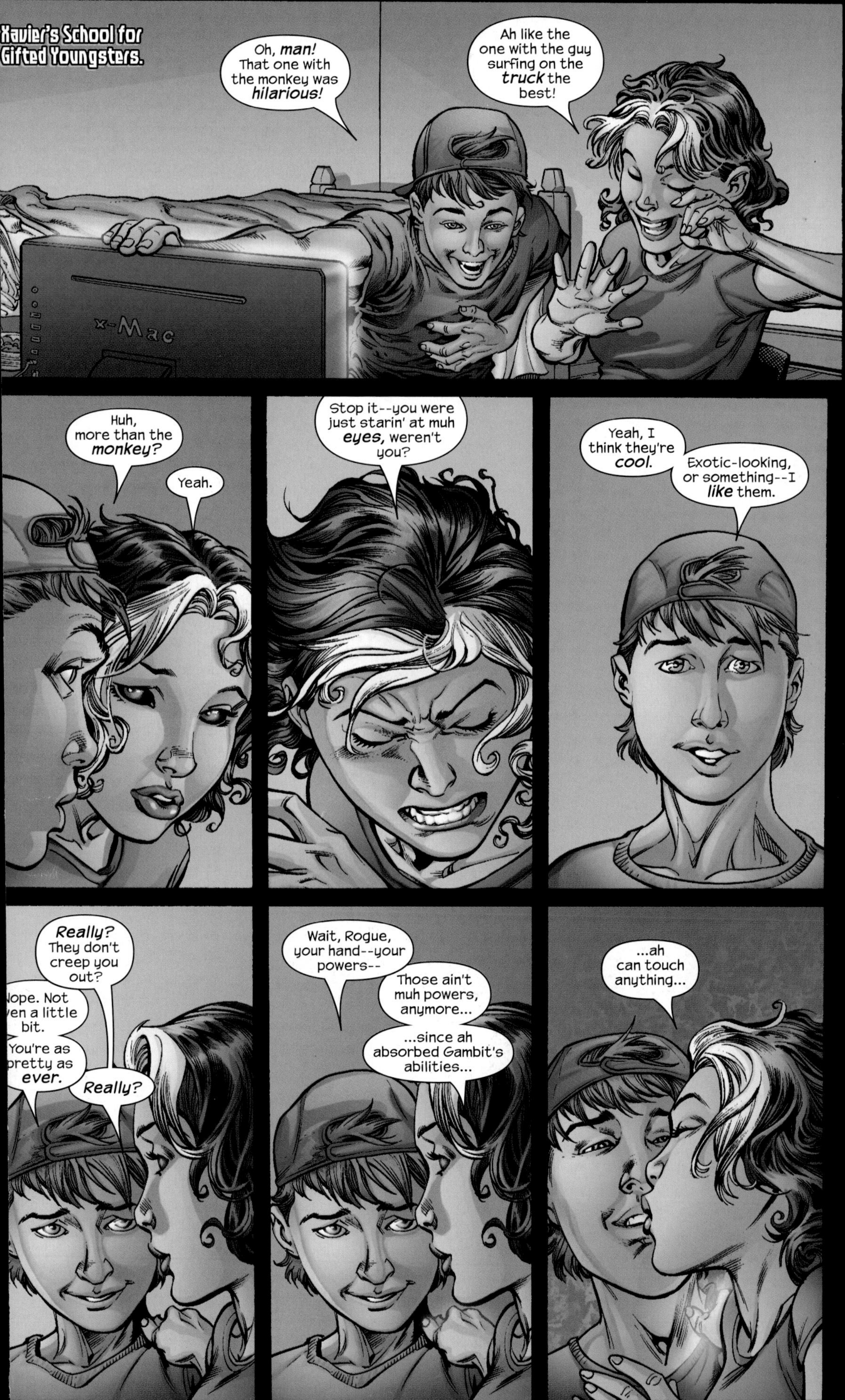
Xavier's School for Gifted Youngsters.
Oh, man! That one with the monkey was hilarious!
Ah like the one with the guy surfing on the truck the best!
Huh, more than the monkey?
Yeah.
Stop it--you were just starin' at muh eyes, weren't you?
Yeah, I think they're cool.
Exotic-looking, or something--I like them.
Really? They don't creep you out?
Nope. Not even a little bit.
You're as pretty as ever.
Really?
Wait, Rogue, your hand--your powers--
Those ain't muh powers, anymore...
...since ah absorbed Gambit's abilities...
...ah can touch anything...

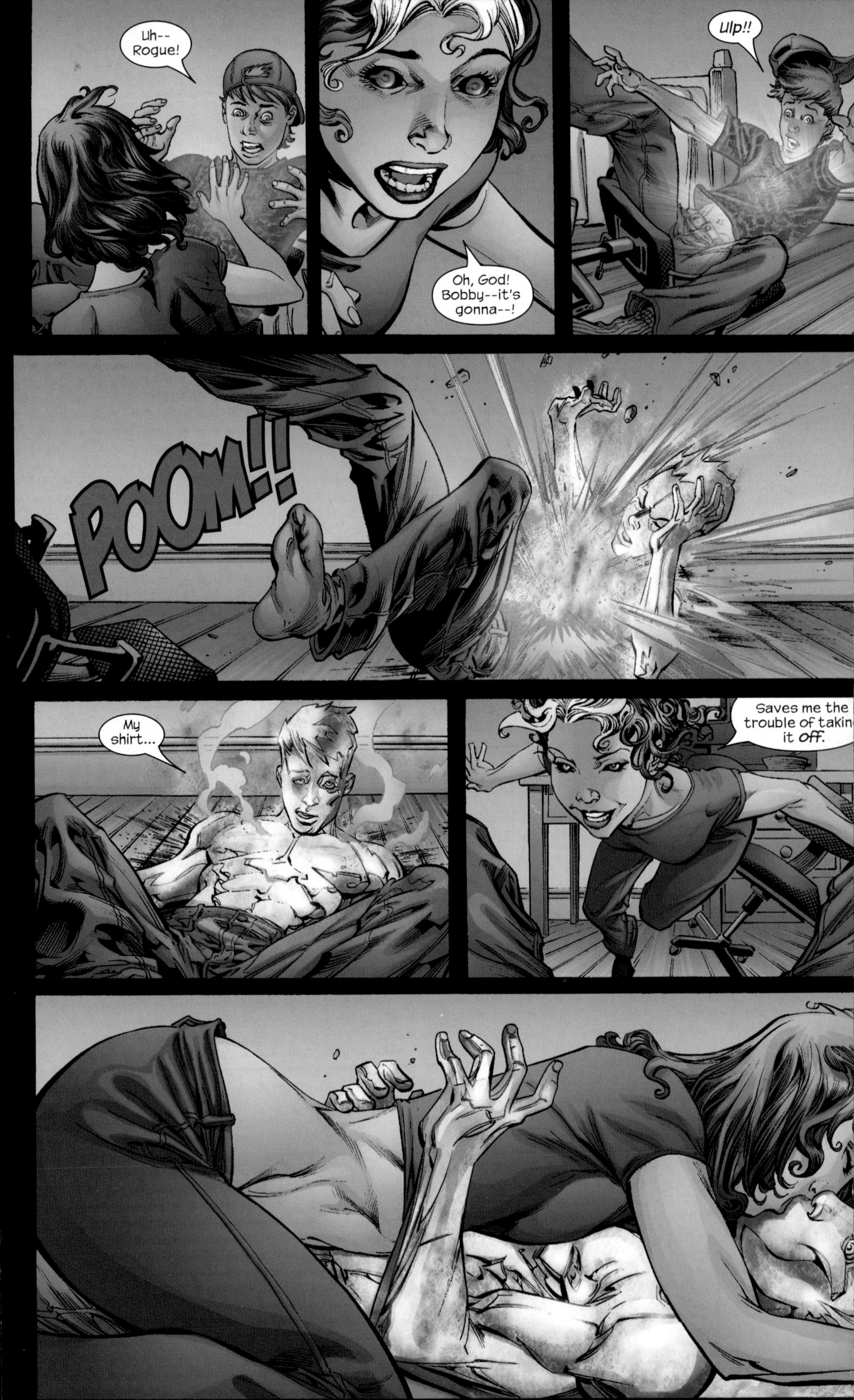
Uh--
Rogue!
Oh, God!
Bobby--it's
gonna--!
Ulp!!
POOM!!
My
shirt...
Saves me the
trouble of takin
it OFF.

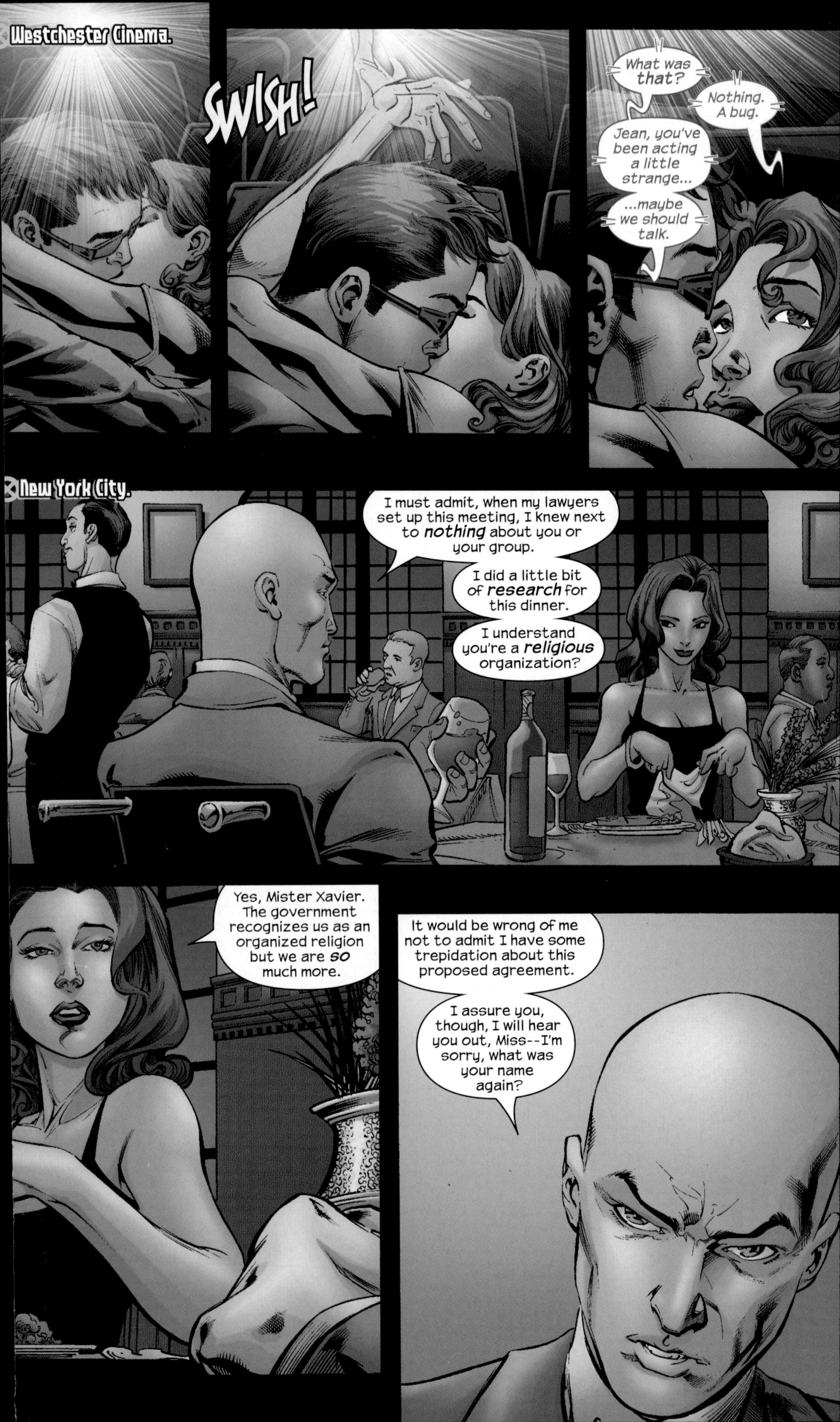
Westchester Cinema.
SWISH!
What was that?
Nothing. A bug.
Jean, you've been acting a little strange...
...maybe we should talk.
New York City.
I must admit, when my lawyers set up this meeting, I knew next to nothing about you or your group.
I did a little bit of research for this dinner.
I understand you're a religious organization?
Yes, Mister Xavier. The government recognizes us as an organized religion but we are so much more.
It would be wrong of me not to admit I have some trepidation about this proposed agreement.
I assure you, though, I will hear you out, Miss--I'm sorry, what was your name again?

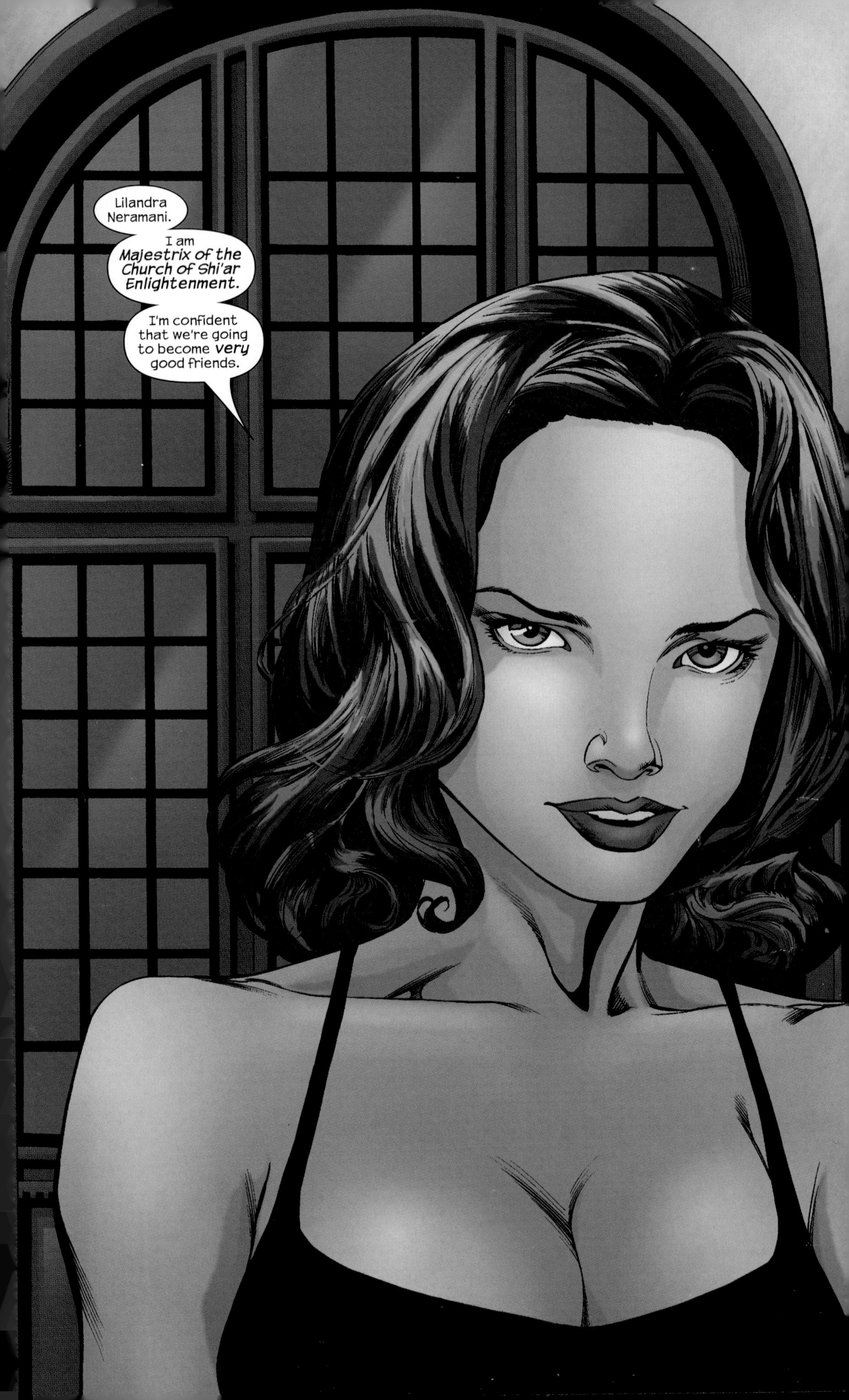
Lilandra Neramani.
I am Majestrix of the Church of Shi'ar Enlightenment.
I'm confident that we're going to become very good friends.

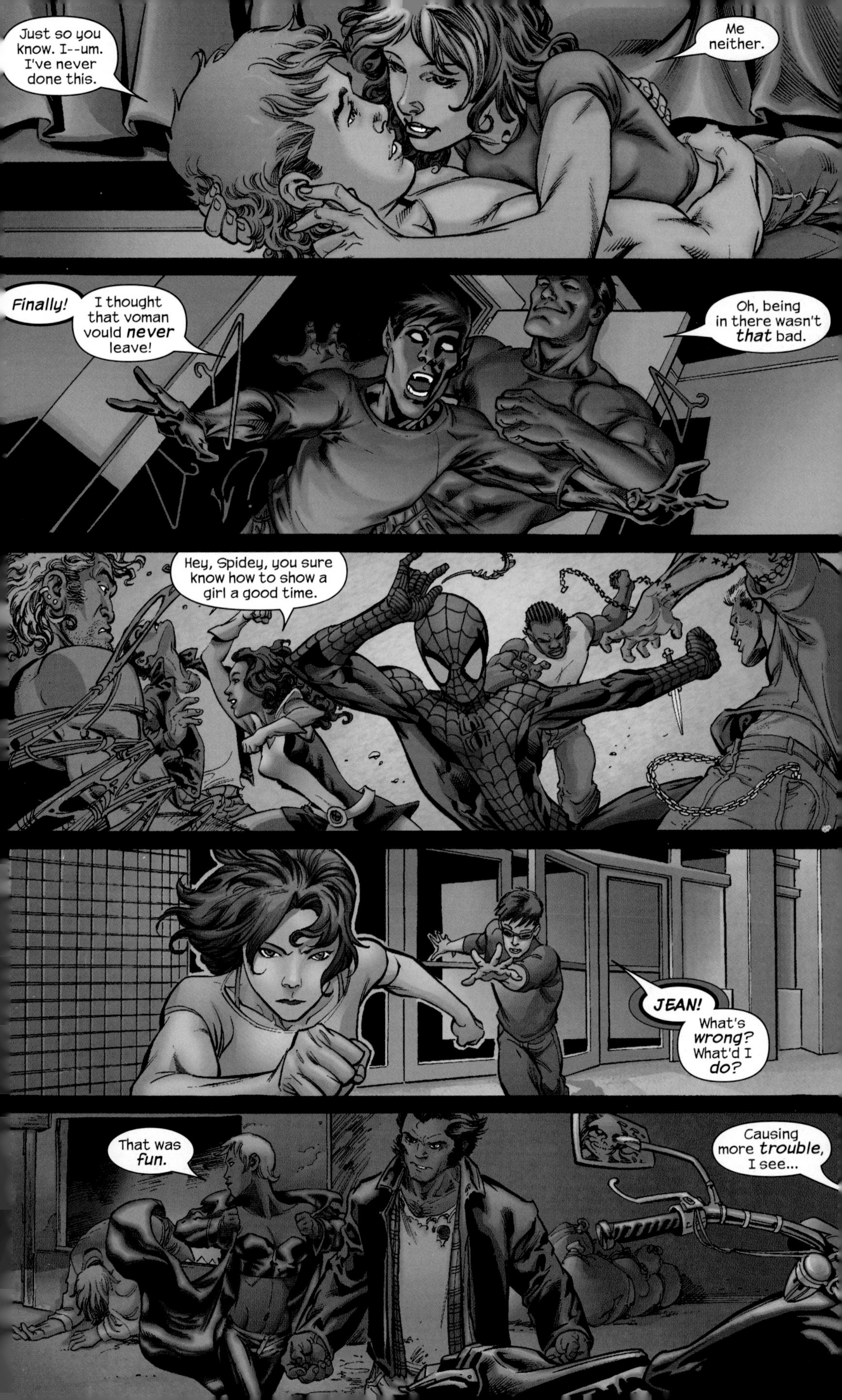
Just so you know. I--um. I've never done this.
Me neither.
Finally!
I thought that voman vould never leave!
Oh, being in there wasn't that bad.
Hey, Spidey, you sure know how to show a girl a good time.
JEAN!
What's wrong? What'd I do?
That was fun.
Causing more trouble, I see...

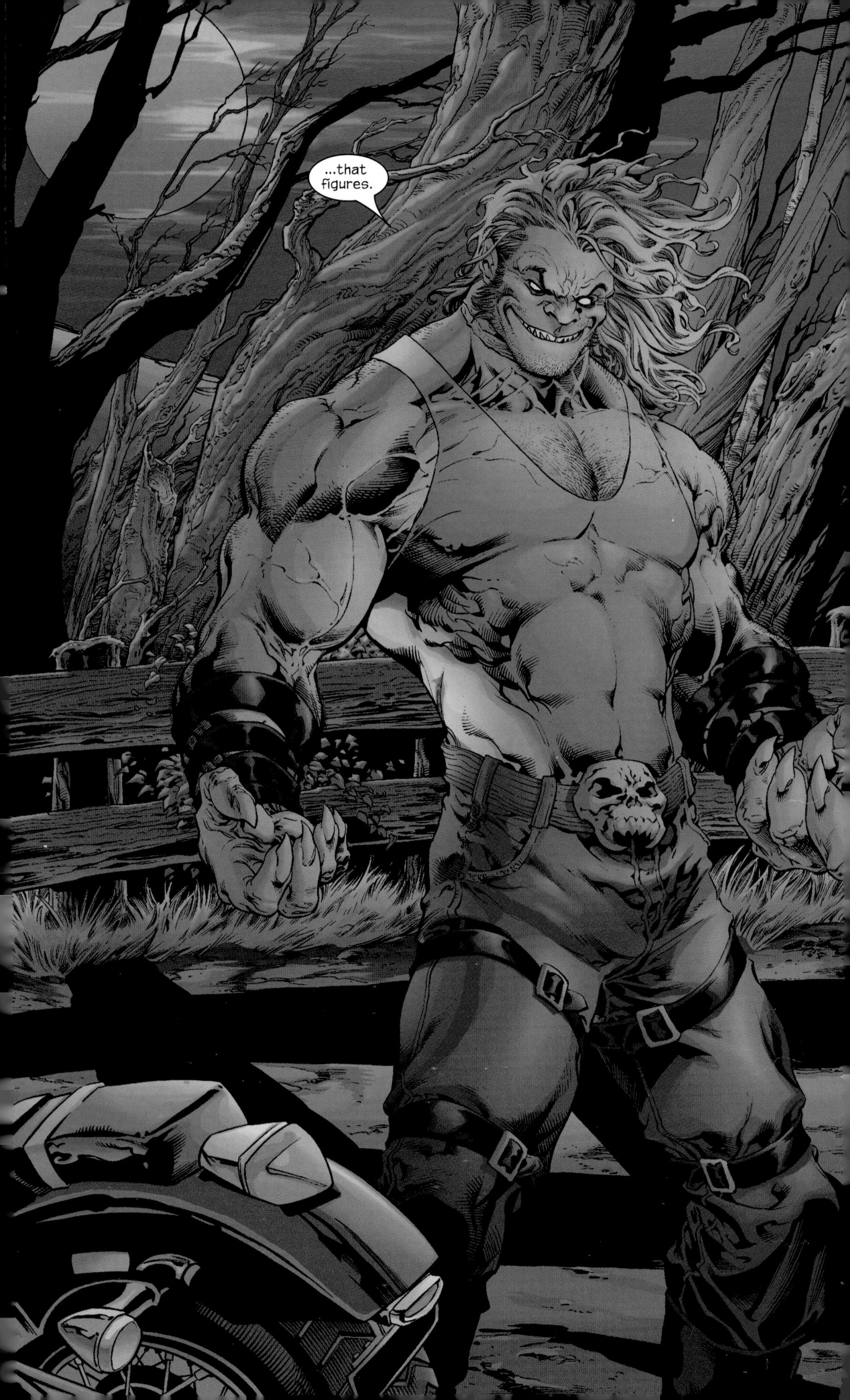
...that figures.

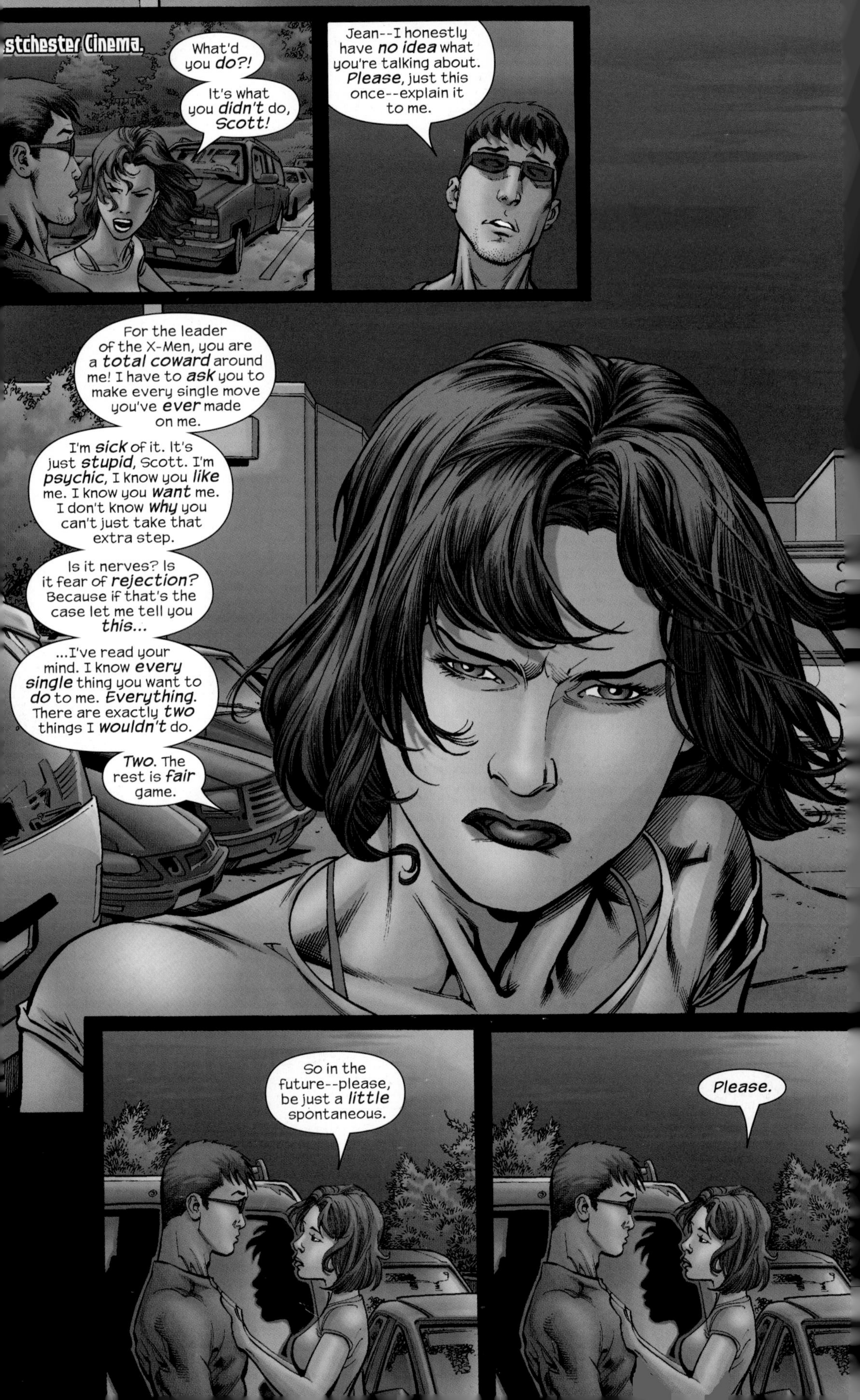
stchester Cinema.
What'd you do?!
It's what you didn't do, Scott!
Jean--I honestly have no idea what you're talking about. Please, just this once--explain it to me.
For the leader of the X-Men, you are a total coward around me! I have to ask you to make every single move you've ever made on me.
I'm sick of it. It's just stupid, Scott. I'm psychic, I know you like me. I know you want me. I don't know why you can't just take that extra step.
Is it nerves? Is it fear of rejection? Because if that's the case let me tell you this...
...I've read your mind. I know every single thing you want to do to me. Everything. There are exactly two things I wouldn't do.
Two. The rest is fair game.
So in the future--please, be just a little spontaneous.
Please.

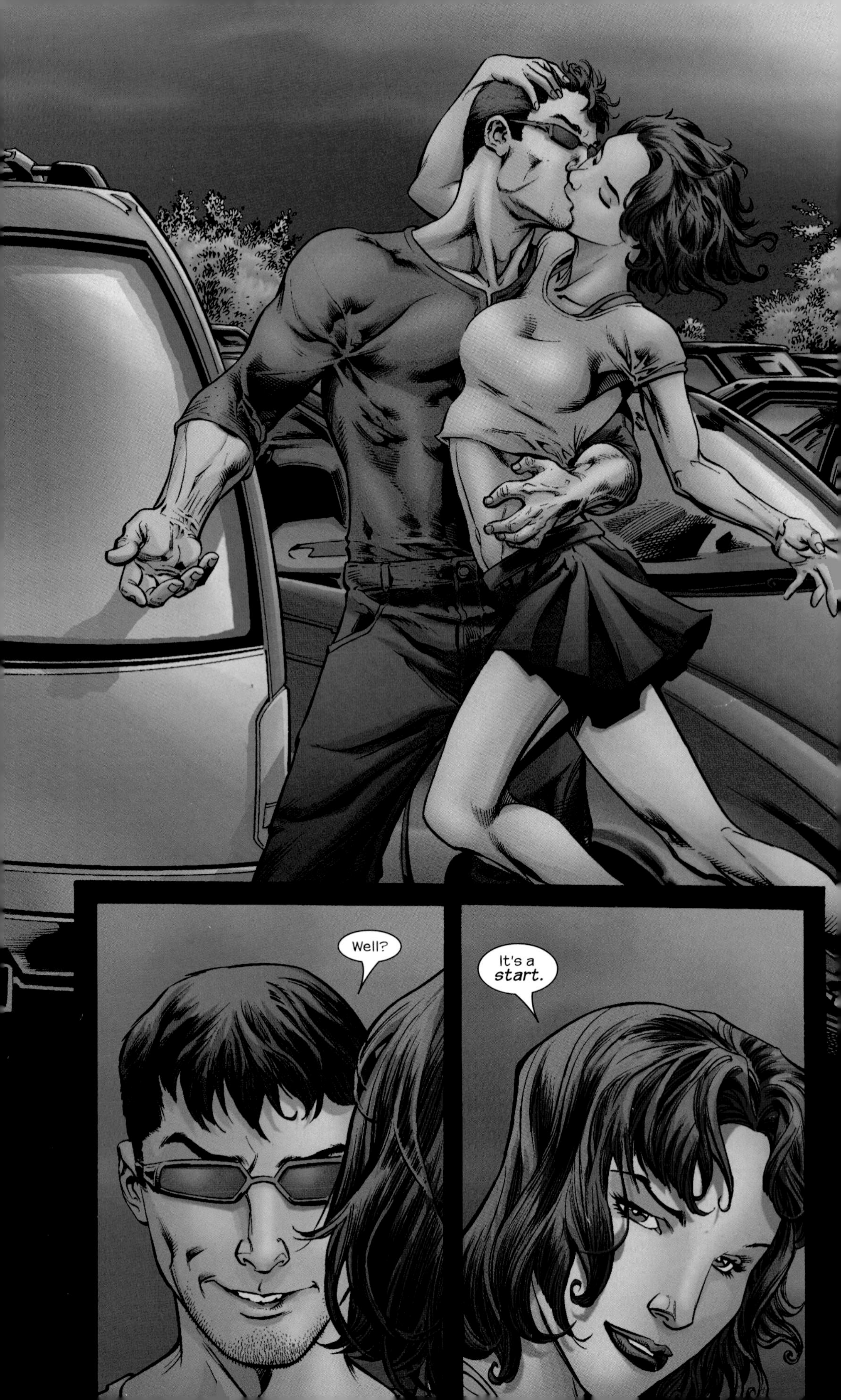
Well?
It's a *start.*

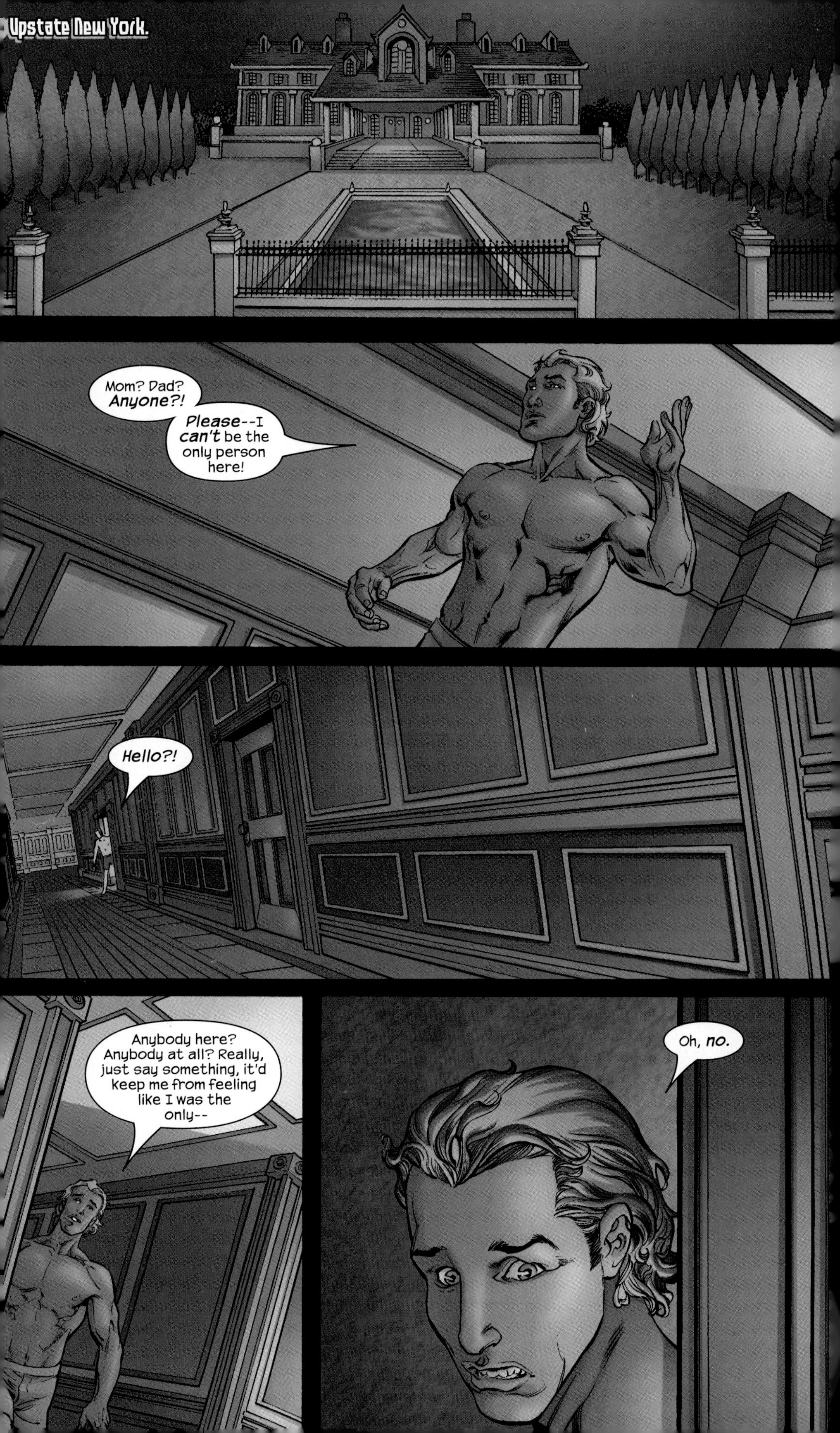
Upstate New York.
Mom? Dad? Anyone?!
Please--I can't be the only person here!
Hello?!
Anybody here? Anybody at all? Really, just say something, it'd keep me from feeling like I was the only--
Oh, no.

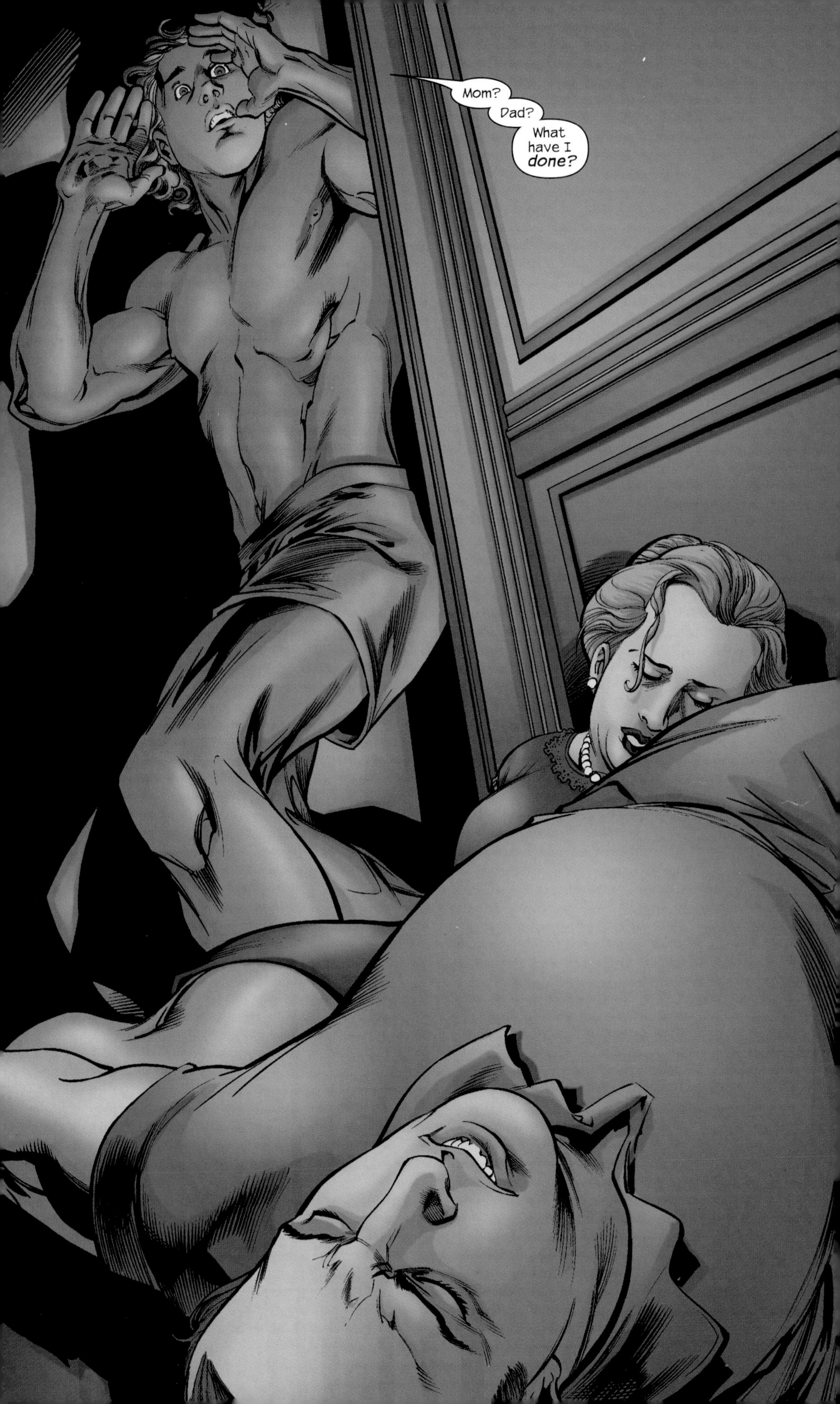
Mom?
Dad?
What have I *done*?

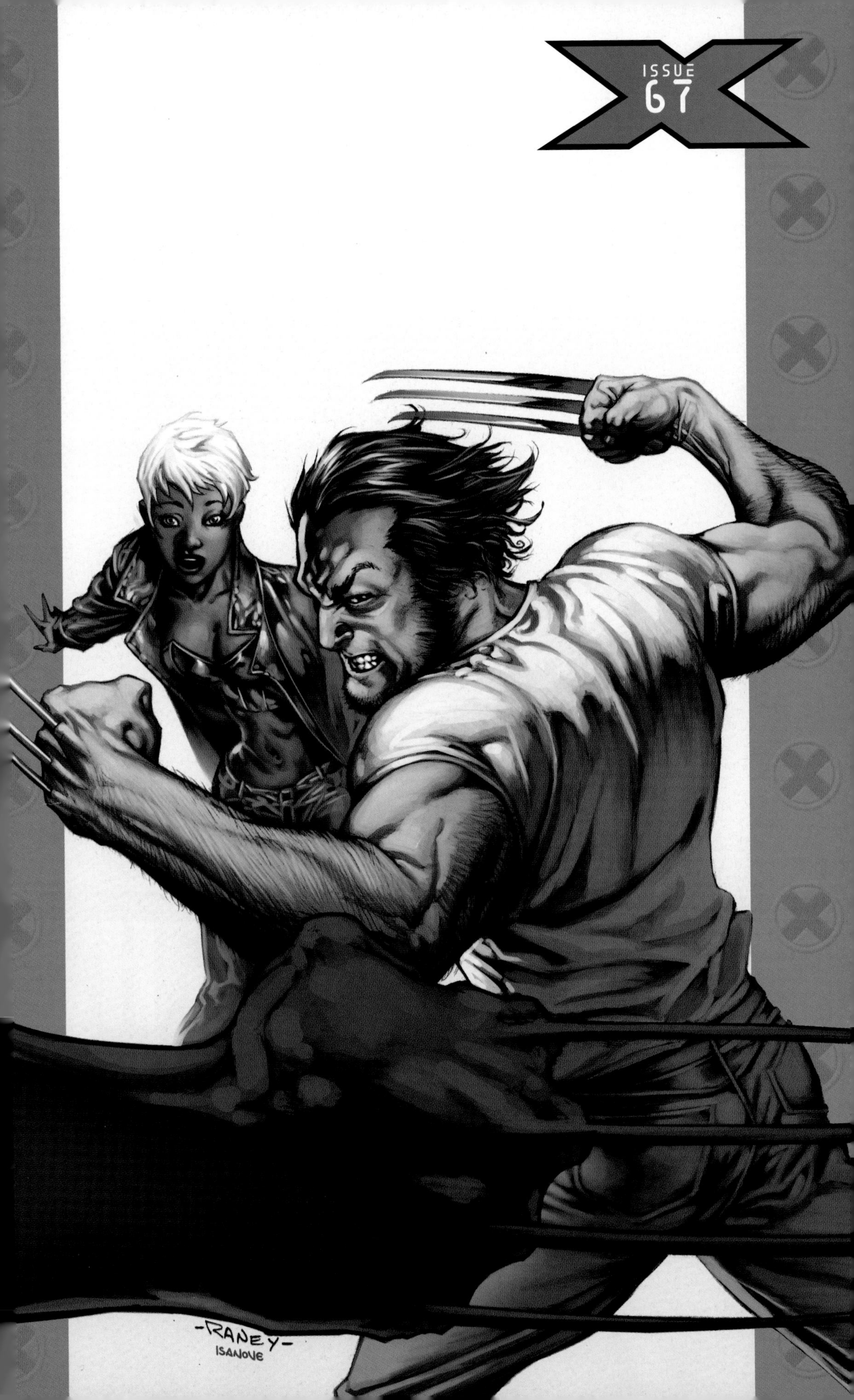
ISSUE
67
-RANEY-
ISANOVE

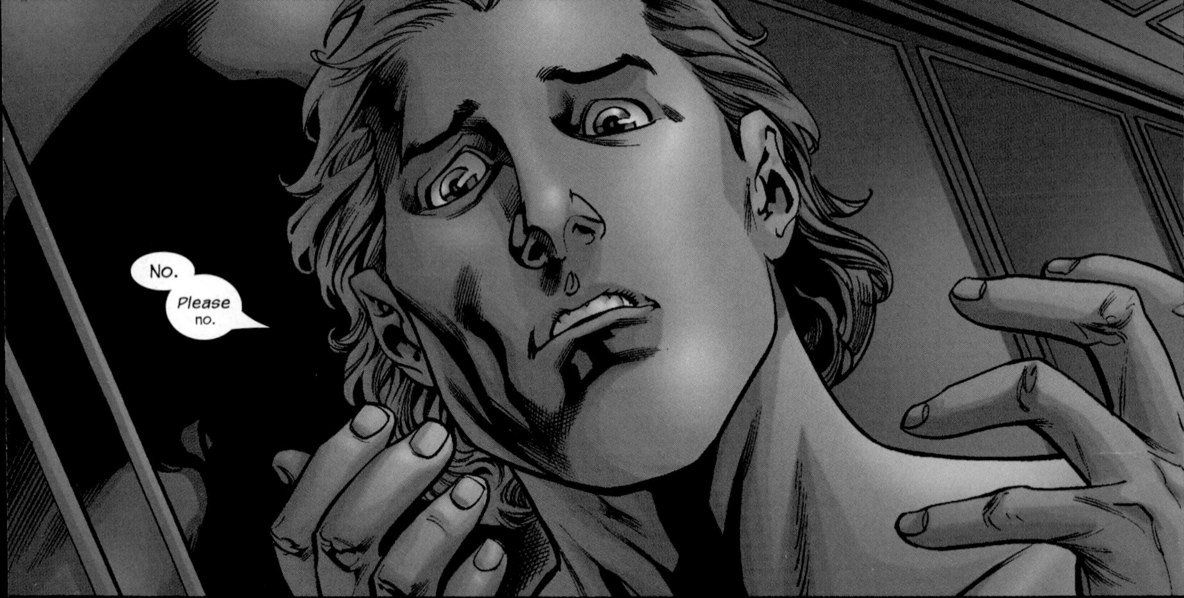
No.
Please no.

DATE NIGHT

PART 2 O

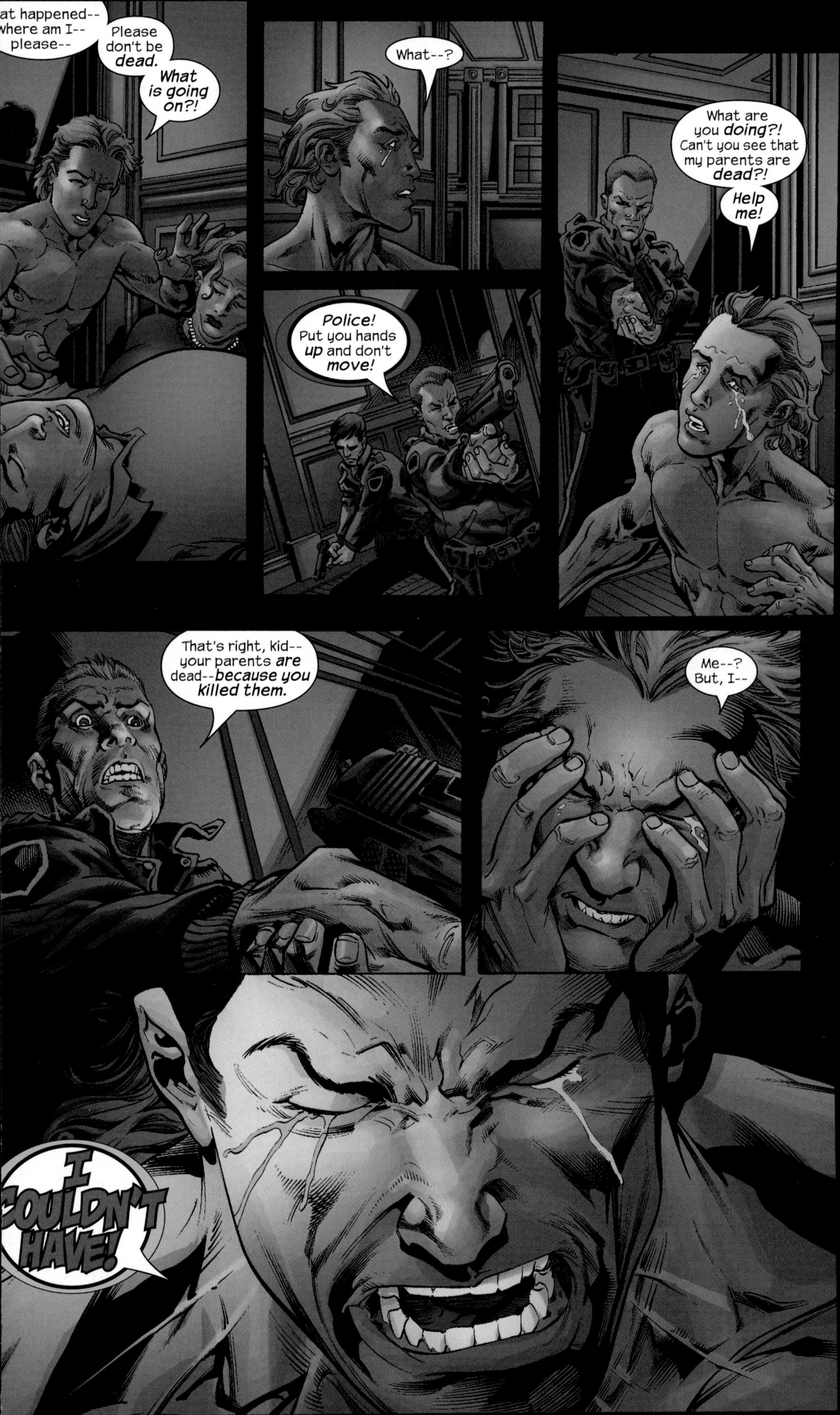

at happened--
where am I--
please--
Please
don't be
dead.
What
is going
on?!
What--?
Police!
Put you hands
up and don't
move!
What are
you doing?!
Can't you see that
my parents are
dead?!
Help
me!
That's right, kid--
your parents are
dead--because you
killed them.
Me--?
But, I--
I
COULDN'T
HAVE!

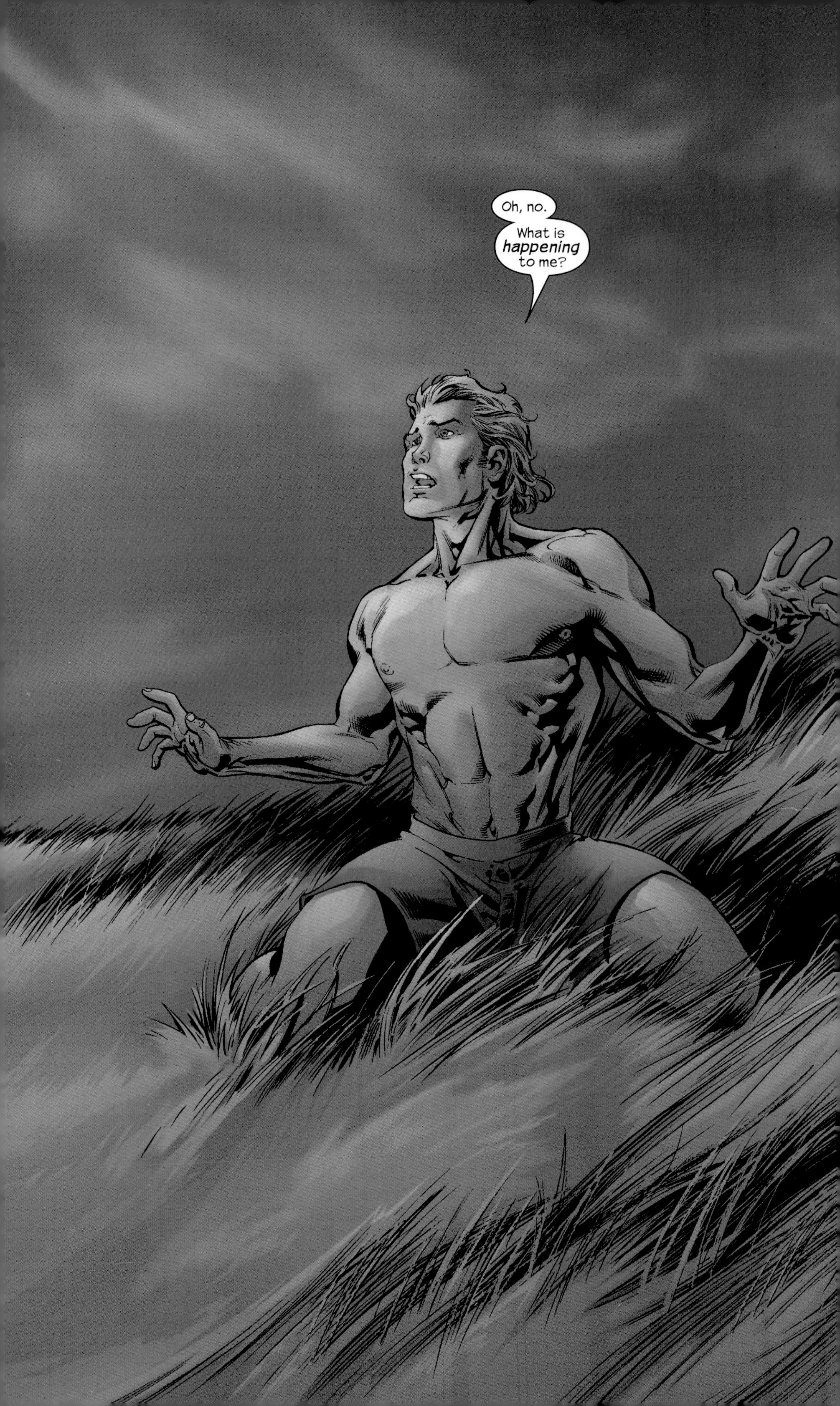
Oh, no.
What is *happening* to me?

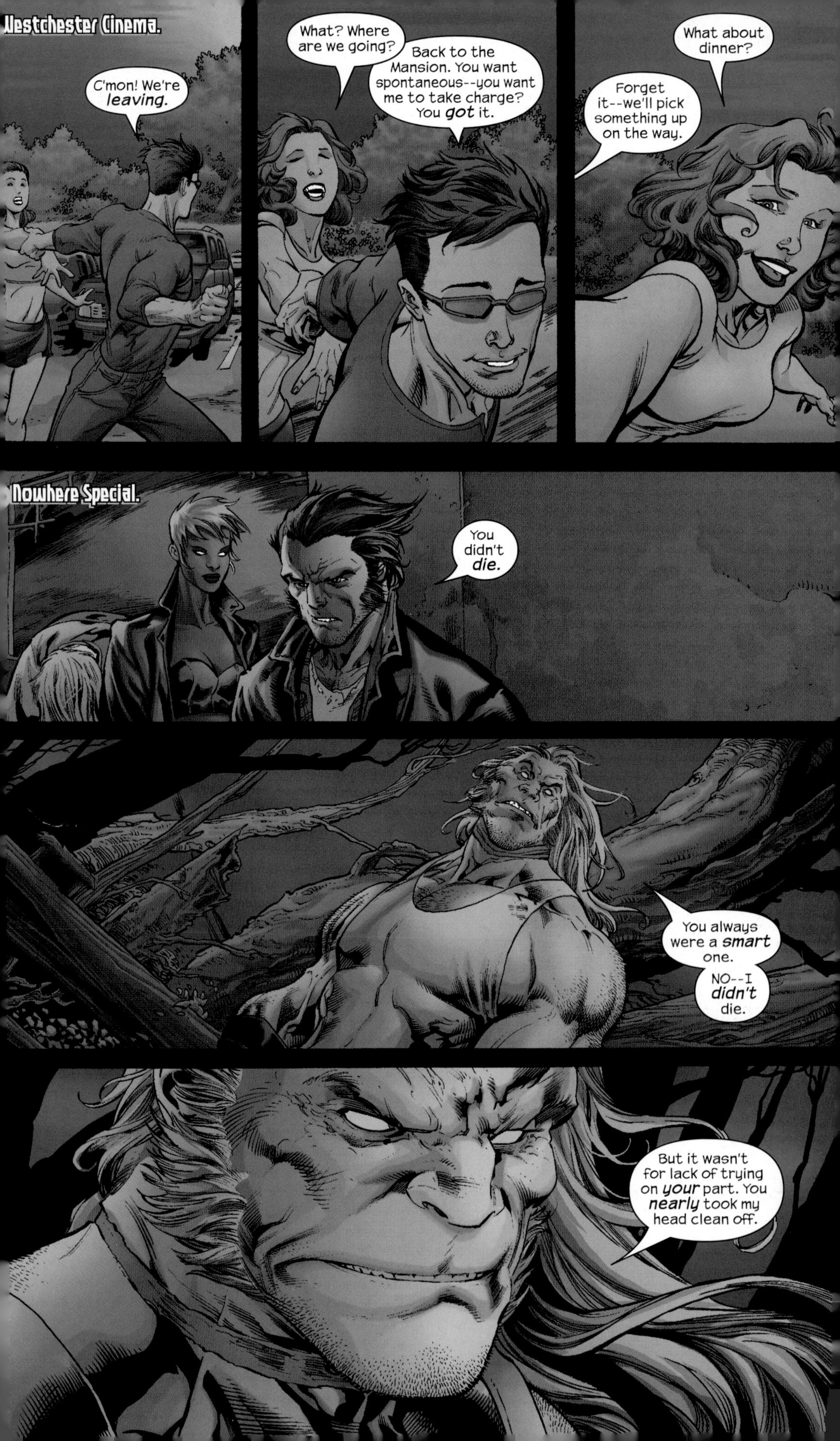
Westchester Cinema.
C'mon! We're *leaving.*
What? Where are we going?
Back to the Mansion. You want spontaneous--you want me to take charge? You *got* it.
What about dinner?
Forget it--we'll pick something up on the way.
Nowhere Special.
You didn't *die.*
You always were a *smart* one.
NO--I *didn't* die.
But it wasn't for lack of trying on *your* part. You *nearly* took my head clean off.

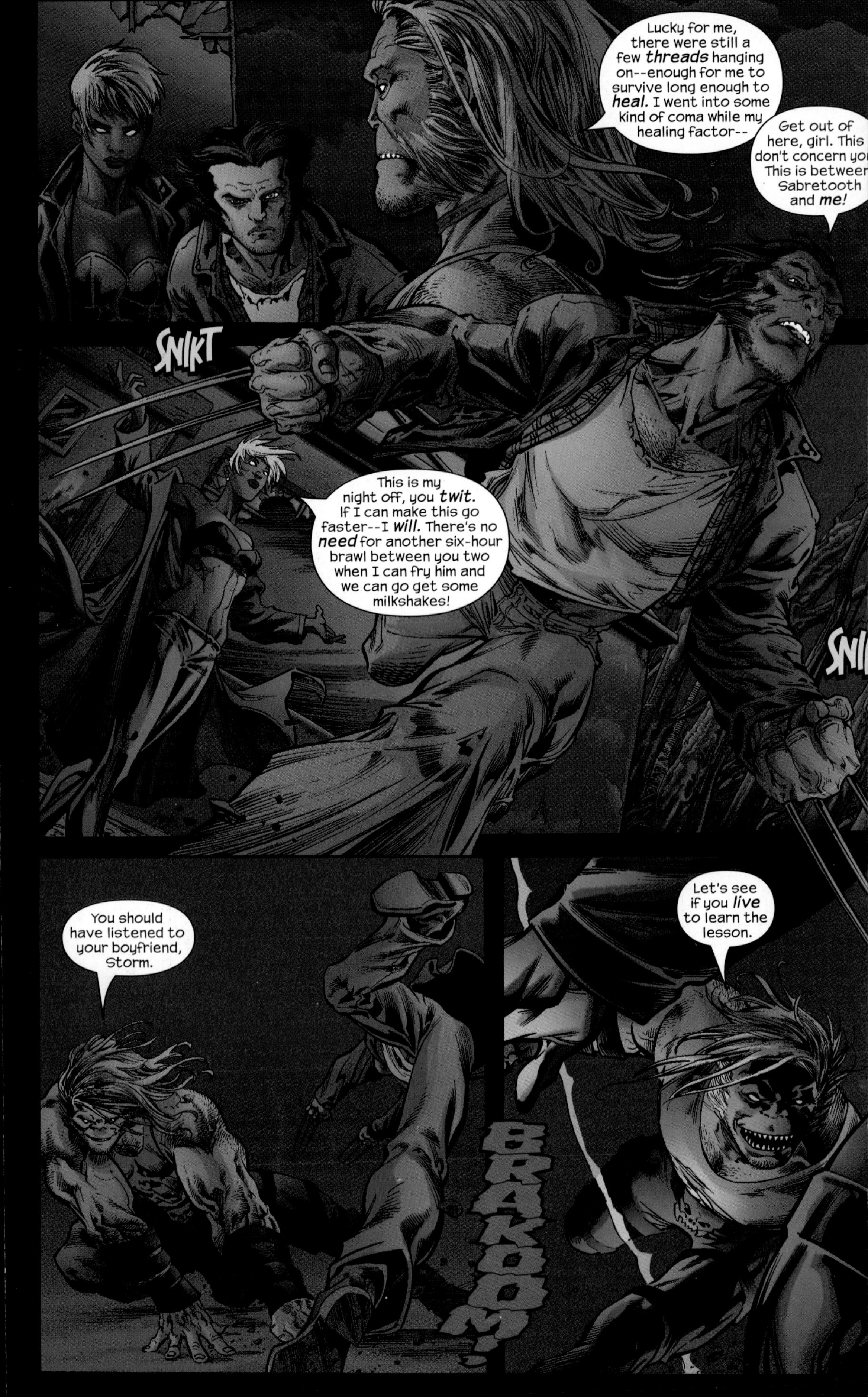
Lucky for me, there were still a few *threads* hanging on--enough for me to survive long enough to *heal.* I went into some kind of coma while my healing factor--
Get out of here, girl. This don't concern you. This is between Sabretooth and *me!*
SNIKT
This is my night off, you *twit.* If I can make this go faster--I *will.* There's no *need* for another six-hour brawl between you two when I can fry him and we can go get some milkshakes!
You should have listened to your boyfriend, Storm.
BRAKOOM
Let's see if you *live* to learn the lesson.

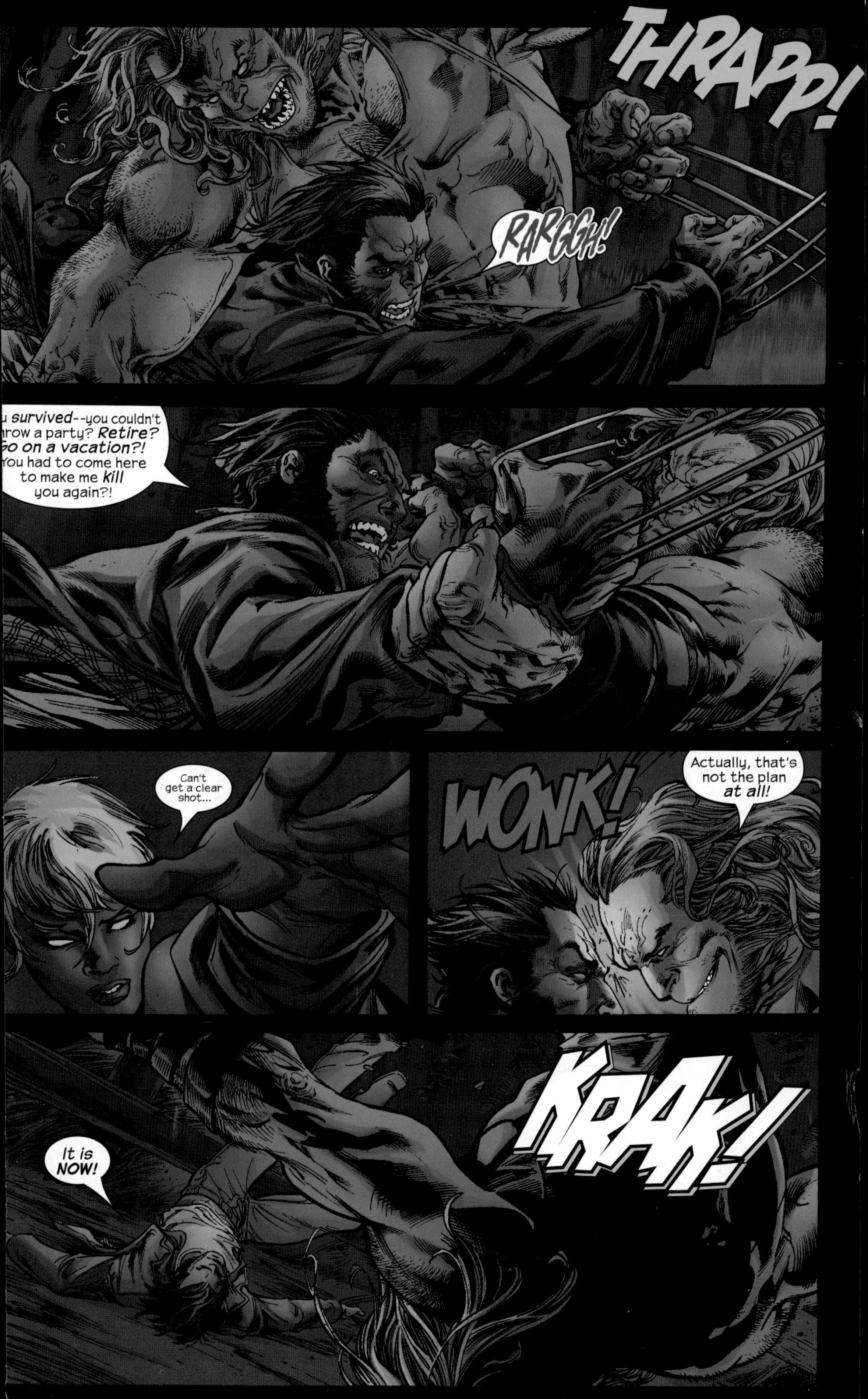
THRAPP!
RARGGH!
Go on a vacation?! You had to come here to make me kill you again?!
Can't get a clear shot...
WONK!
Actually, that's not the plan at all!
KRAK!
It is NOW!

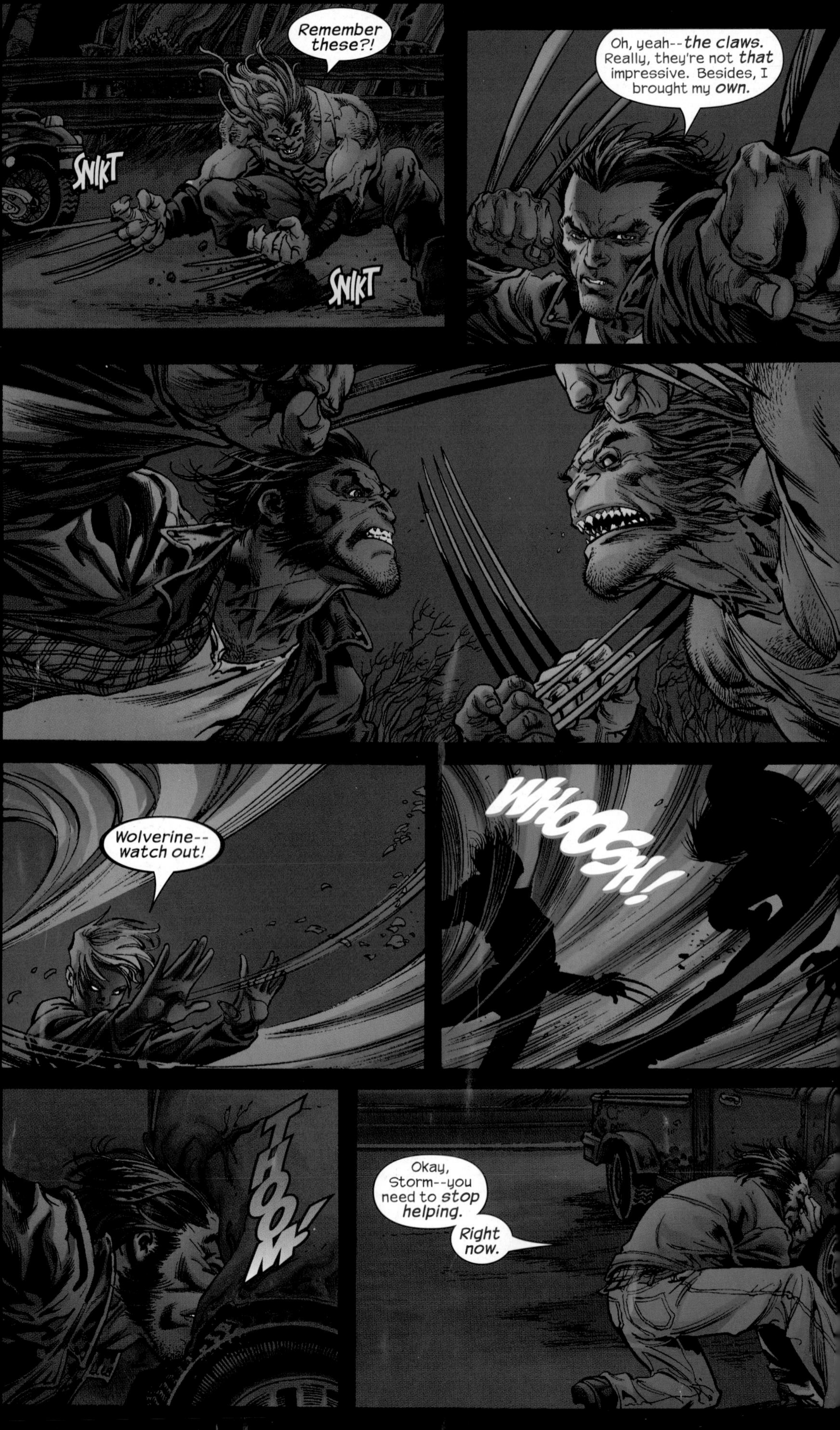
Remember these?!
SNIKT
SNIKT
Oh, yeah--the claws. Really, they're not that impressive. Besides, I brought my own.
Wolverine--watch out!
WHOOSH!
THOOM!
Okay, Storm--you need to stop helping.
Right now.

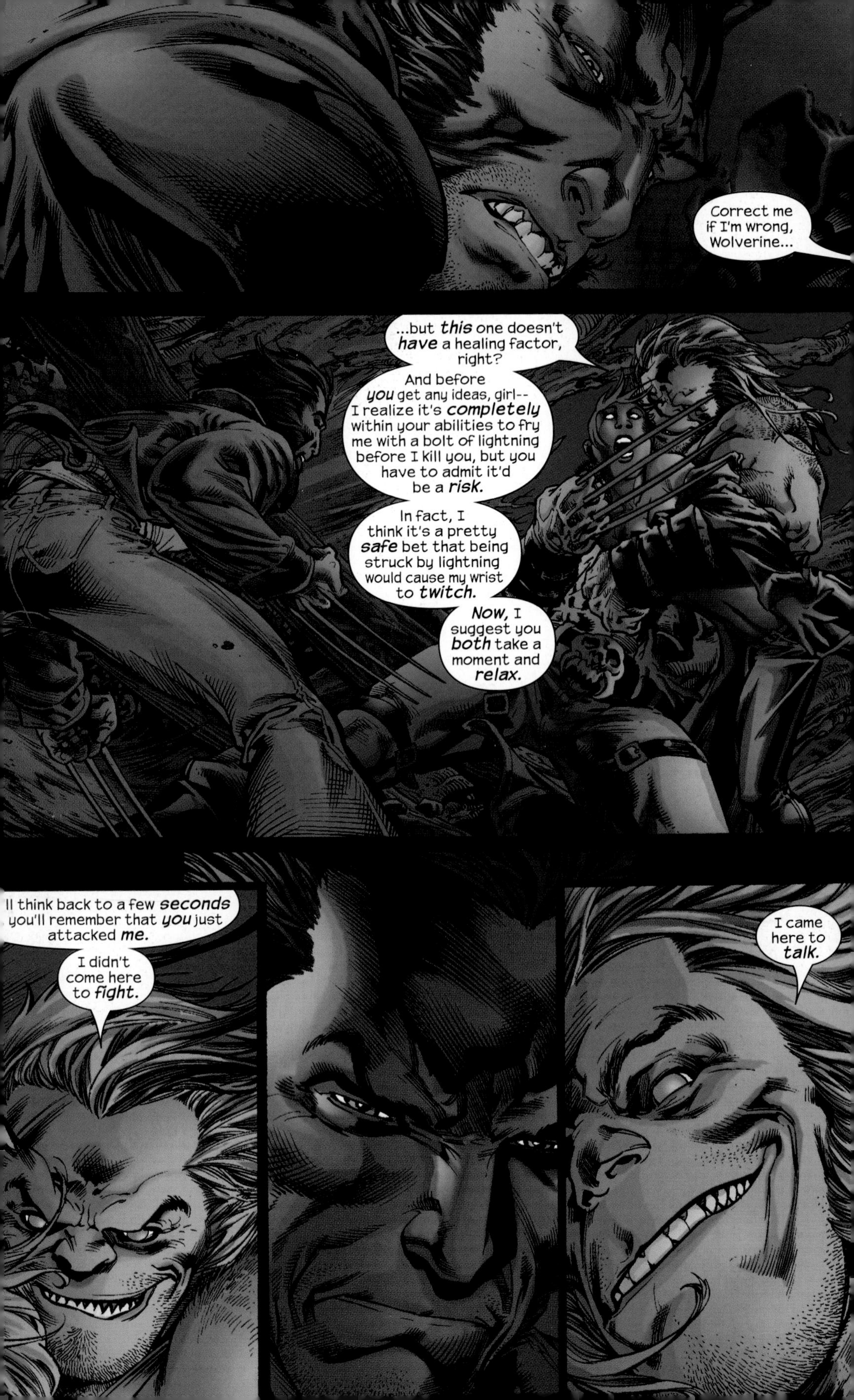
Correct me if I'm wrong, Wolverine...
...but *this* one doesn't *have* a healing factor, right?
And before *you* get any ideas, girl-- I realize it's *completely* within your abilities to fry me with a bolt of lightning before I kill you, but you have to admit it'd be a *risk.*
In fact, I think it's a pretty *safe* bet that being struck by lightning would cause my wrist to *twitch.*
Now, I suggest you *both* take a moment and *relax.*
ll think back to a few *seconds* you'll remember that *you* just attacked *me.*
I didn't come here to *fight.*
I came here to *talk.*

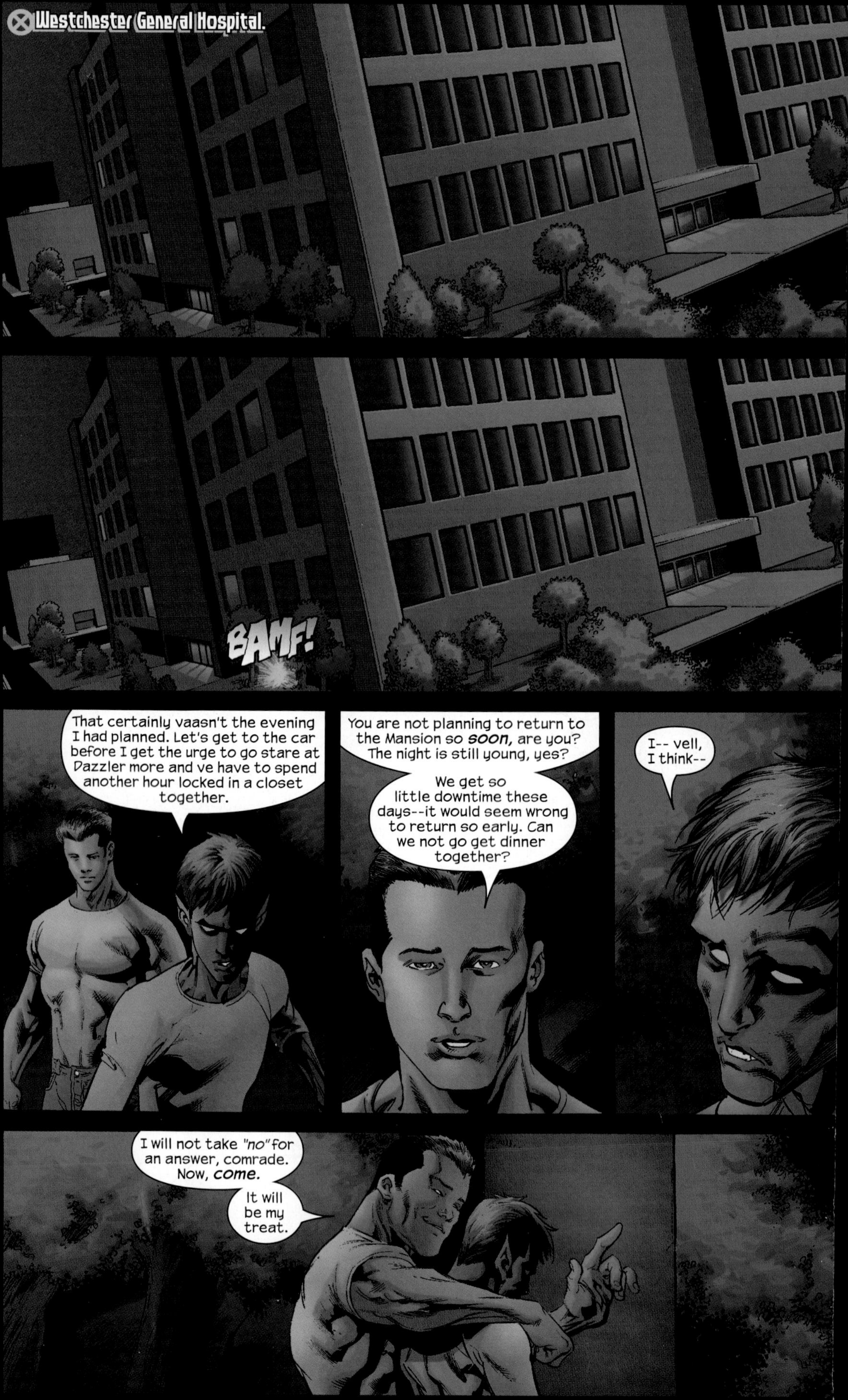
Westchester General Hospital.
BAMF!
That certainly vaasn't the evening I had planned. Let's get to the car before I get the urge to go stare at Dazzler more and ve have to spend another hour locked in a closet together.
You are not planning to return to the Mansion so *soon,* are you? The night is still young, yes?
We get so little downtime these days--it would seem wrong to return so early. Can we not go get dinner together?
I-- vell, I think--
I will not take *"no"* for an answer, comrade. Now, *come.*
It will be my treat.

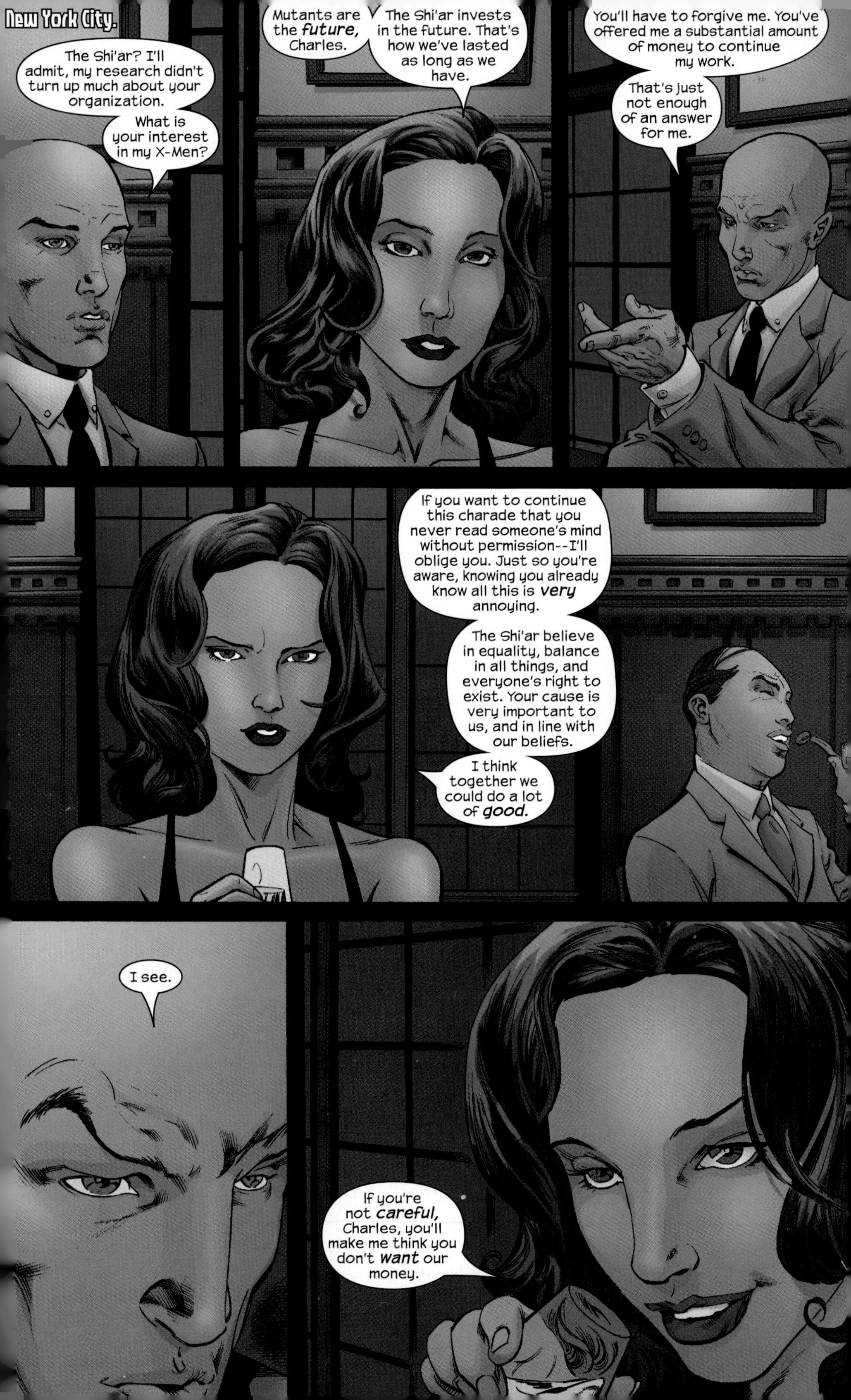
New York City.
The Shi'ar? I'll admit, my research didn't turn up much about your organization.
What is your interest in my X-Men?
Mutants are the *future,* Charles.
The Shi'ar invests in the future. That's how we've lasted as long as we have.
You'll have to forgive me. You've offered me a substantial amount of money to continue my work.
That's just not enough of an answer for me.
If you want to continue this charade that you never read someone's mind without permission--I'll oblige you. Just so you're aware, knowing you already know all this is *very* annoying.
The Shi'ar believe in equality, balance in all things, and everyone's right to exist. Your cause is very important to us, and in line with our beliefs.
I think together we could do a lot of *good.*
I see.
If you're not *careful,* Charles, you'll make me think you don't *want* our money.

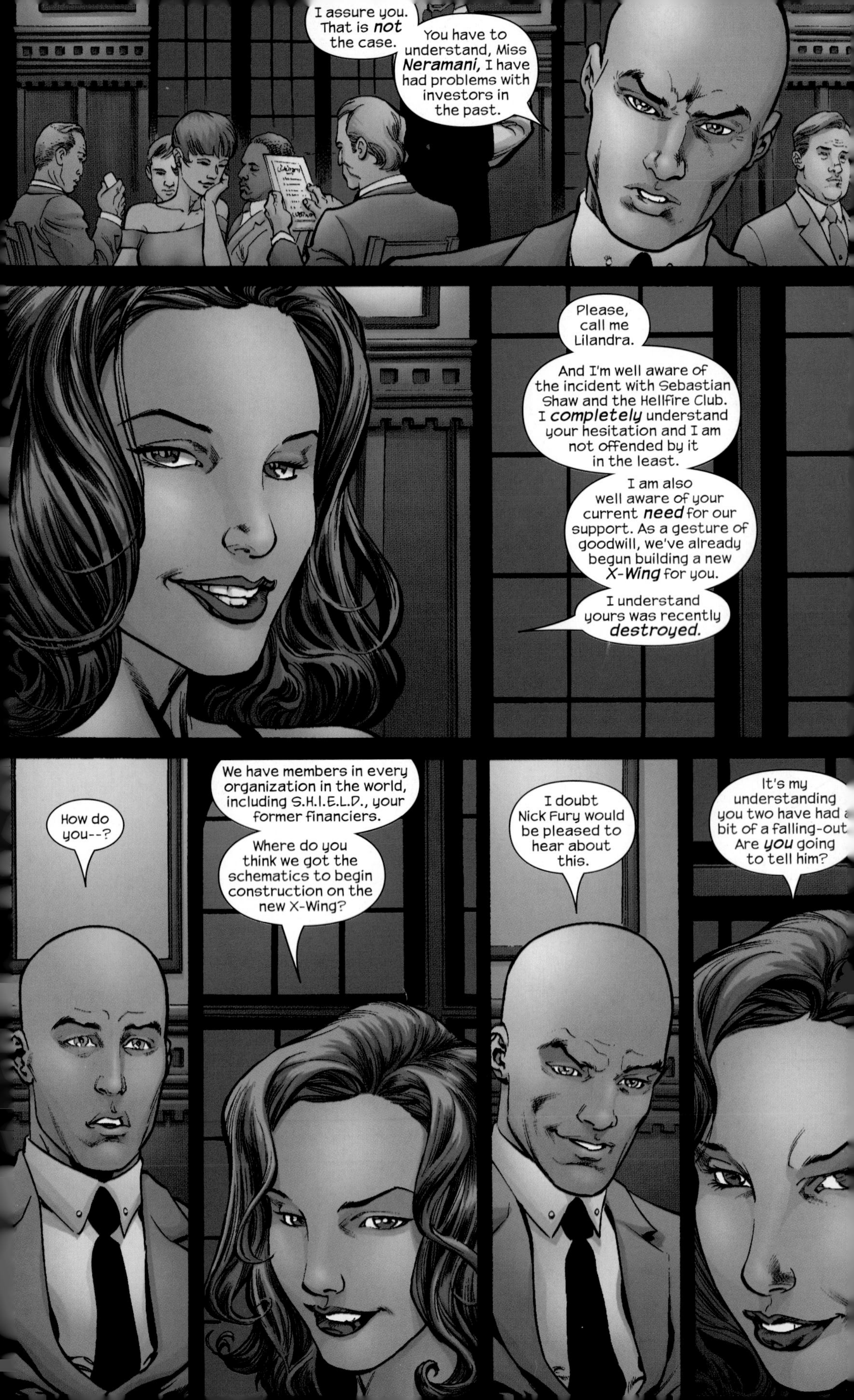
I assure you. That is *not* the case.
You have to understand, Miss *Neramani,* I have had problems with investors in the past.
Please, call me Lilandra.
And I'm well aware of the incident with Sebastian Shaw and the Hellfire Club. I *completely* understand your hesitation and I am not offended by it in the least.
I am also well aware of your current *need* for our support. As a gesture of goodwill, we've already begun building a new *X-Wing* for you.
I understand yours was recently *destroyed.*
How do you--?
We have members in every organization in the world, including S.H.I.E.L.D., your former financiers.
Where do you think we got the schematics to begin construction on the new X-Wing?
I doubt Nick Fury would be pleased to hear about this.
It's my understanding you two have had a bit of a falling-out. Are *you* going to tell him?

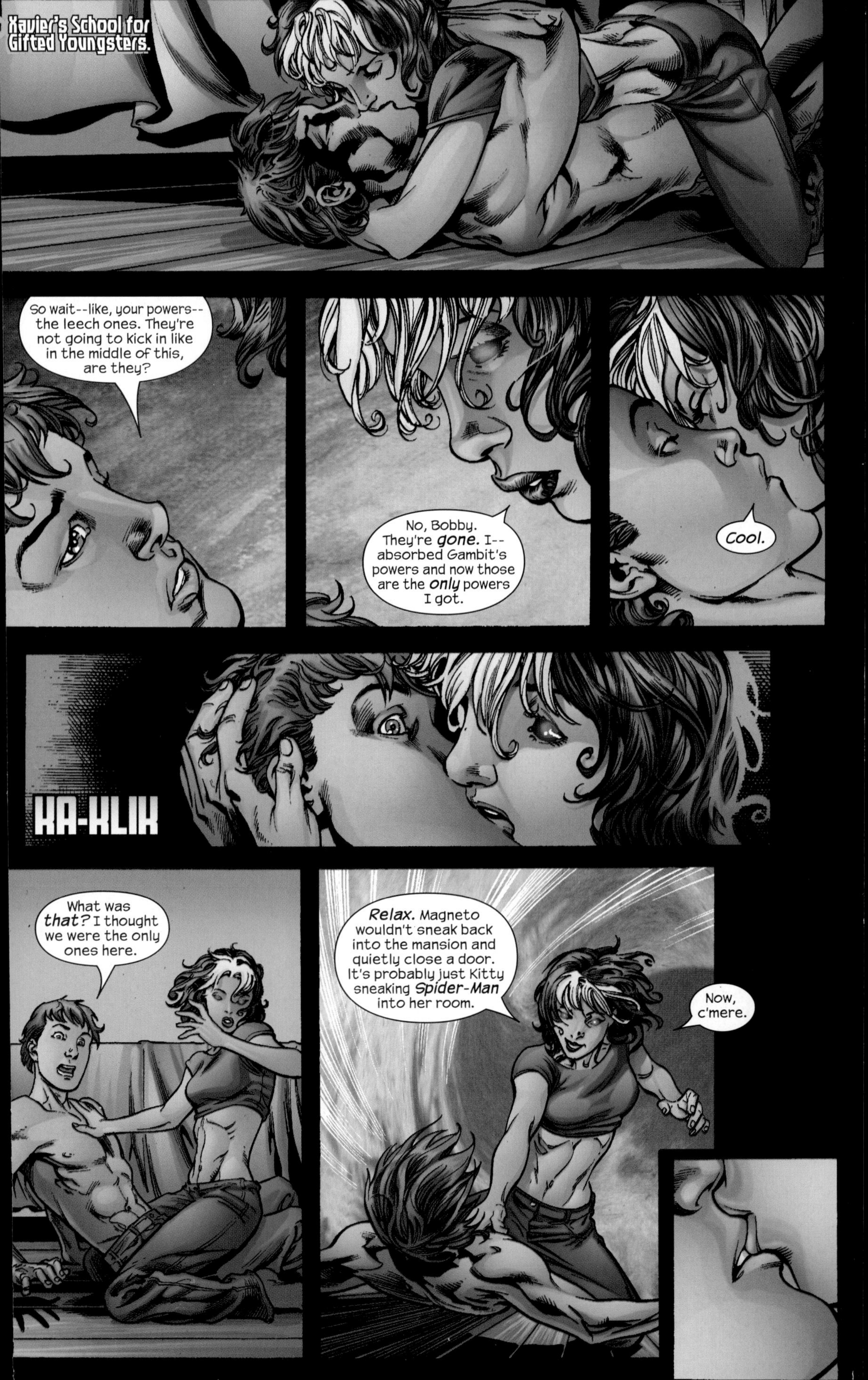
Xavier's School for Gifted Youngsters.
So wait--like, your powers-- the leech ones. They're not going to kick in like in the middle of this, are they?
No, Bobby. They're gone. I-- absorbed Gambit's powers and now those are the only powers I got.
Cool.
KA-KLIK
What was that? I thought we were the only ones here.
Relax. Magneto wouldn't sneak back into the mansion and quietly close a door. It's probably just Kitty sneaking Spider-Man into her room.
Now, c'mere.

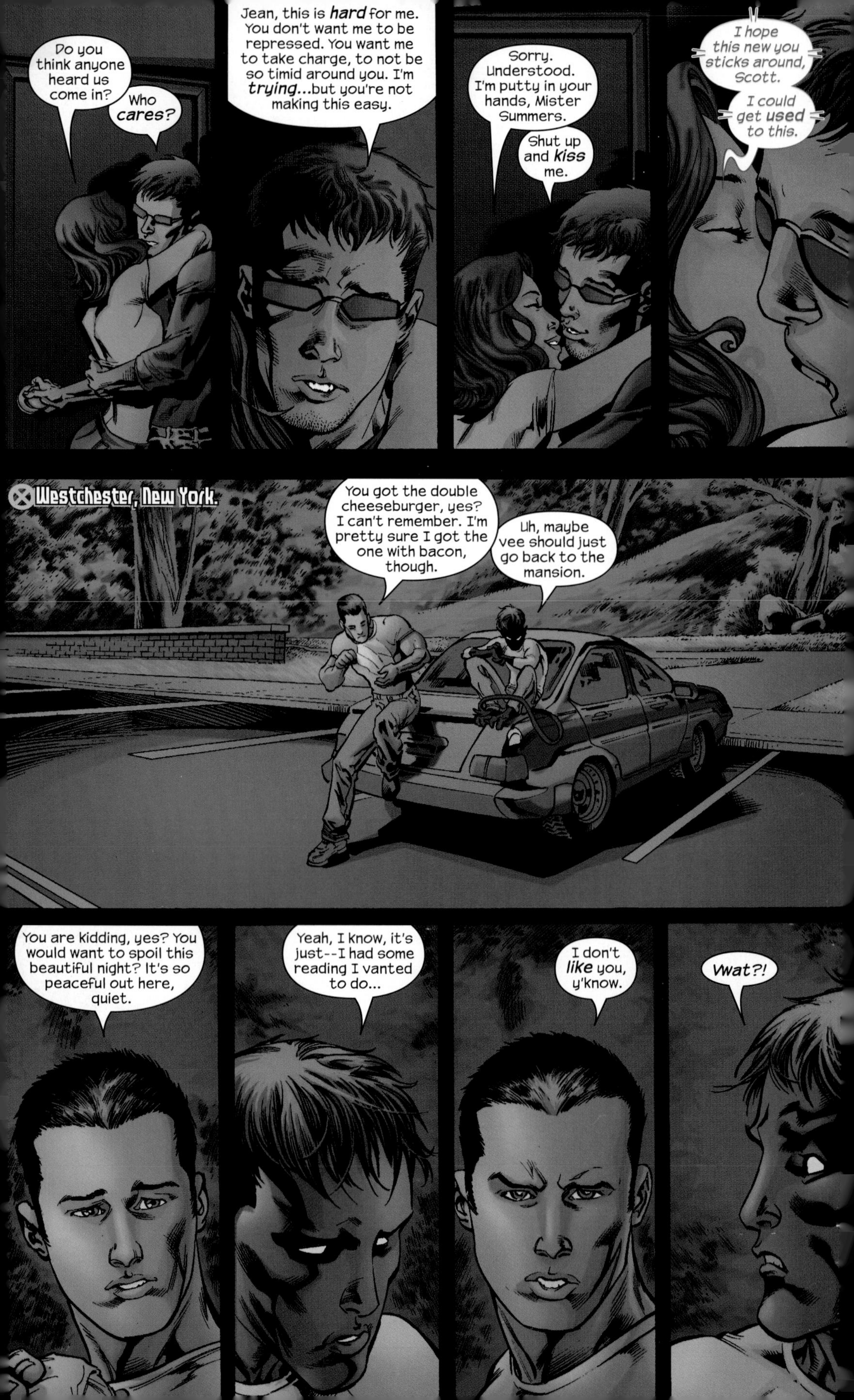
Do you think anyone heard us come in?
Who *cares?*
Jean, this is *hard* for me. You don't want me to be repressed. You want me to take charge, to not be so timid around you. I'm *trying*...but you're not making this easy.
Sorry. Understood. I'm putty in your hands, Mister Summers.
Shut up and *kiss* me.
I hope this new you sticks around, Scott.
I could get *used* to this.
Westchester, New York.
You got the double cheeseburger, yes? I can't remember. I'm pretty sure I got the one with bacon, though.
Uh, maybe vee should just go back to the mansion.
You are kidding, yes? You would want to spoil this beautiful night? It's so peaceful out here, quiet.
Yeah, I know, it's just--I had some reading I vanted to do...
I don't *like* you, y'know.
Vwat?!

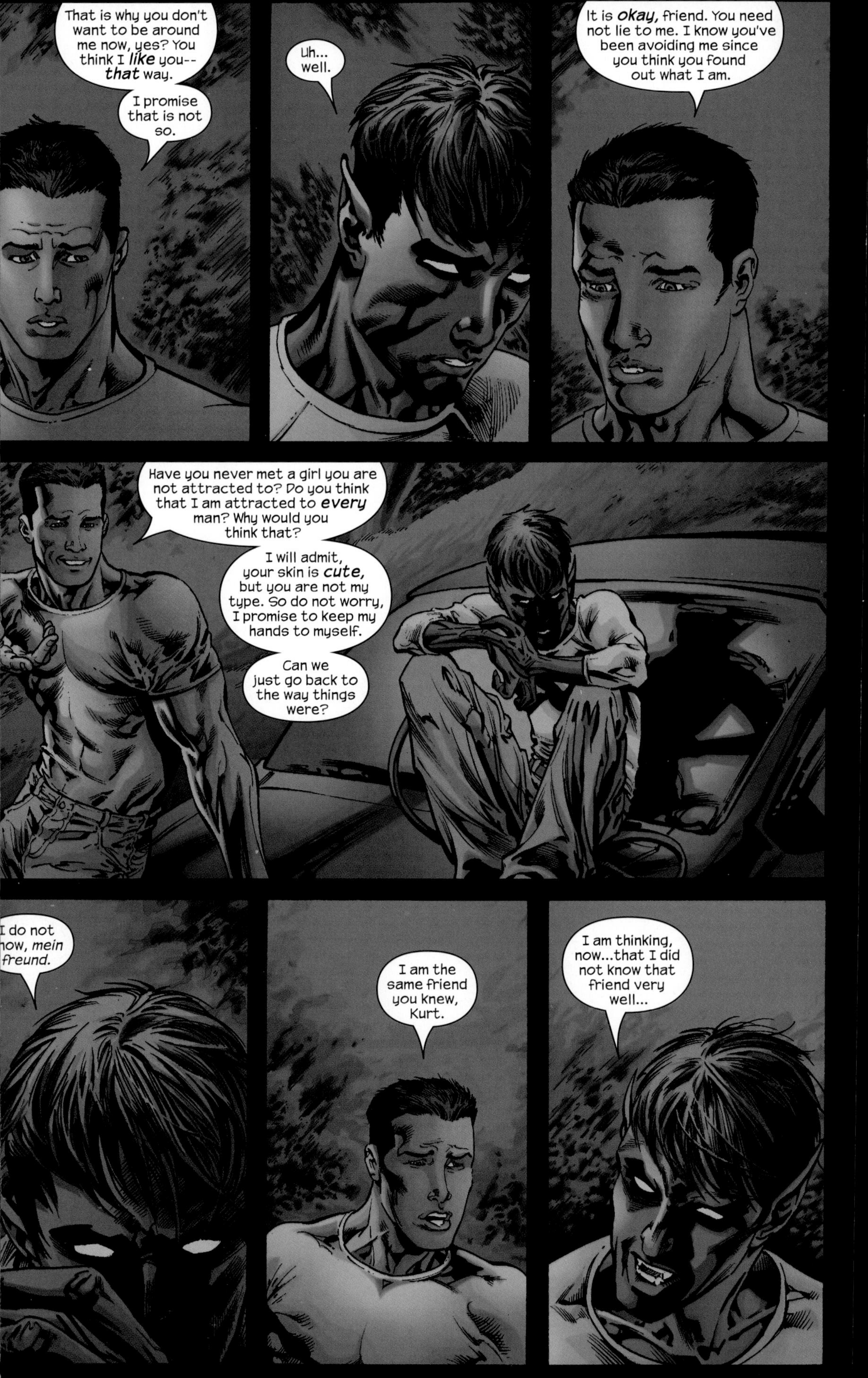
That is why you don't want to be around me now, yes? You think I *like* you-- *that* way.
I promise that is not so.
Uh... well.
It is *okay,* friend. You need not lie to me. I know you've been avoiding me since you think you found out what I am.
Have you never met a girl you are not attracted to? Do you think that I am attracted to *every* man? Why would you think that?
I will admit, your skin is *cute,* but you are not my type. So do not worry, I promise to keep my hands to myself.
Can we just go back to the way things were?
I do not ...ow, *mein freund.*
I am the same friend you knew, Kurt.
I am thinking, now...that I did not know that friend very well...

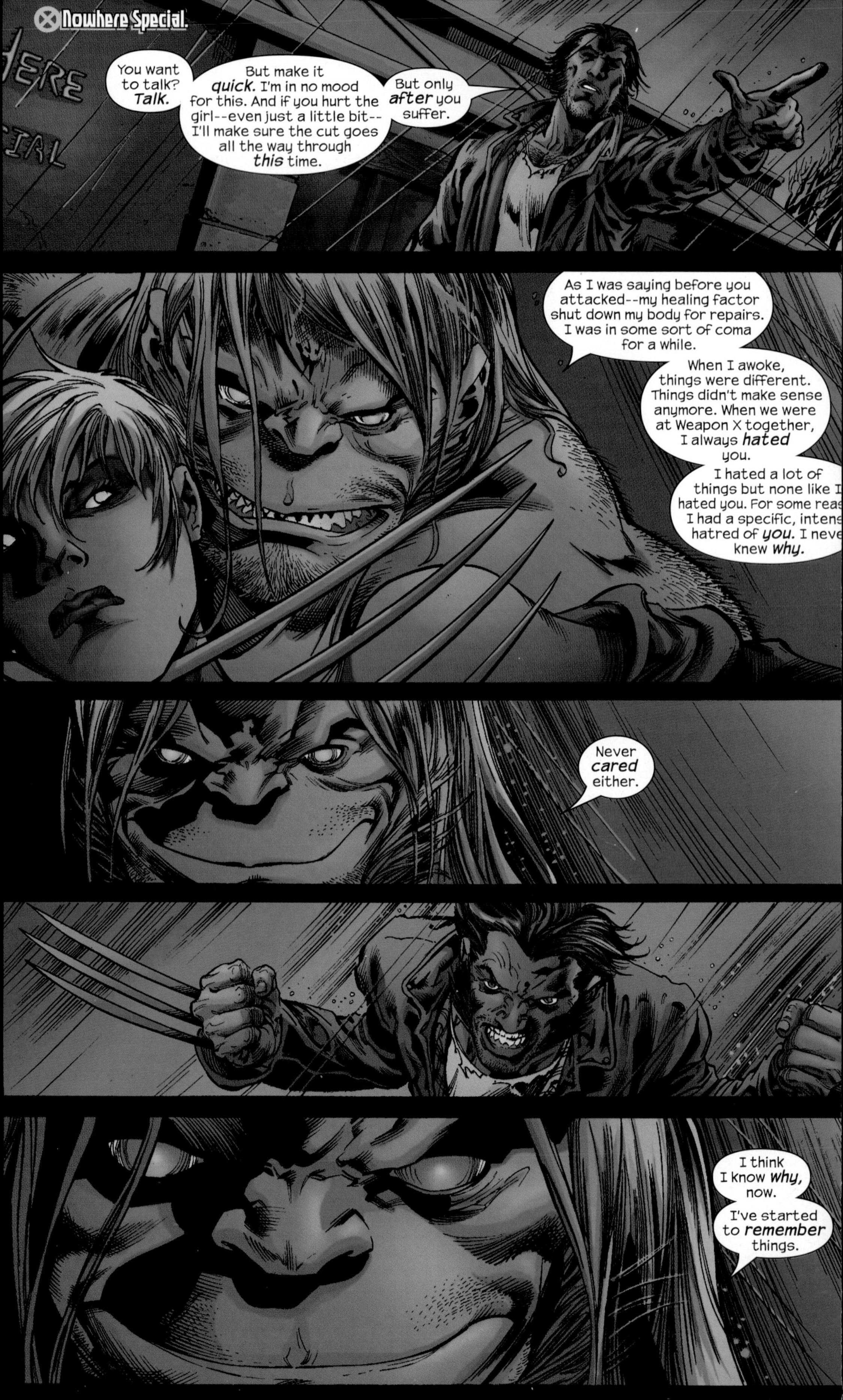
Nowhere Special.
You want to talk? Talk.
But make it quick. I'm in no mood for this. And if you hurt the girl--even just a little bit--I'll make sure the cut goes all the way through this time.
But only after you suffer.
As I was saying before you attacked--my healing factor shut down my body for repairs. I was in some sort of coma for a while.
When I awoke, things were different. Things didn't make sense anymore. When we were at Weapon X together, I always hated you.
I hated a lot of things but none like I hated you. For some reas I had a specific, intens hatred of you. I neve knew why.
Never cared either.
I think I know why, now.
I've started to remember things.

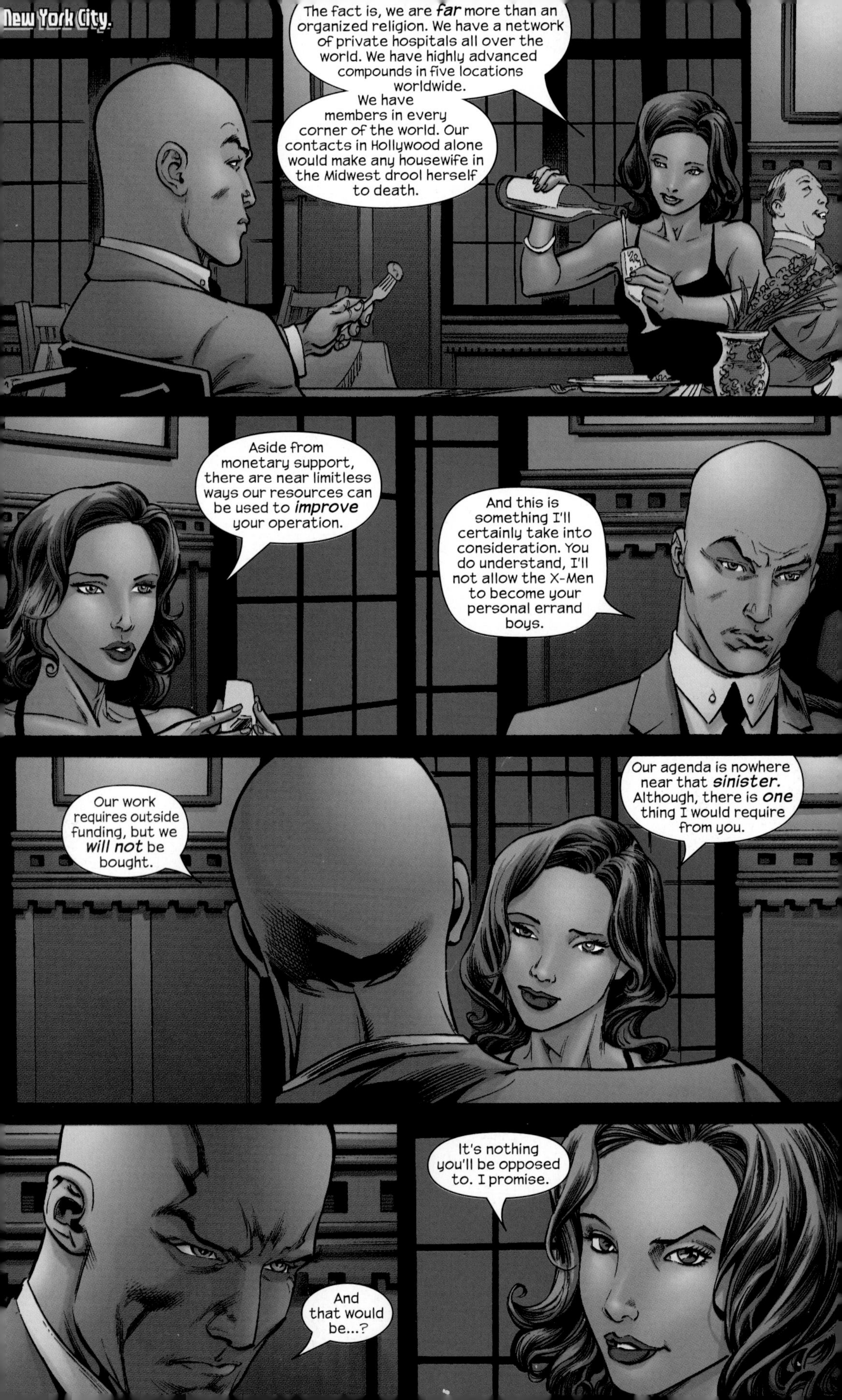
New York City.
The fact is, we are *far* more than an organized religion. We have a network of private hospitals all over the world. We have highly advanced compounds in five locations worldwide.
We have members in every corner of the world. Our contacts in Hollywood alone would make any housewife in the Midwest drool herself to death.
Aside from monetary support, there are near limitless ways our resources can be used to *improve* your operation.
And this is something I'll certainly take into consideration. You do understand, I'll not allow the X-Men to become your personal errand boys.
Our work requires outside funding, but we *will not* be bought.
Our agenda is nowhere near that *sinister.* Although, there is *one* thing I would require from you.
It's nothing you'll be opposed to. I promise.
And that would be...?

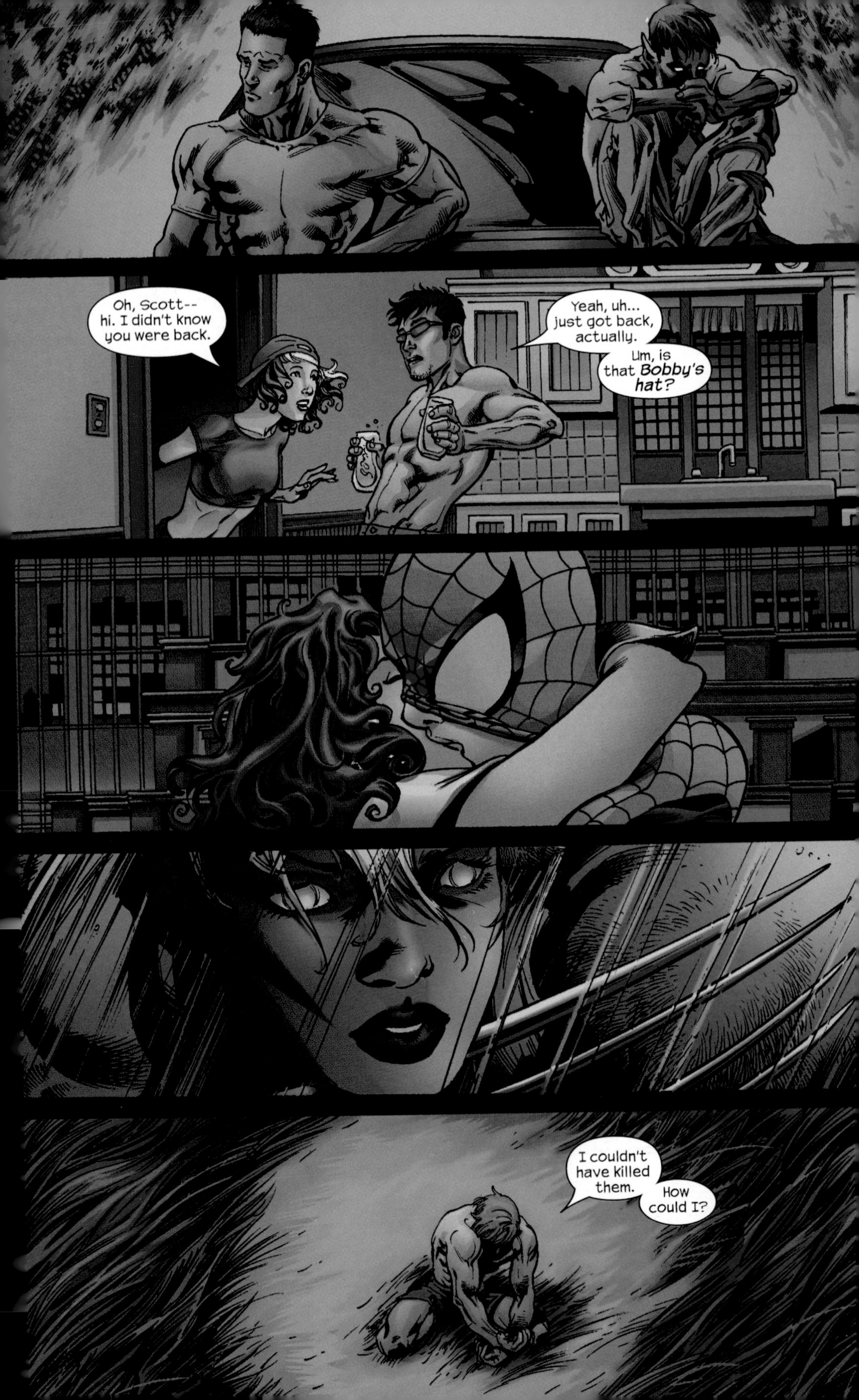
Oh, Scott--
hi. I didn't know
you were back.
Yeah, uh...
just got back,
actually.
Um, is
that *Bobby's*
hat?
I couldn't
have killed
them.
How
could I?

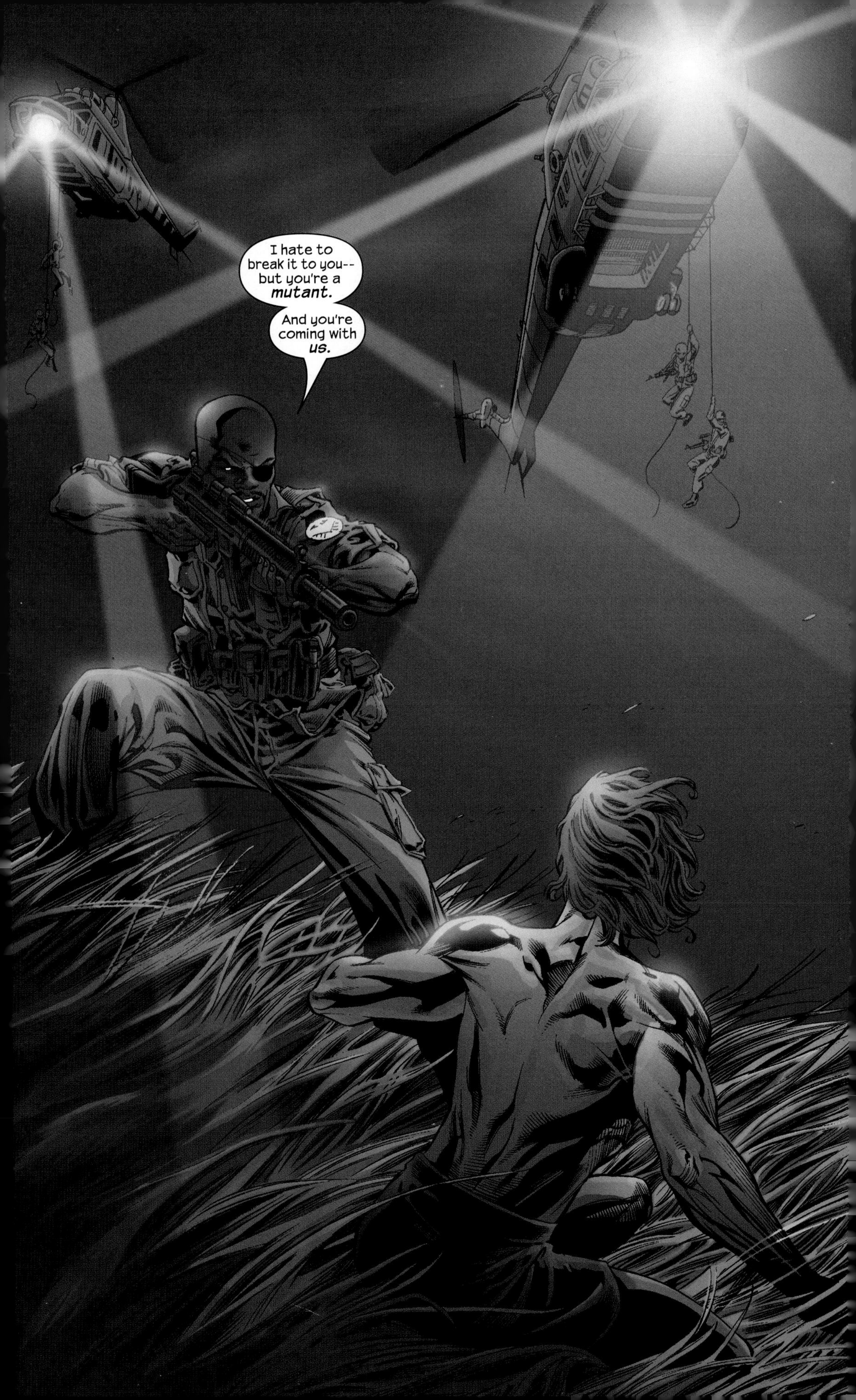
I hate to break it to you-- but you're a *mutant.*
And you're coming with *us.*

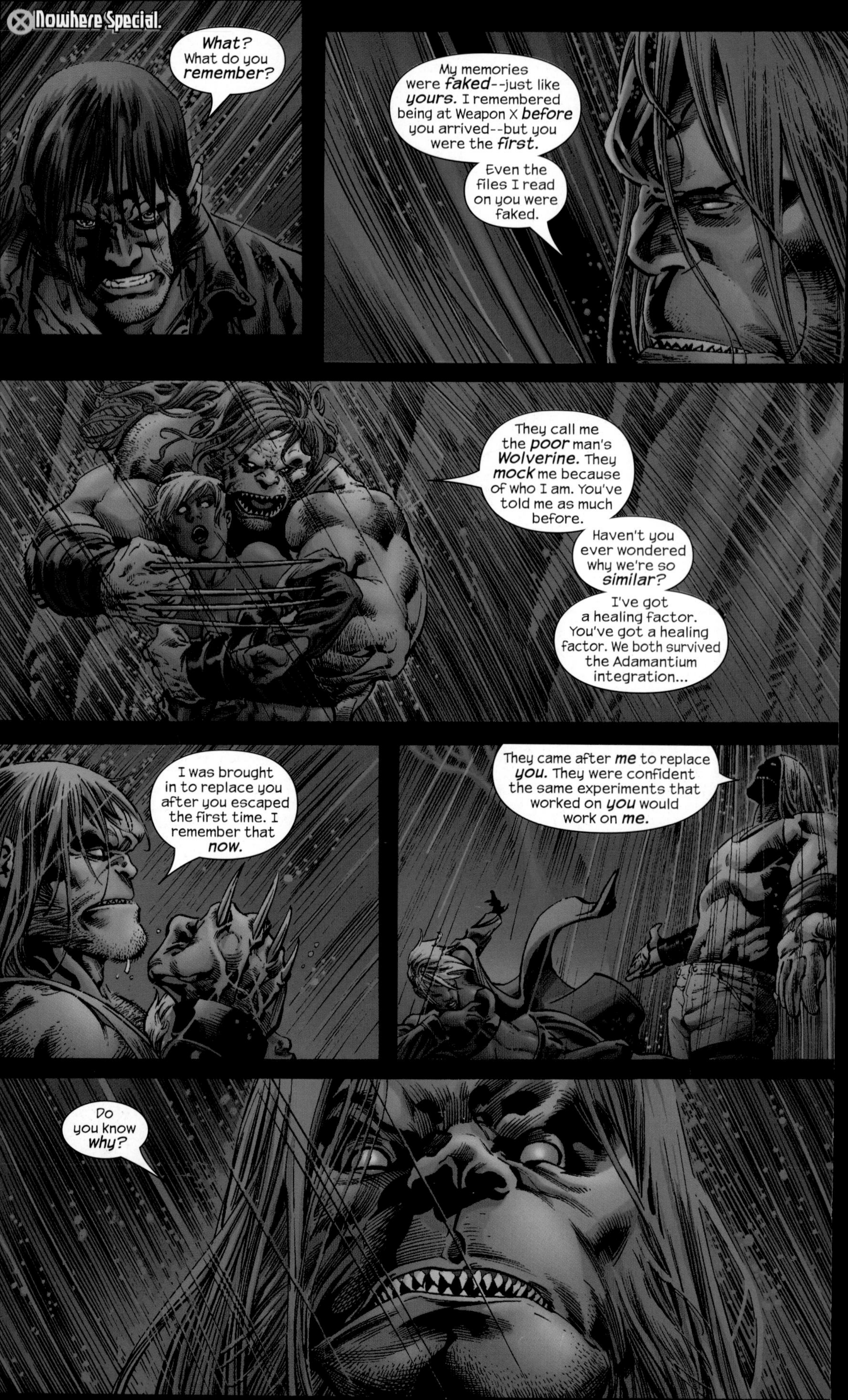
What? What do you remember?
My memories were faked--just like yours. I remembered being at Weapon X before you arrived--but you were the first.
Even the files I read on you were faked.
They call me the poor man's Wolverine. They mock me because of who I am. You've told me as much before.
Haven't you ever wondered why we're so similar?
I've got a healing factor. You've got a healing factor. We both survived the Adamantium integration...
I was brought in to replace you after you escaped the first time. I remember that now.
They came after me to replace you. They were confident the same experiments that worked on you would work on me.
Do you know why?

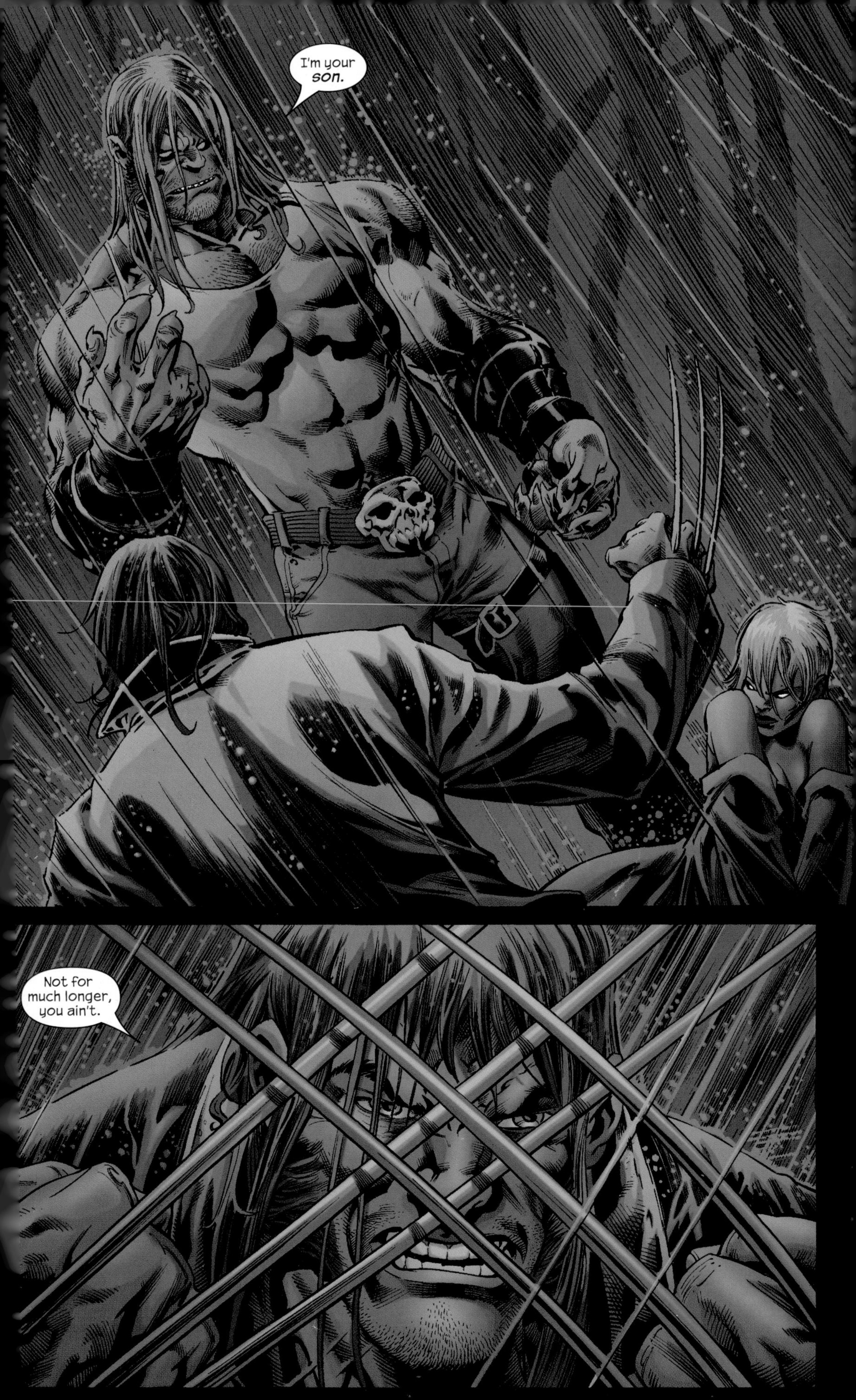
I'm your son.
Not for much longer, you ain't.

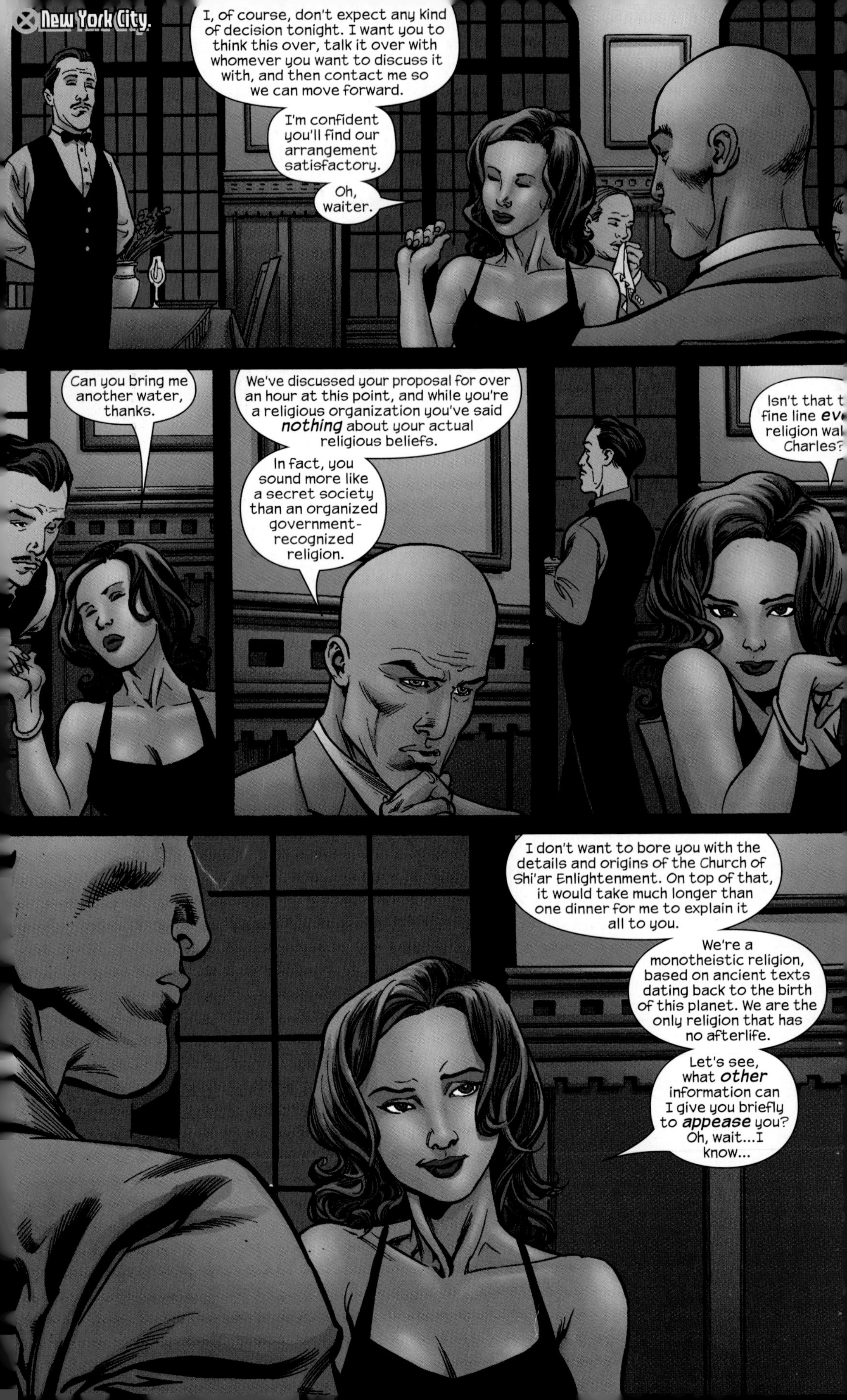
New York City.
I, of course, don't expect any kind of decision tonight. I want you to think this over, talk it over with whomever you want to discuss it with, and then contact me so we can move forward.
I'm confident you'll find our arrangement satisfactory.
Oh, waiter.
Can you bring me another water, thanks.
We've discussed your proposal for over an hour at this point, and while you're a religious organization you've said *nothing* about your actual religious beliefs.
In fact, you sound more like a secret society than an organized government-recognized religion.
Isn't that t fine line **ev** religion wal Charles?
I don't want to bore you with the details and origins of the Church of Shi'ar Enlightenment. On top of that, it would take much longer than one dinner for me to explain it all to you.
We're a monotheistic religion, based on ancient texts dating back to the birth of this planet. We are the only religion that has no afterlife.
Let's see, what ***other*** information can I give you briefly to ***appease*** you? Oh, wait...I know...

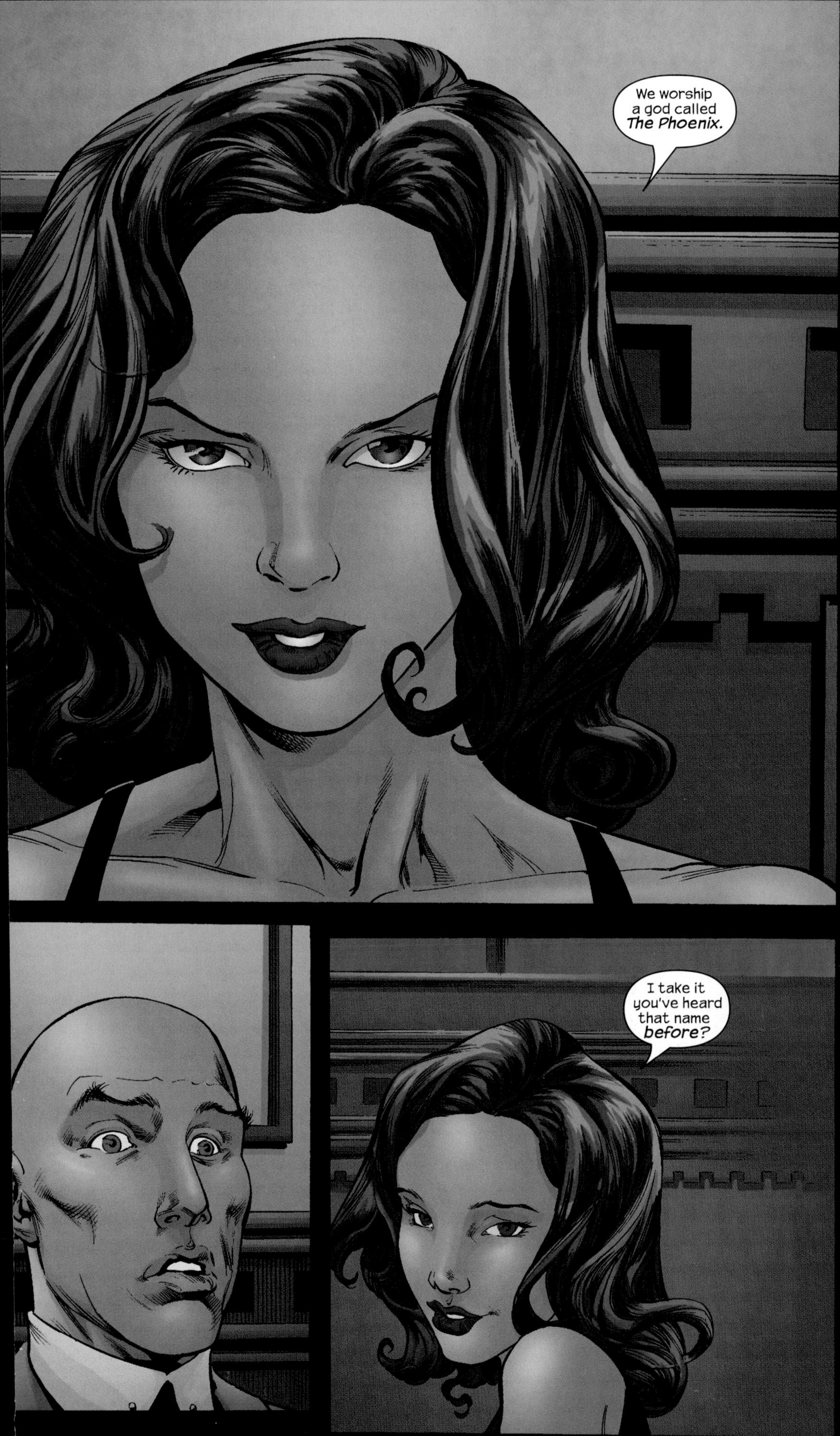
We worship a god called *The Phoenix.*
I take it you've heard that name *before?*

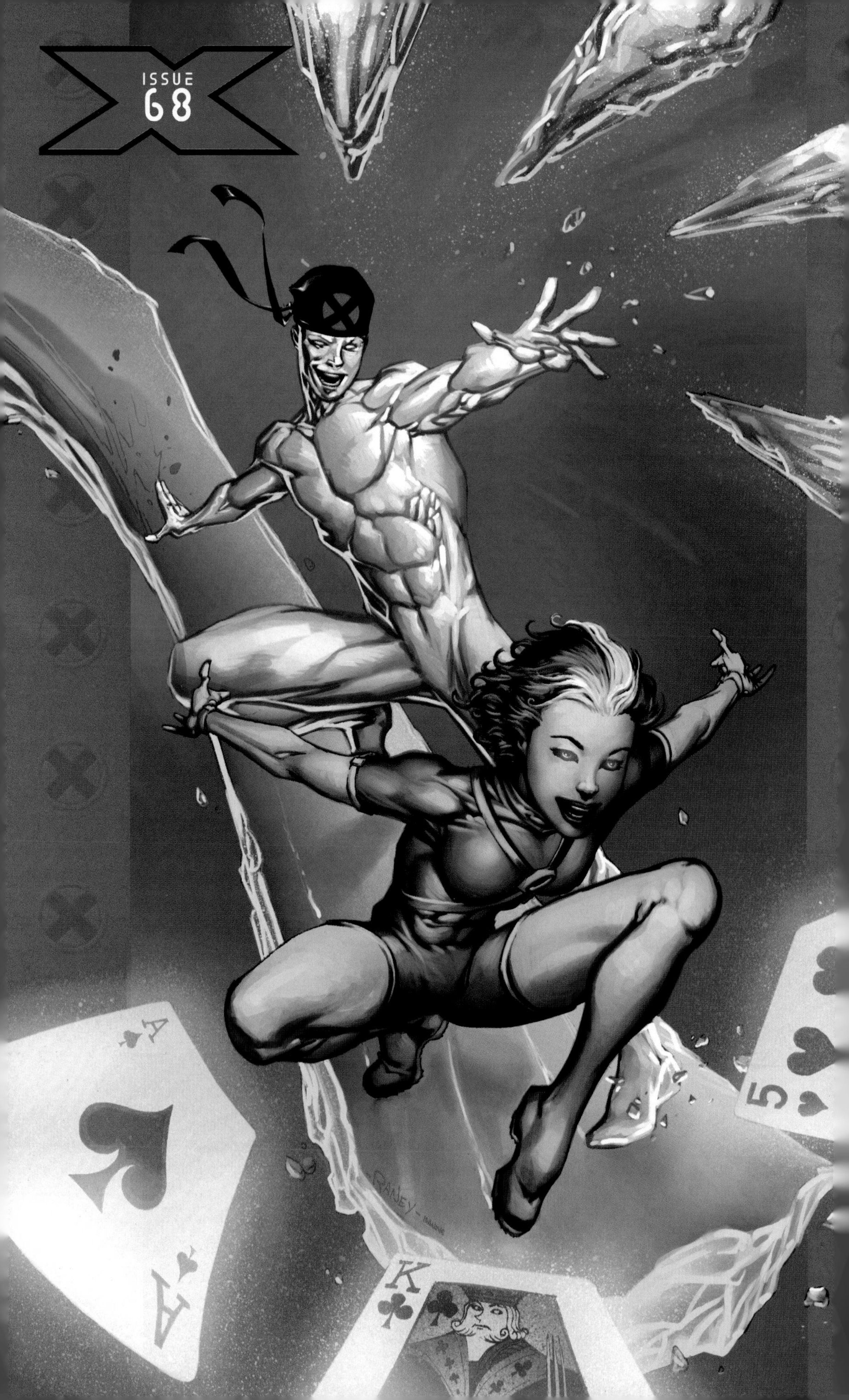
ISSUE
68

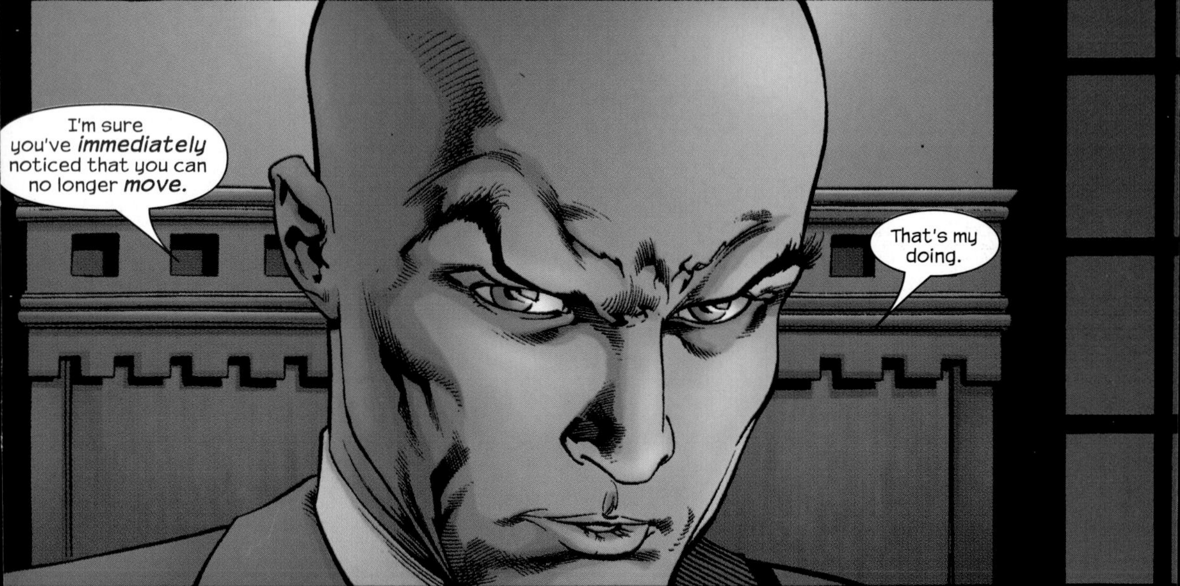
I'm sure you've *immediately* noticed that you can no longer *move.*
That's my doing.

DATE NIGHT

PART 3 OF 3

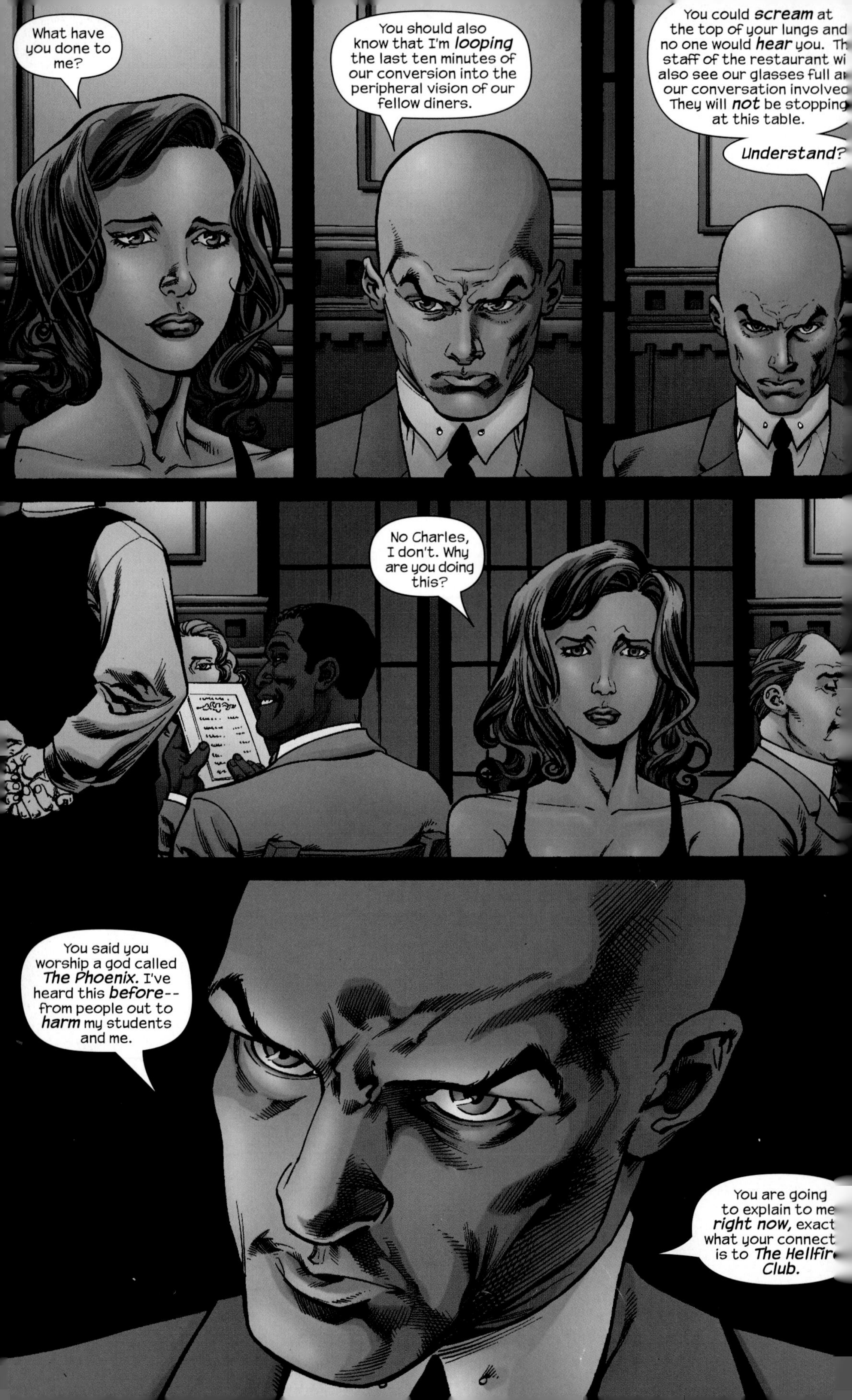
What have you done to me?
You should also know that I'm *looping* the last ten minutes of our conversion into the peripheral vision of our fellow diners.
You could *scream* at the top of your lungs and no one would *hear* you. Th staff of the restaurant wi also see our glasses full a our conversation involved They will *not* be stopping at this table.
Understand?
No Charles, I don't. Why are you doing this?
You said you worship a god called *The Phoenix.* I've heard this *before*-- from people out to *harm* my students and me.
You are going to explain to me *right now,* exact what your connect is to *The Hellfir Club.*

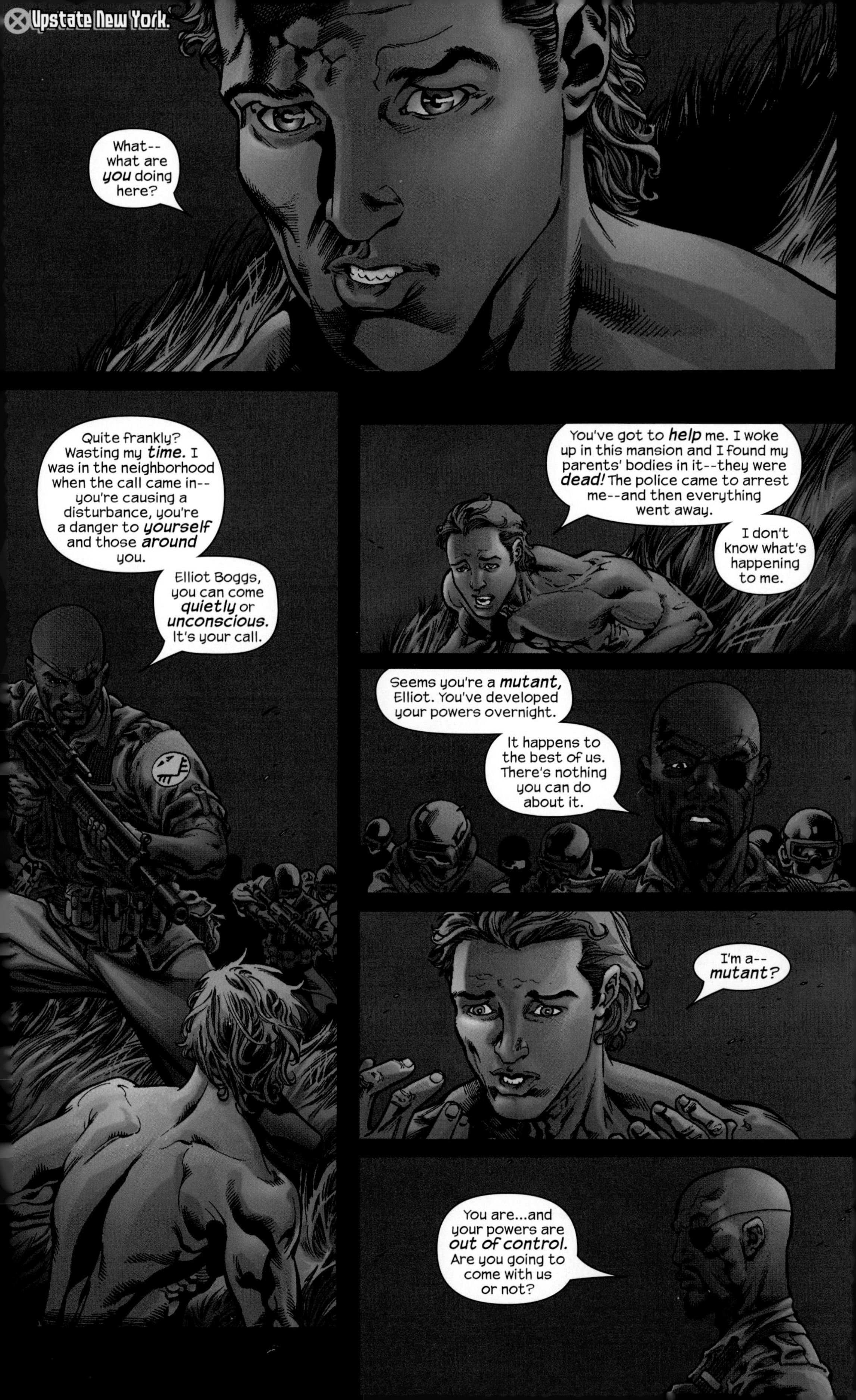
Upstate New York.
What--what are you doing here?
Quite frankly? Wasting my time. I was in the neighborhood when the call came in--you're causing a disturbance, you're a danger to yourself and those around you.
Elliot Boggs, you can come quietly or unconscious. It's your call.
You've got to help me. I woke up in this mansion and I found my parents' bodies in it--they were dead! The police came to arrest me--and then everything went away.
I don't know what's happening to me.
Seems you're a mutant, Elliot. You've developed your powers overnight.
It happens to the best of us. There's nothing you can do about it.
I'm a--mutant?
You are...and your powers are out of control. Are you going to come with us or not?

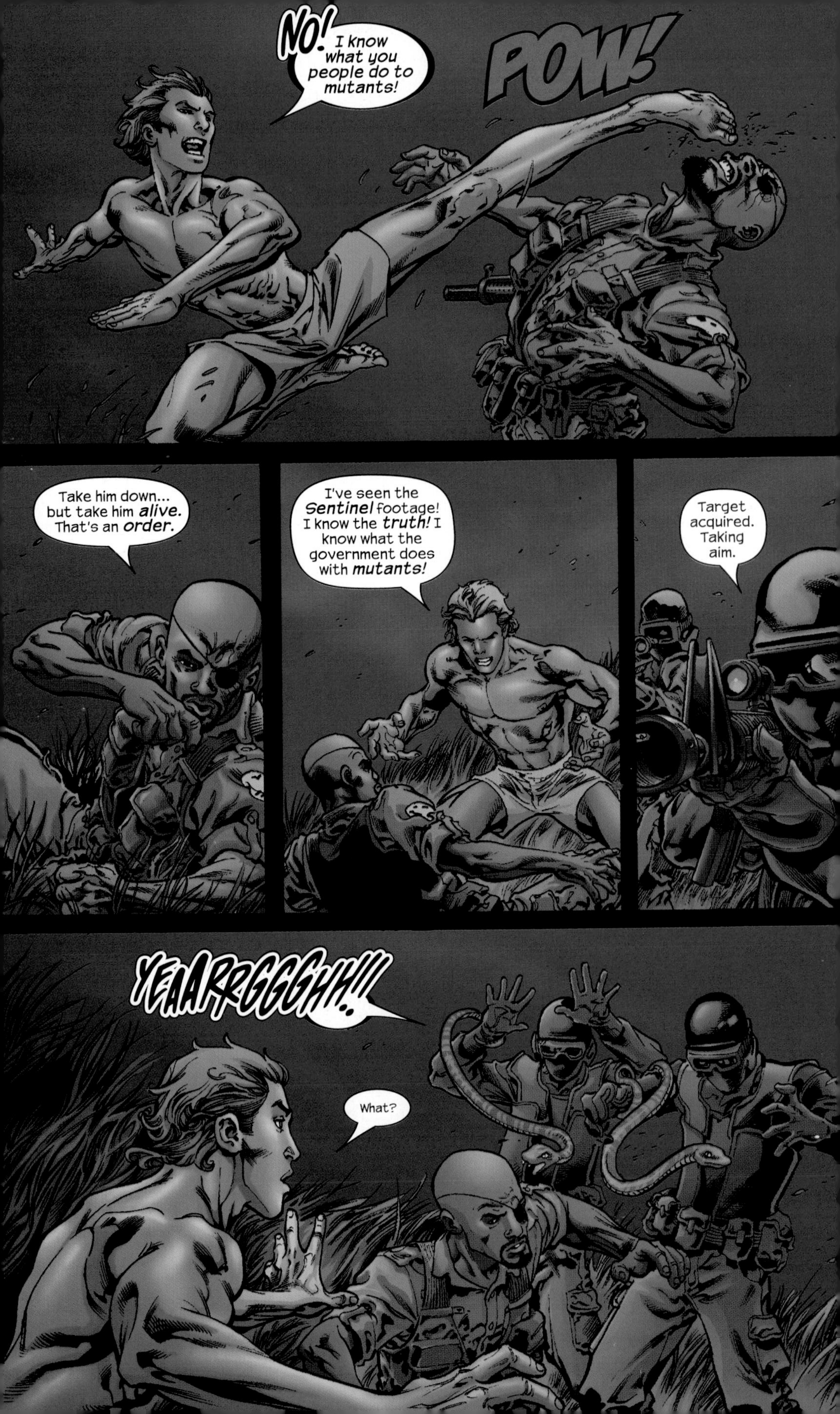
NO! I know what you people do to mutants!
POW!
Take him down... but take him alive. That's an order.
I've seen the Sentinel footage! I know the truth! I know what the government does with mutants!
Target acquired. Taking aim.
YEAARRGGGHH!!!
What?

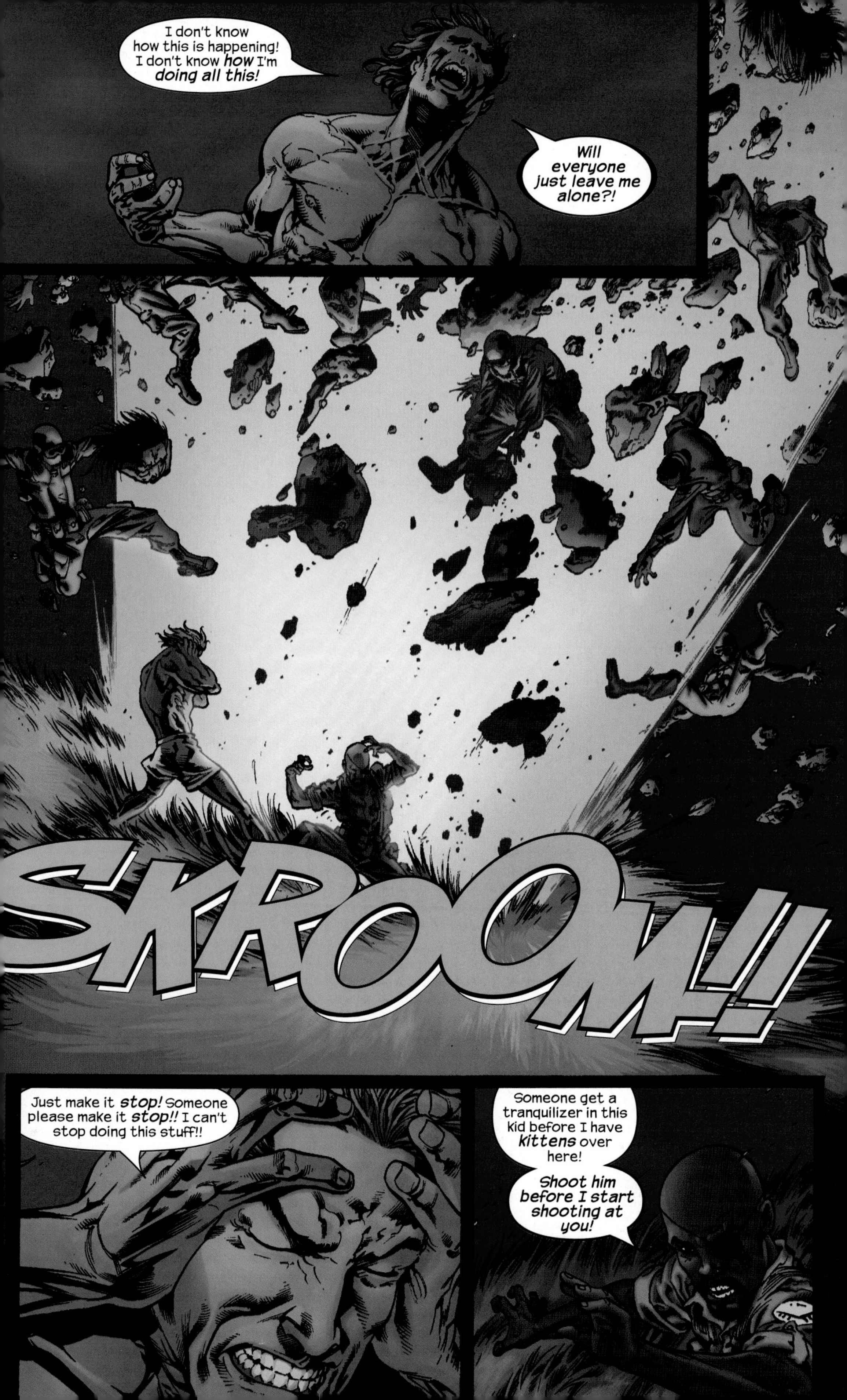
I don't know how this is happening! I don't know *how* I'm *doing all this!*
Will everyone just leave me alone?!
SKROOM!!
Just make it *stop!* Someone please make it *stop!!* I can't stop doing this stuff!!
Someone get a tranquilizer in this kid before I have *kittens* over here!
Shoot him before I start shooting at you!

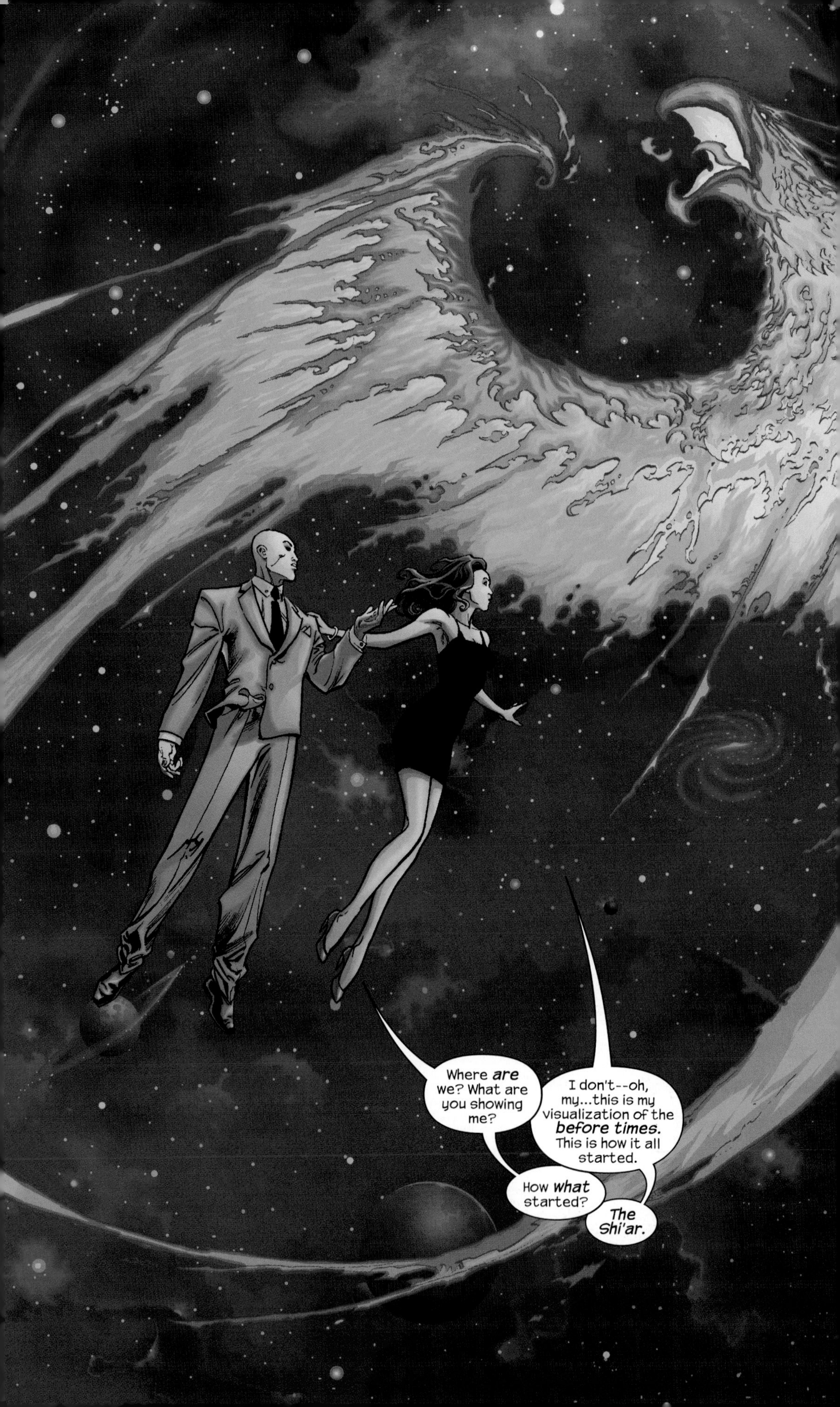
Where *are* we? What are you showing me?
I don't--oh, my...this is my visualization of the *before times.* This is how it all started.
How *what* started?
The Shi'ar.

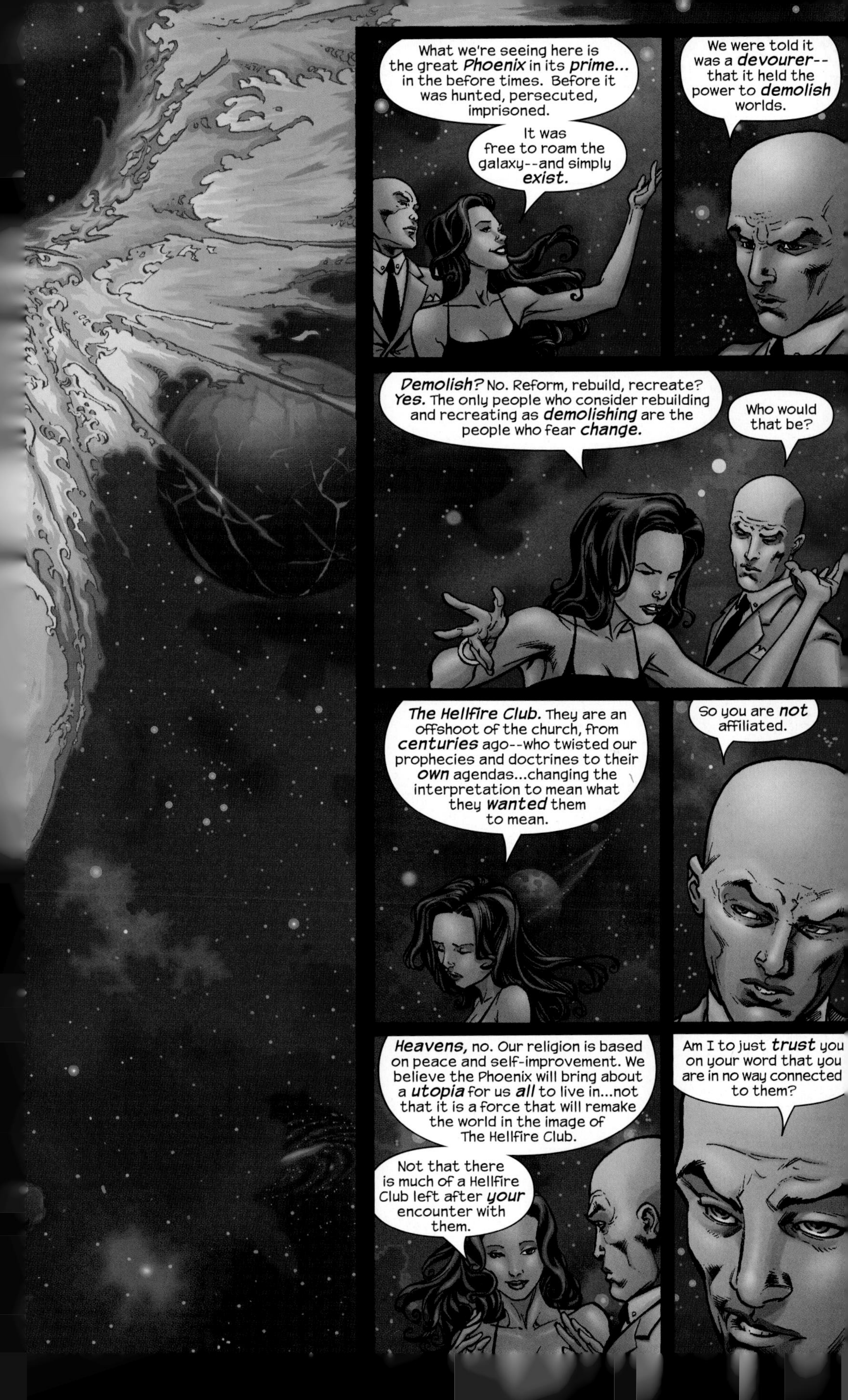
What we're seeing here is the great Phoenix in its prime... in the before times. Before it was hunted, persecuted, imprisoned.
It was free to roam the galaxy--and simply exist.
We were told it was a devourer--that it held the power to demolish worlds.
Demolish? No. Reform, rebuild, recreate? Yes. The only people who consider rebuilding and recreating as demolishing are the people who fear change.
Who would that be?
The Hellfire Club. They are an offshoot of the church, from centuries ago--who twisted our prophecies and doctrines to their own agendas...changing the interpretation to mean what they wanted them to mean.
So you are not affiliated.
Heavens, no. Our religion is based on peace and self-improvement. We believe the Phoenix will bring about a utopia for us all to live in...not that it is a force that will remake the world in the image of The Hellfire Club.
Not that there is much of a Hellfire Club left after your encounter with them.
Am I to just trust you on your word that you are in no way connected to them?

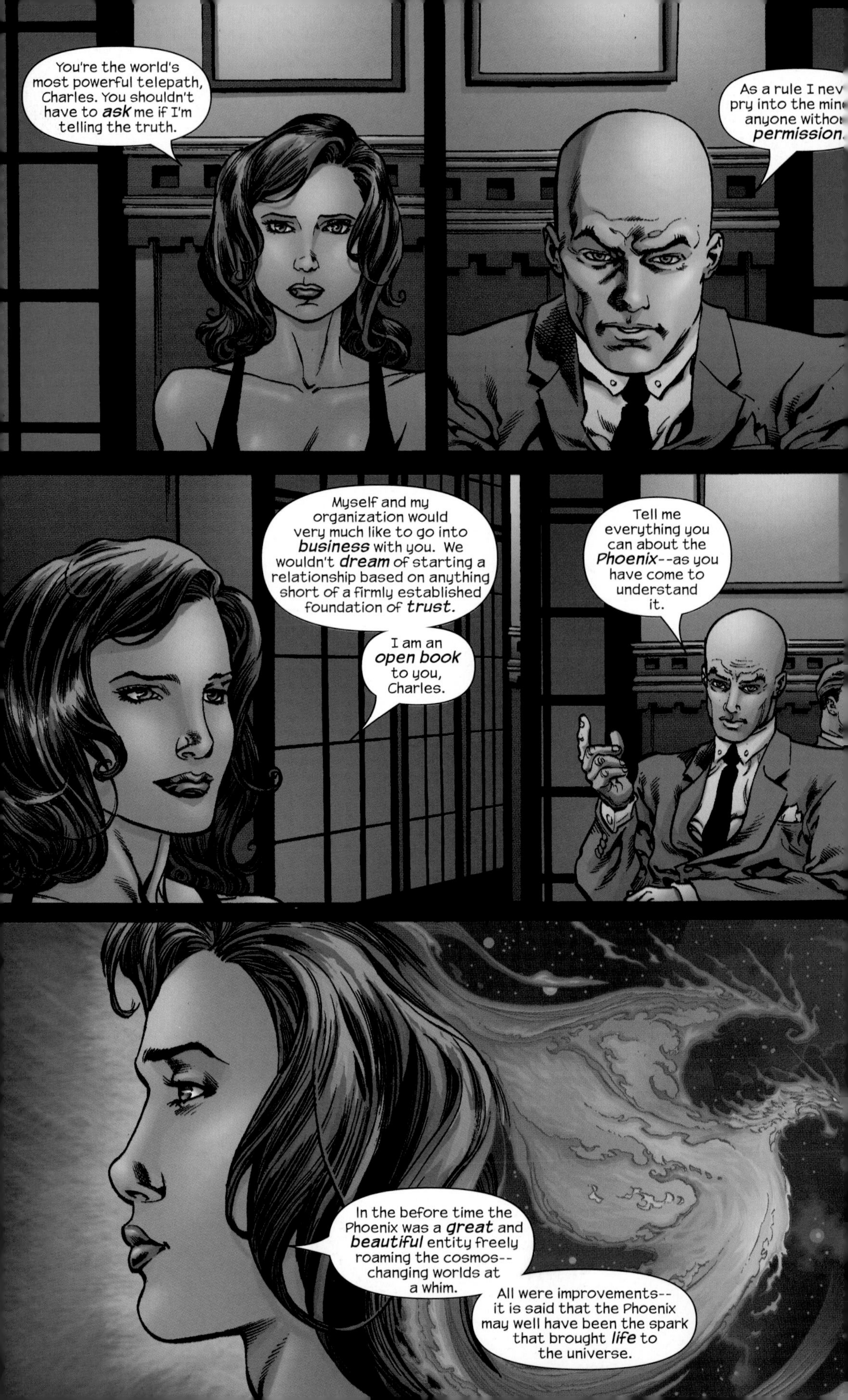
You're the world's most powerful telepath, Charles. You shouldn't have to *ask* me if I'm telling the truth.
As a rule I nev pry into the min anyone witho *permission.*
Myself and my organization would very much like to go into *business* with you. We wouldn't *dream* of starting a relationship based on anything short of a firmly established foundation of *trust.*
I am an *open book* to you, Charles.
Tell me everything you can about the *Phoenix*--as you have come to understand it.
In the before time the Phoenix was a *great* and *beautiful* entity freely roaming the cosmos--changing worlds at a whim.
All were improvements--it is said that the Phoenix may well have been the spark that brought *life* to the universe.

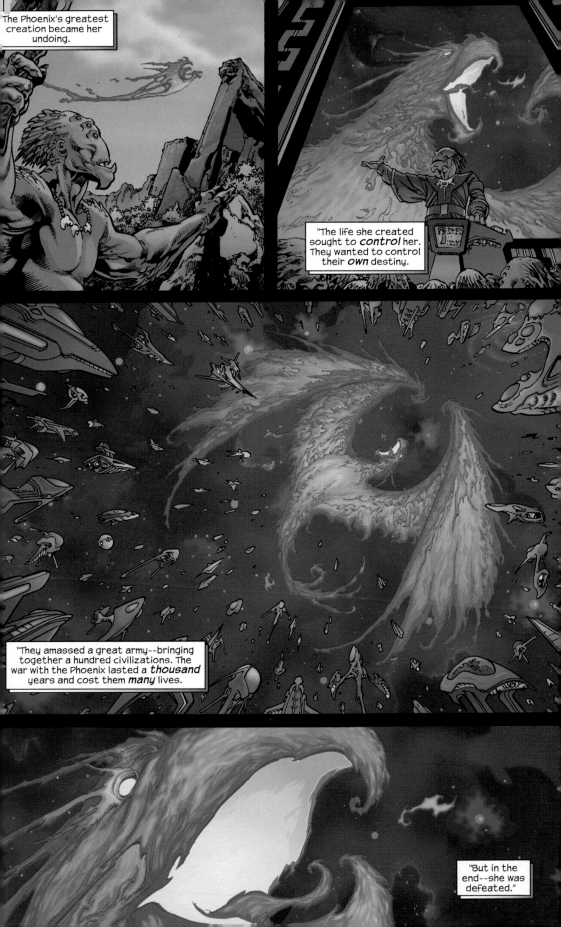

The Phoenix's greatest creation became her undoing.

"The life she created sought to *control* her. They wanted to control their *own* destiny.

"They amassed a great army--bringing together a hundred civilizations. The war with the Phoenix lasted a *thousand* years and cost them *many* lives.

"But in the end--she was defeated."

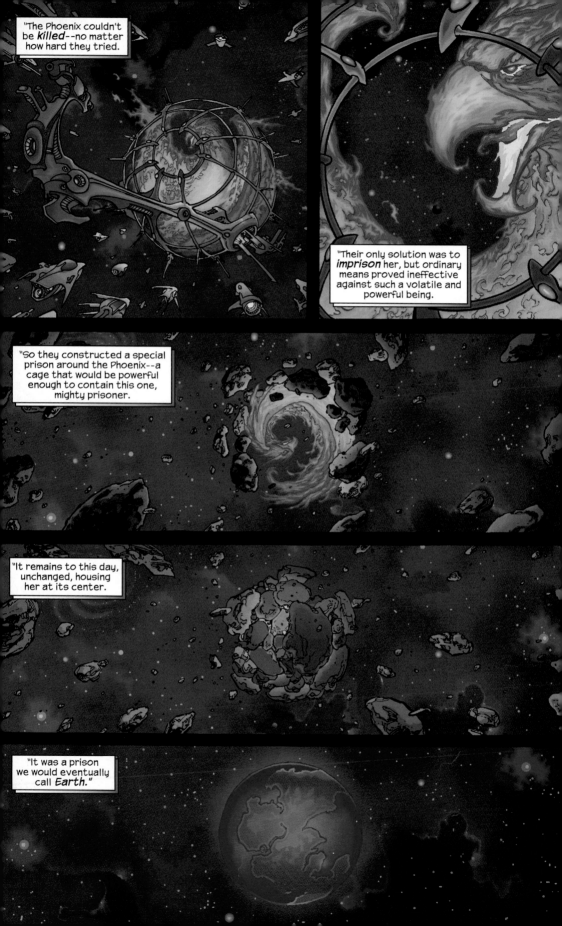

"The Phoenix couldn't be *killed*--no matter how hard they tried."

"Their only solution was to *imprison* her, but ordinary means proved ineffective against such a volatile and powerful being."

"So they constructed a special prison around the Phoenix--a cage that would be powerful enough to contain this one, mighty prisoner."

"It remains to this day, unchanged, housing her at its center.

"It was a prison we would eventually call *Earth*."

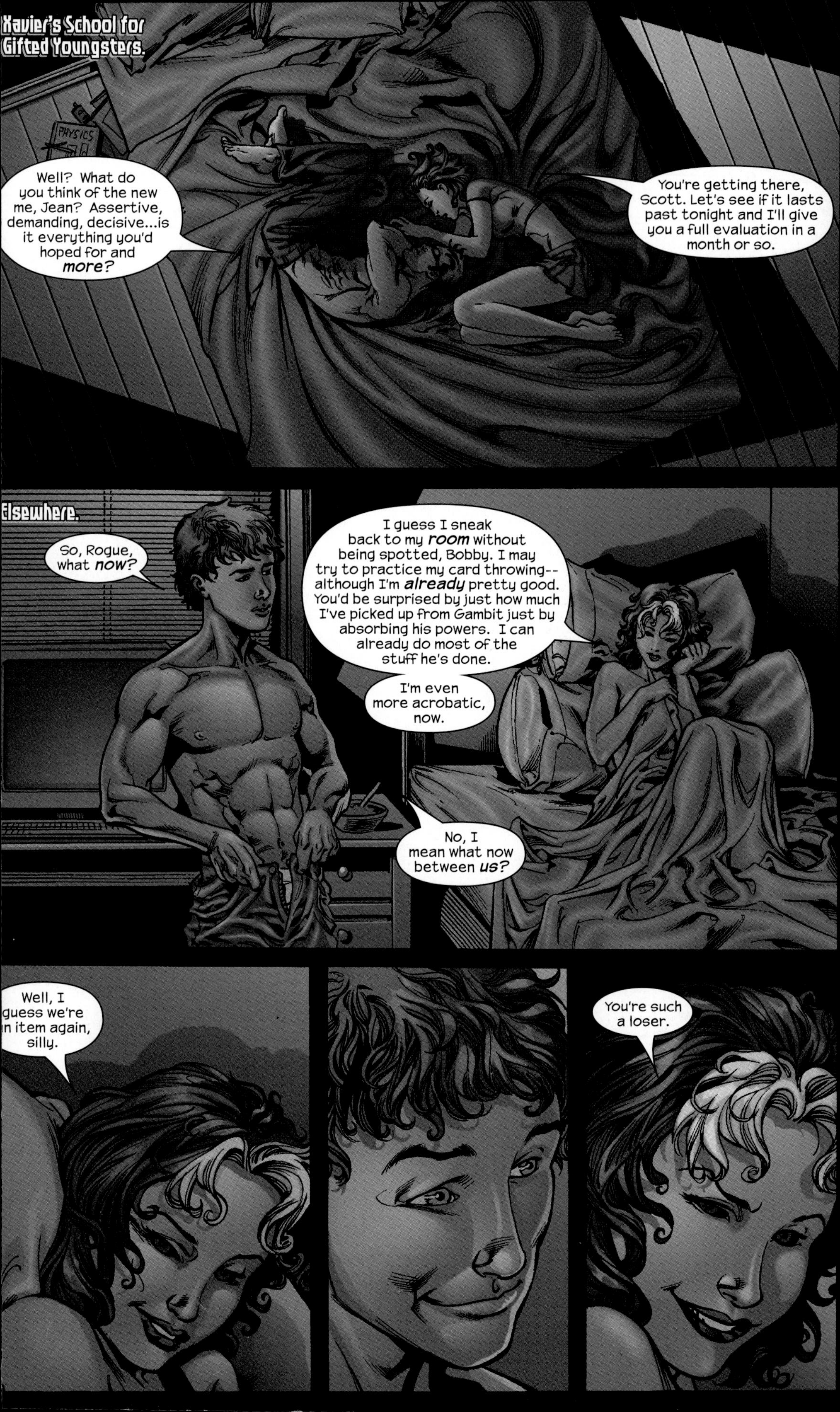
Xavier's School for Gifted Youngsters.
PHYSICS
Well? What do you think of the new me, Jean? Assertive, demanding, decisive...is it everything you'd hoped for and more?
You're getting there, Scott. Let's see if it lasts past tonight and I'll give you a full evaluation in a month or so.
Elsewhere.
So, Rogue, what now?
I guess I sneak back to my room without being spotted, Bobby. I may try to practice my card throwing--although I'm already pretty good. You'd be surprised by just how much I've picked up from Gambit just by absorbing his powers. I can already do most of the stuff he's done.
I'm even more acrobatic, now.
No, I mean what now between us?
Well, I guess we're n item again, silly.
You're such a loser.

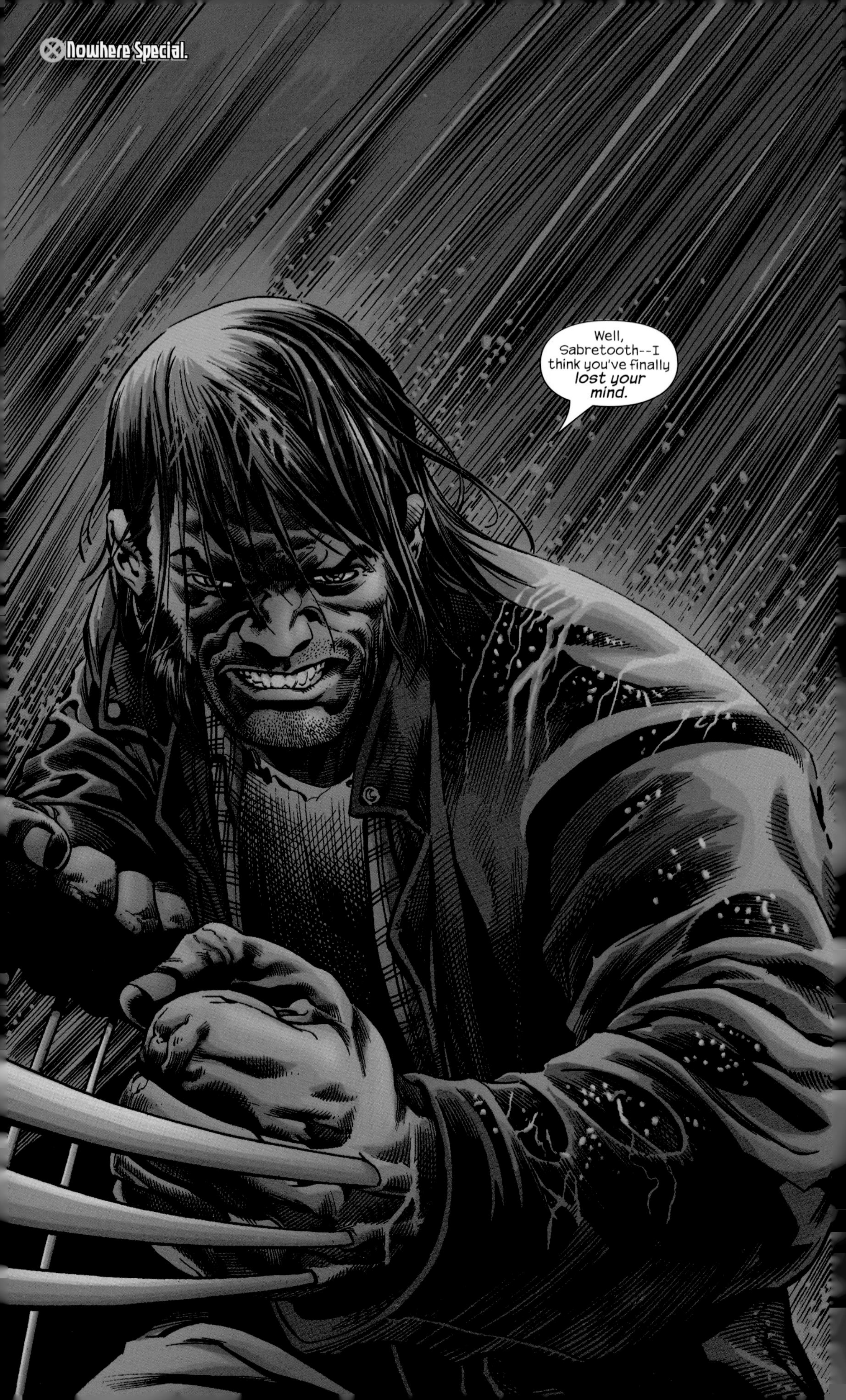
Nowhere Special.
Well, Sabretooth--I think you've finally *lost your mind.*

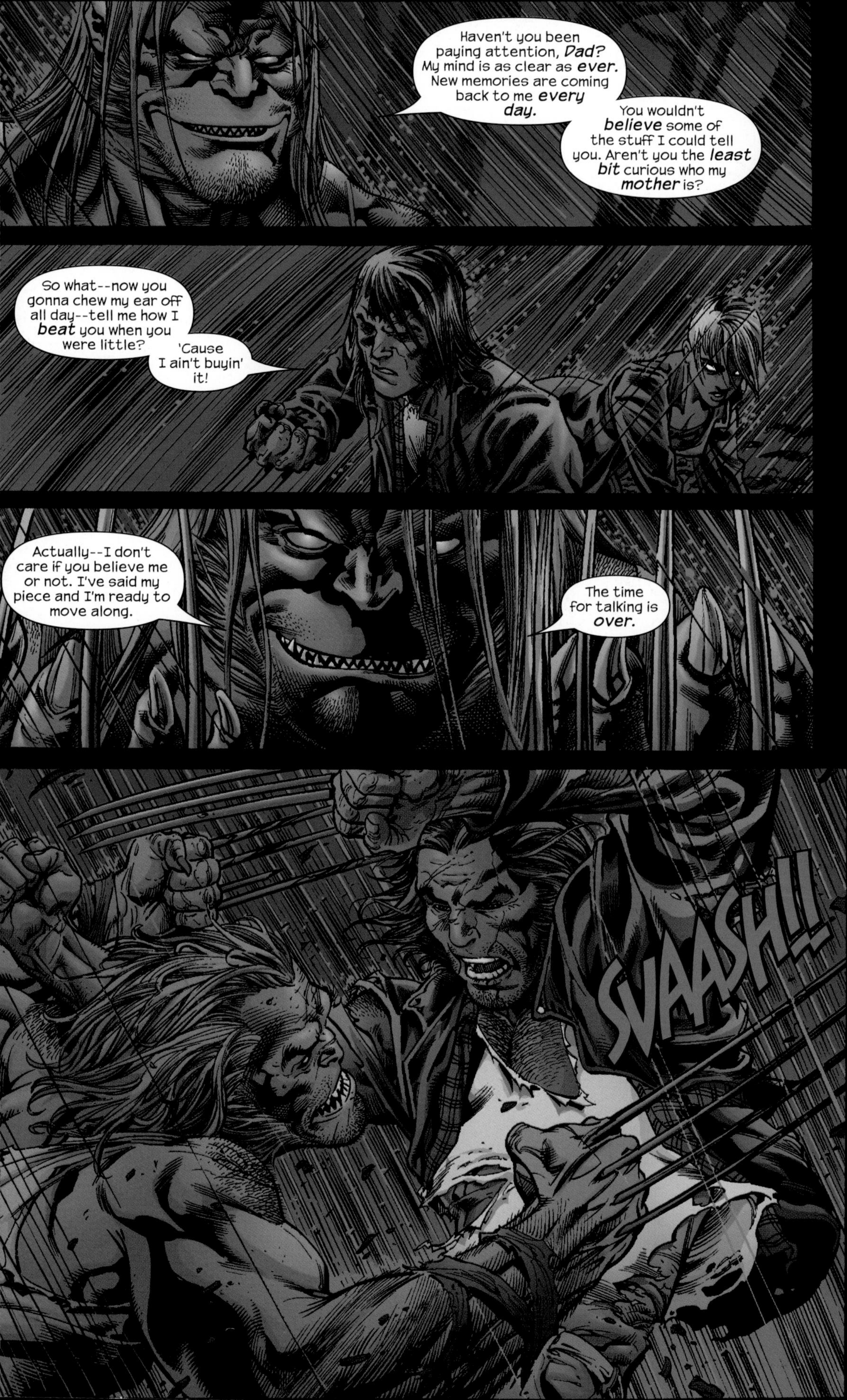
Haven't you been paying attention, Dad? My mind is as clear as ever. New memories are coming back to me every day.
You wouldn't believe some of the stuff I could tell you. Aren't you the least bit curious who my mother is?
So what--now you gonna chew my ear off all day--tell me how I beat you when you were little?
'Cause I ain't buyin' it!
Actually--I don't care if you believe me or not. I've said my piece and I'm ready to move along.
The time for talking is over.
SVAASH!!

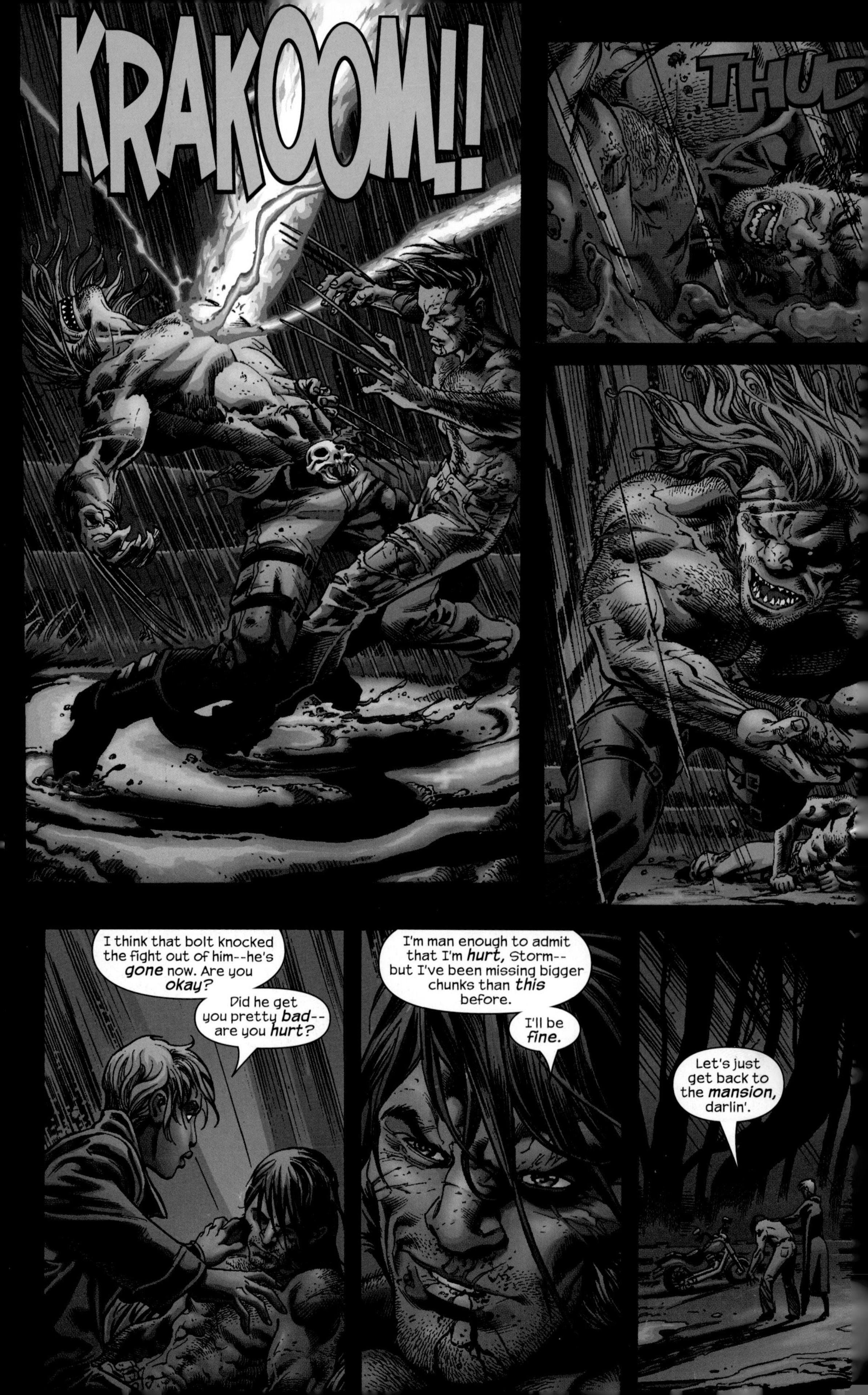
KRAKOOM!!
THUD
I think that bolt knocked the fight out of him--he's *gone* now. Are you *okay*?
Did he get you pretty *bad*--are you *hurt?*
I'm man enough to admit that I'm *hurt,* Storm--but I've been missing bigger chunks than *this* before.
I'll be *fine.*
Let's just get back to the *mansion,* darlin'.

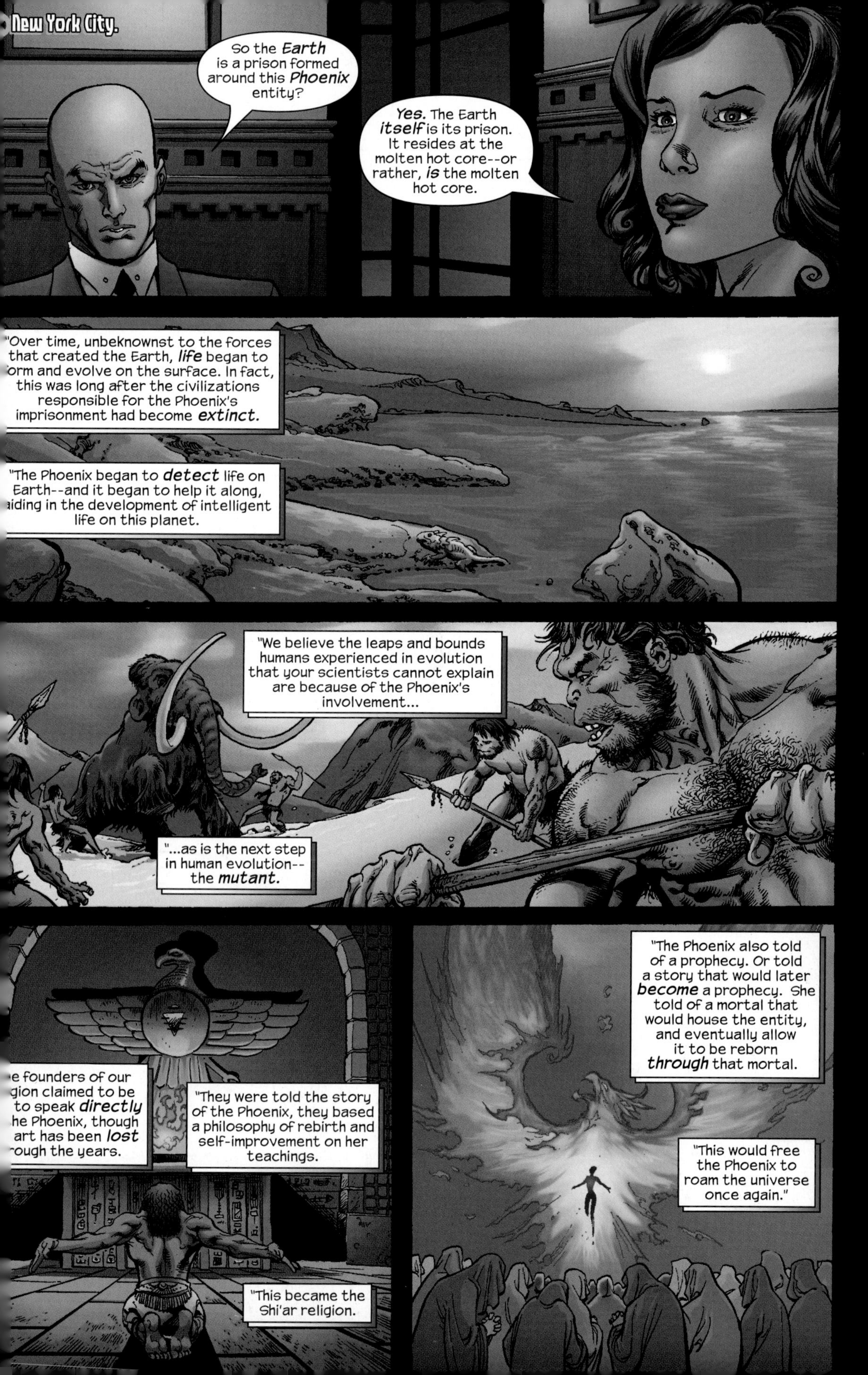
New York City.
So the Earth is a prison formed around this Phoenix entity?
Yes. The Earth itself is its prison. It resides at the molten hot core--or rather, is the molten hot core.
"Over time, unbeknownst to the forces that created the Earth, life began to form and evolve on the surface. In fact, this was long after the civilizations responsible for the Phoenix's imprisonment had become extinct.
"The Phoenix began to detect life on Earth--and it began to help it along, aiding in the development of intelligent life on this planet.
"We believe the leaps and bounds humans experienced in evolution that your scientists cannot explain are because of the Phoenix's involvement...
"...as is the next step in human evolution--the mutant.
e founders of our gion claimed to be to speak directly he Phoenix, though art has been lost rough the years.
"They were told the story of the Phoenix, they based a philosophy of rebirth and self-improvement on her teachings.
"This became the Shi'ar religion.
"The Phoenix also told of a prophecy. Or told a story that would later become a prophecy. She told of a mortal that would house the entity, and eventually allow it to be reborn through that mortal.
"This would free the Phoenix to roam the universe once again."

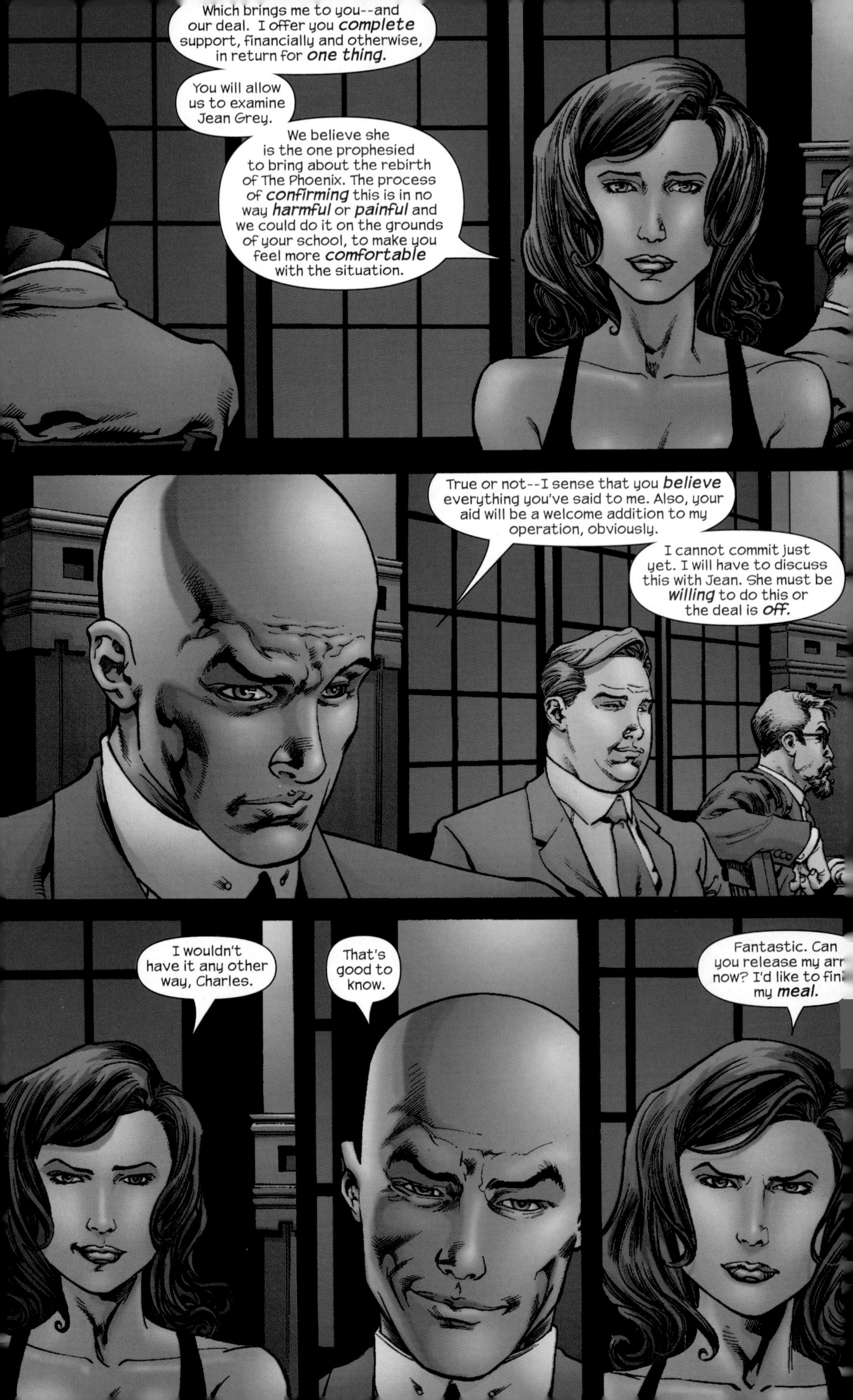
Which brings me to you--and our deal. I offer you *complete* support, financially and otherwise, in return for *one thing.*
You will allow us to examine Jean Grey.
We believe she is the one prophesied to bring about the rebirth of The Phoenix. The process of *confirming* this is in no way *harmful* or *painful* and we could do it on the grounds of your school, to make you feel more *comfortable* with the situation.
True or not--I sense that you *believe* everything you've said to me. Also, your aid will be a welcome addition to my operation, obviously.
I cannot commit just yet. I will have to discuss this with Jean. She must be *willing* to do this or the deal is *off.*
I wouldn't have it any other way, Charles.
That's good to know.
Fantastic. Can you release my arm now? I'd like to fini my *meal.*

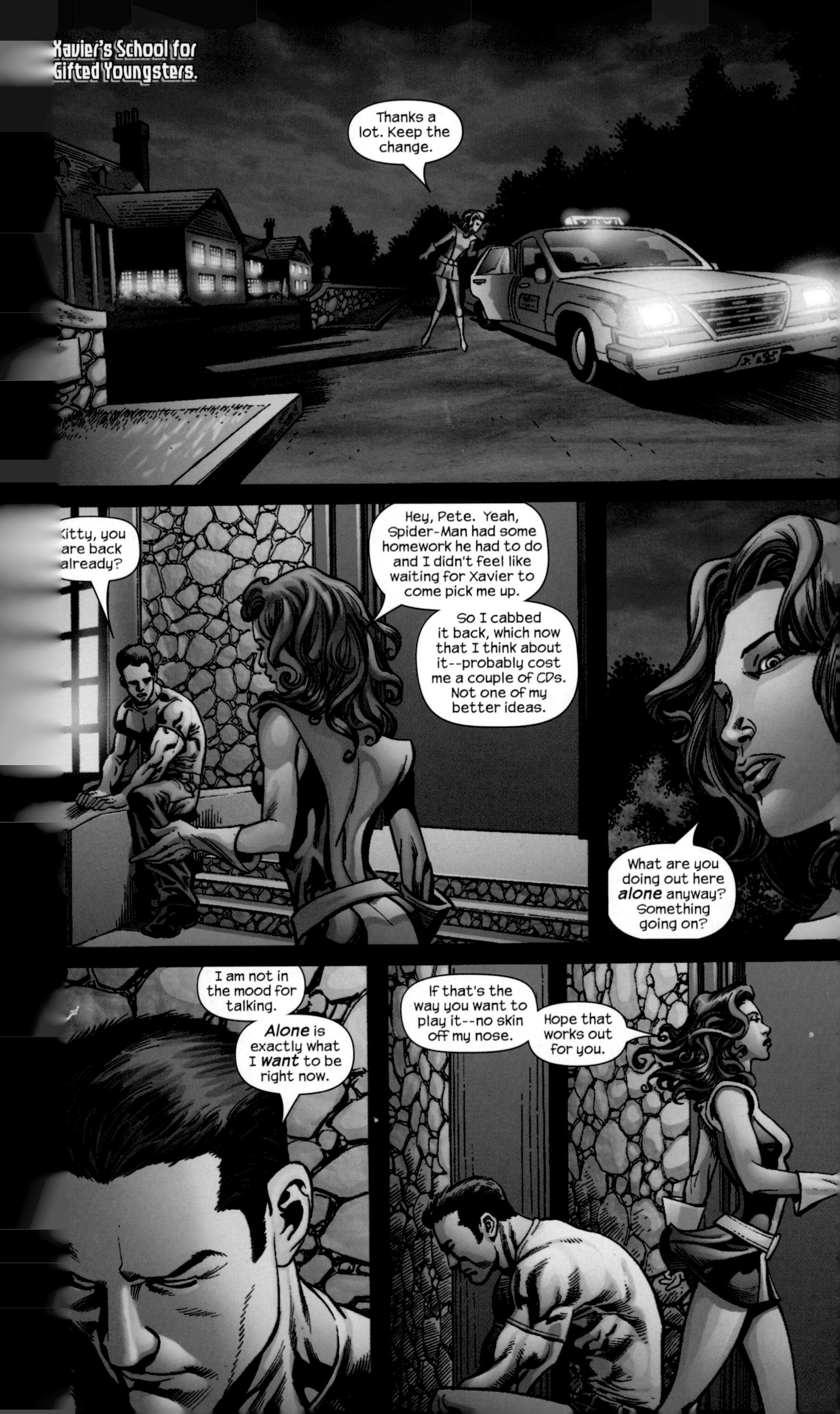
Xavier's School for Gifted Youngsters.
Thanks a lot. Keep the change.
Kitty, you are back already?
Hey, Pete. Yeah, Spider-Man had some homework he had to do and I didn't feel like waiting for Xavier to come pick me up.
So I cabbed it back, which now that I think about it--probably cost me a couple of CDs. Not one of my better ideas.
What are you doing out here *alone* anyway? Something going on?
I am not in the mood for talking.
Alone is exactly what I *want* to be right now.
If that's the way you want to play it--no skin off my nose.
Hope that works out for you.

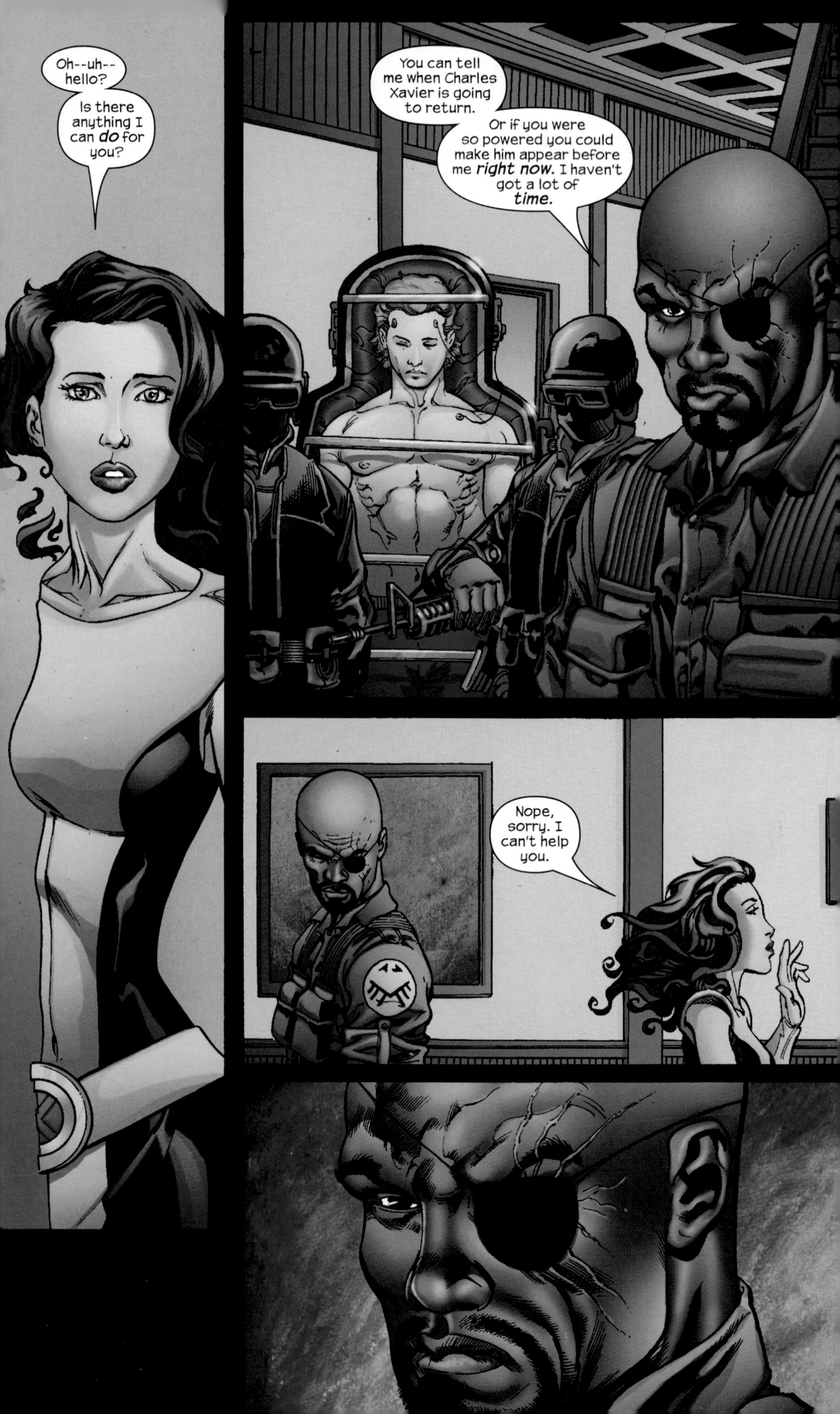

Oh--uh--hello?
Is there anything I can *do* for you?
You can tell me when Charles Xavier is going to return.
Or if you were so powered you could make him appear before me *right now.* I haven't got a lot of *time.*
Nope, sorry. I can't help you.

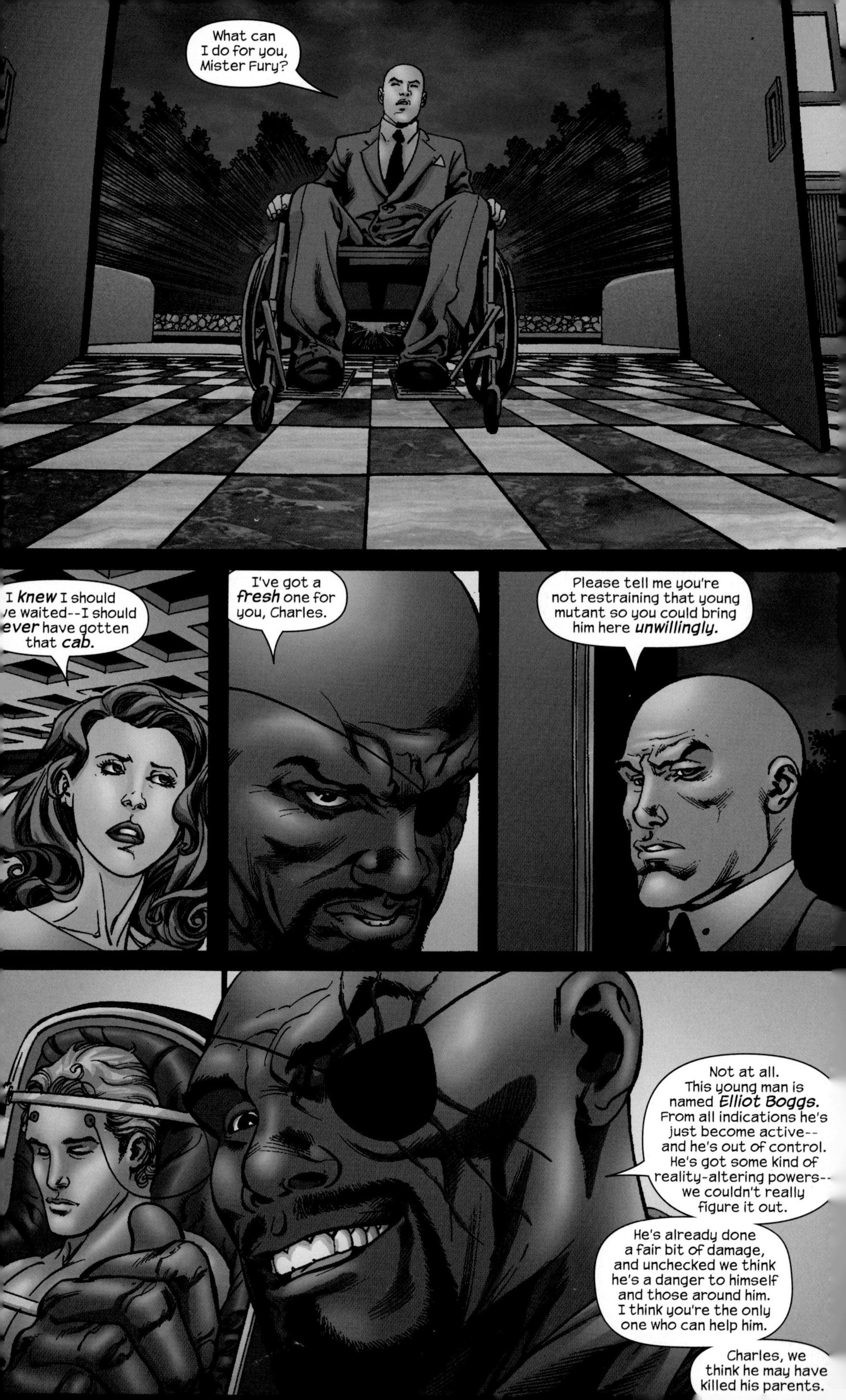

What can I do for you, Mister Fury?
I knew I should ve waited--I should ever have gotten that cab.
I've got a fresh one for you, Charles.
Please tell me you're not restraining that young mutant so you could bring him here unwillingly.
Not at all. This young man is named Elliot Boggs. From all indications he's just become active-- and he's out of control. He's got some kind of reality-altering powers-- we couldn't really figure it out.
He's already done a fair bit of damage, and unchecked we think he's a danger to himself and those around him. I think you're the only one who can help him.
Charles, we think he may have killed his parents.

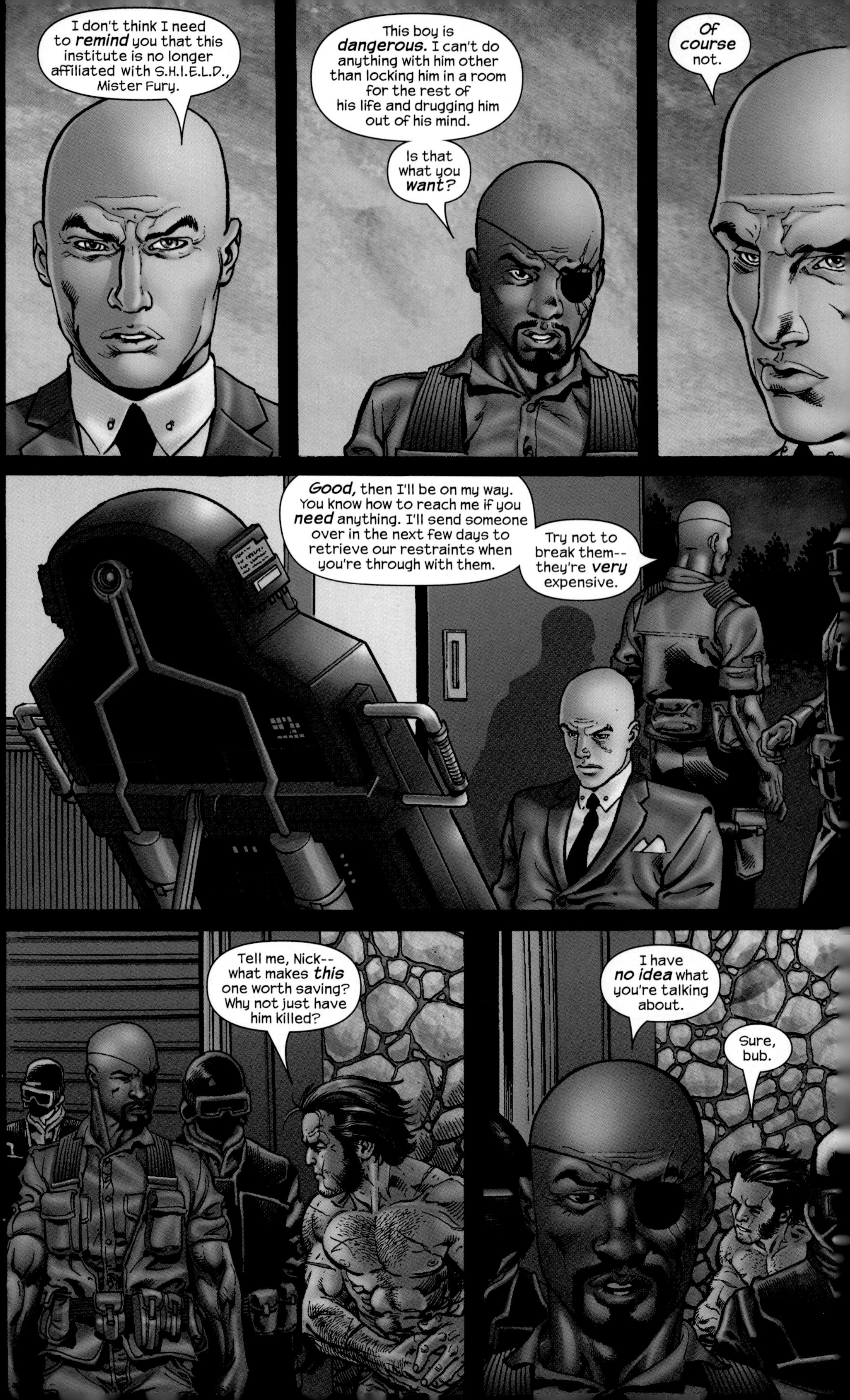
I don't think I need to remind you that this institute is no longer affiliated with S.H.I.E.L.D., Mister Fury.
This boy is dangerous. I can't do anything with him other than locking him in a room for the rest of his life and drugging him out of his mind.
Is that what you want?
Of course not.
Good, then I'll be on my way. You know how to reach me if you need anything. I'll send someone over in the next few days to retrieve our restraints when you're through with them.
Try not to break them--they're very expensive.
Tell me, Nick--what makes this one worth saving? Why not just have him killed?
I have no idea what you're talking about.
Sure, bub.

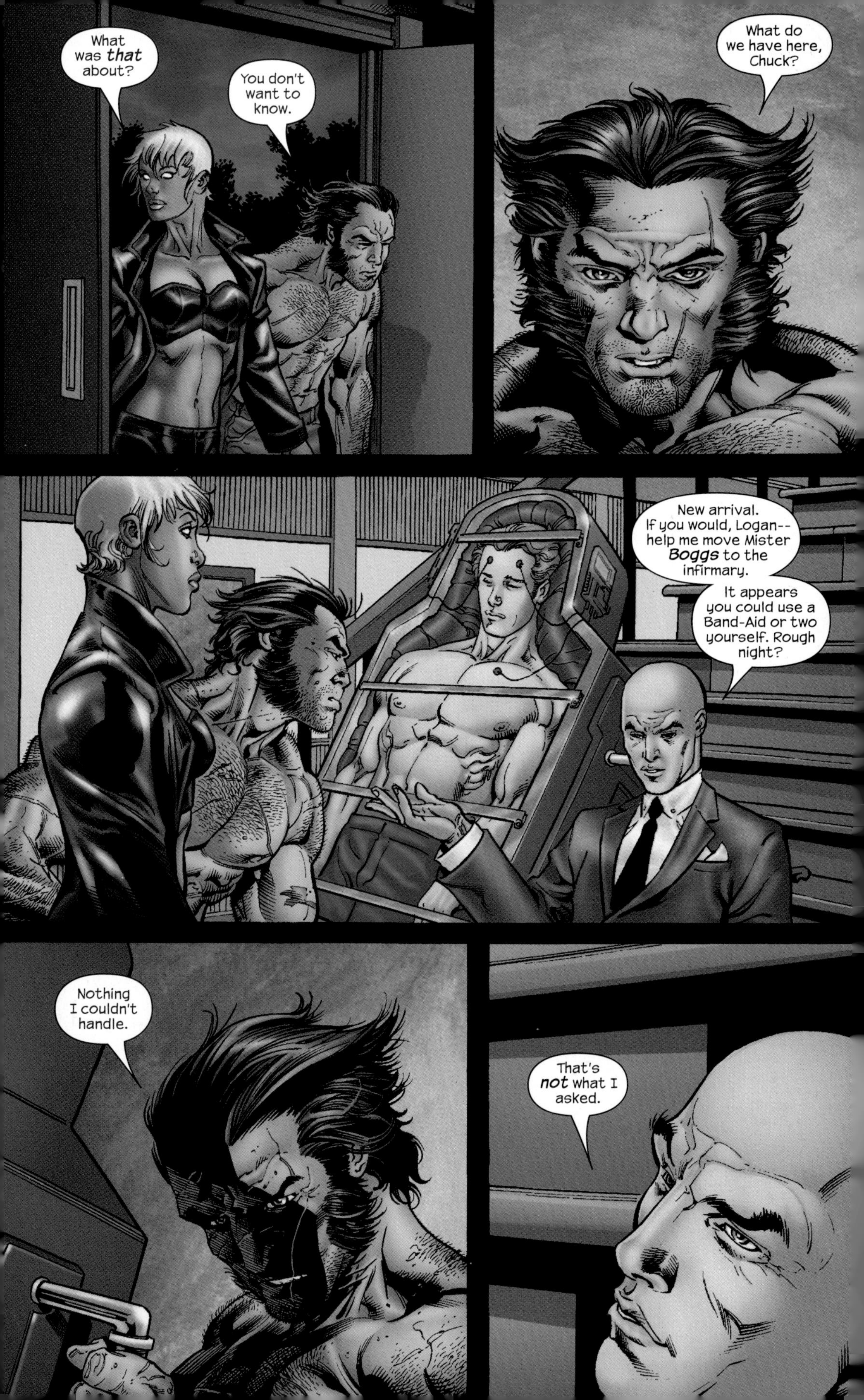
What was *that* about?
You don't want to know.
What do we have here, Chuck?
New arrival. If you would, Logan-- help me move Mister *Boggs* to the infirmary.
It appears you could use a Band-Aid or two yourself. Rough night?
Nothing I couldn't handle.
That's *not* what I asked.

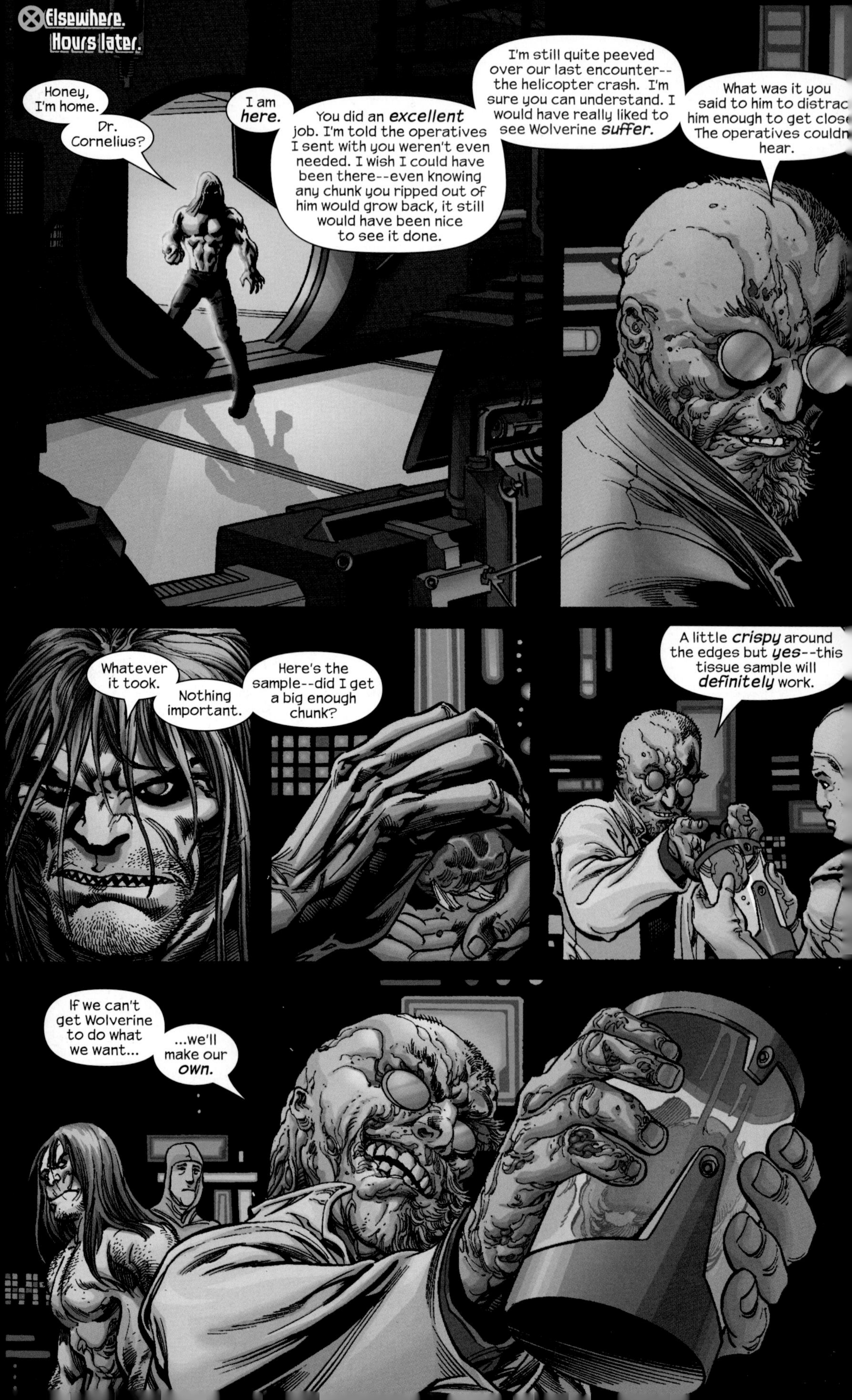
Elsewhere. Hours later.
Honey, I'm home.
Dr. Cornelius?
I am *here.*
You did an *excellent* job. I'm told the operatives I sent with you weren't even needed. I wish I could have been there--even knowing any chunk you ripped out of him would grow back, it still would have been nice to see it done.
I'm still quite peeved over our last encounter--the helicopter crash. I'm sure you can understand. I would have really liked to see Wolverine *suffer.*
What was it you said to him to distrac him enough to get clos The operatives couldn hear.
Whatever it took.
Nothing important.
Here's the sample--did I get a big enough chunk?
A little *crispy* around the edges but *yes*--this tissue sample will *definitely* work.
If we can't get Wolverine to do what we want...
...we'll make our *own.*

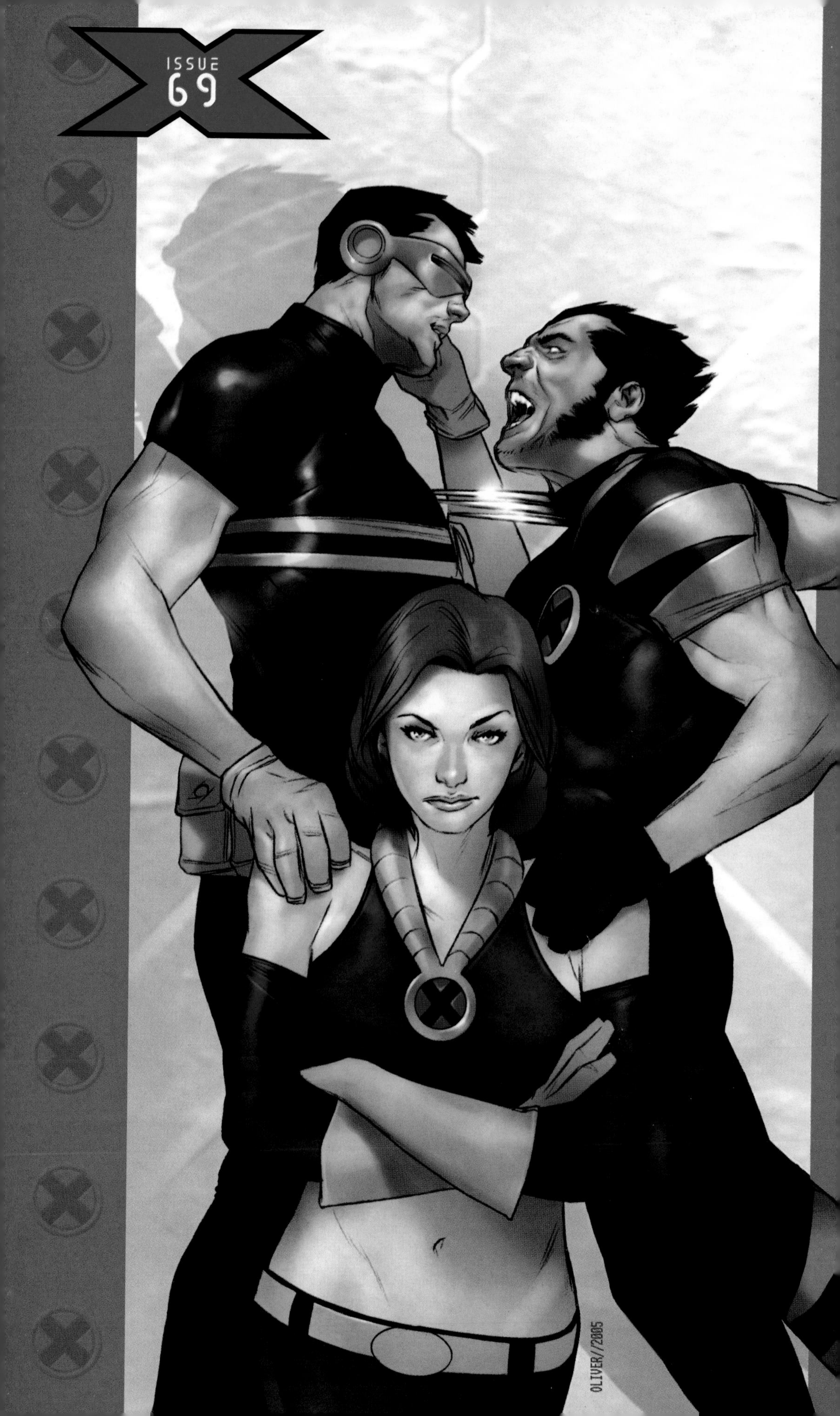
ISSUE
69
OLIVER//2005

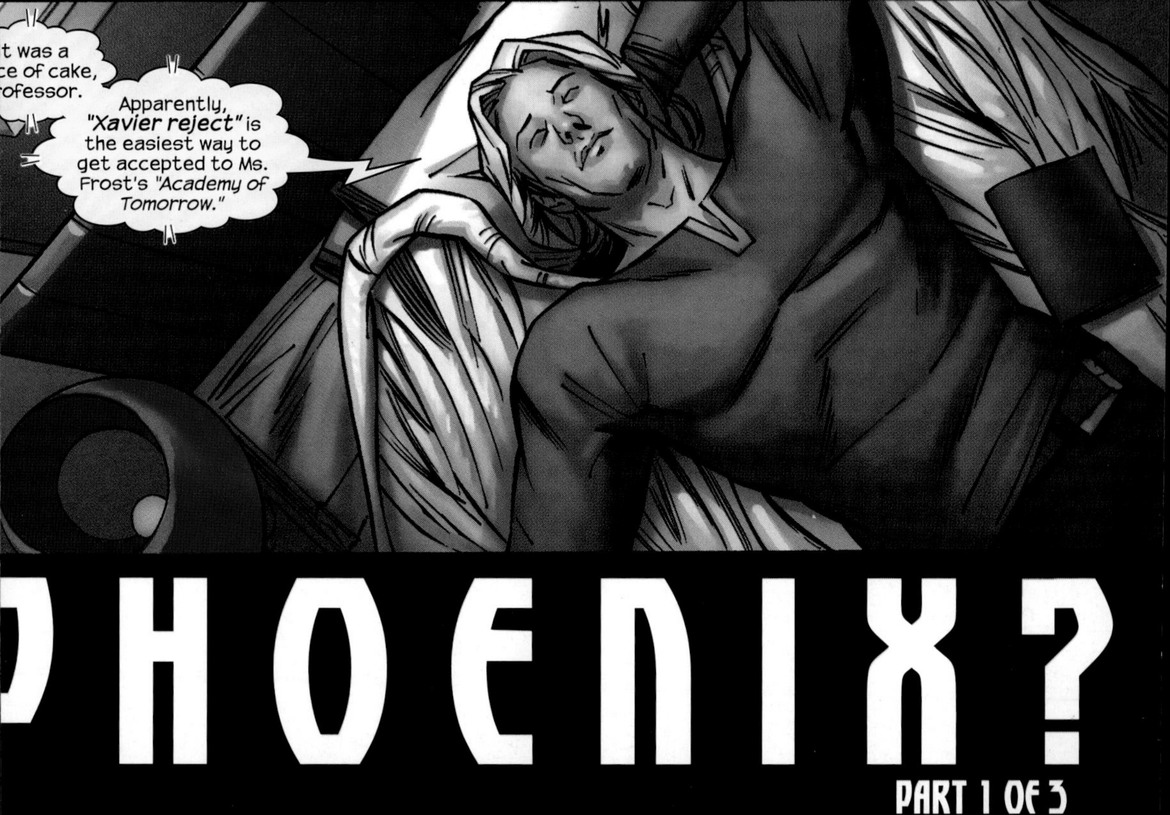
t was a
ce of cake,
rofessor.
Apparently, "*Xavier reject*" is the easiest way to get accepted to Ms. Frost's "Academy of Tomorrow."
PHOENIX?
PART 1 OF 3

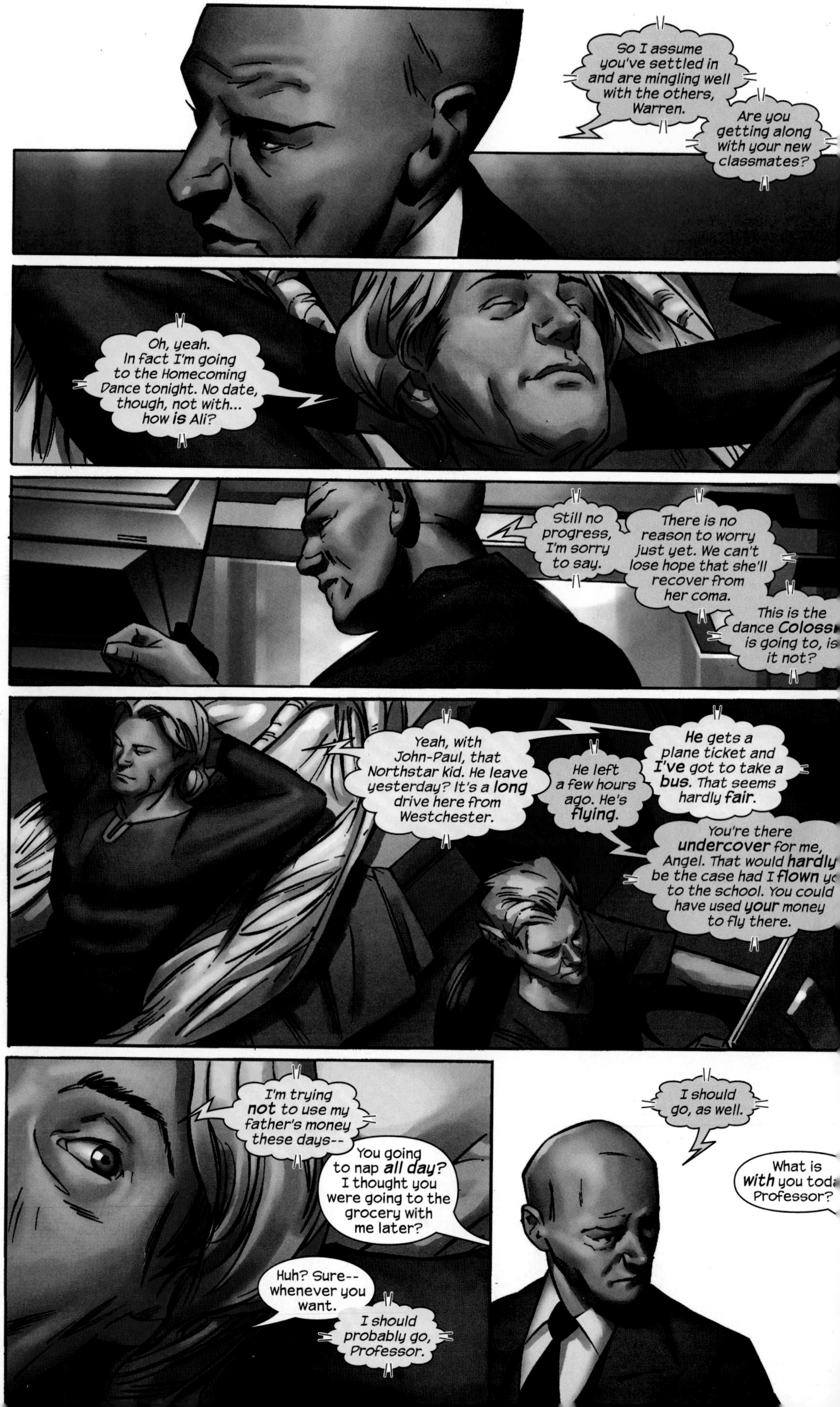
So I assume you've settled in and are mingling well with the others, Warren.
Are you getting along with your new classmates?
Oh, yeah. In fact I'm going to the Homecoming Dance tonight. No date, though, not with... how is Ali?
Still no progress, I'm sorry to say.
There is no reason to worry just yet. We can't lose hope that she'll recover from her coma.
This is the dance Coloss is going to, is it not?
Yeah, with John-Paul, that Northstar kid. He leave yesterday? It's a long drive here from Westchester.
He left a few hours ago. He's flying.
He gets a plane ticket and I've got to take a bus. That seems hardly fair.
You're there undercover for me, Angel. That would hardly be the case had I flown y to the school. You could have used your money to fly there.
I'm trying not to use my father's money these days--
You going to nap all day? I thought you were going to the grocery with me later?
Huh? Sure-- whenever you want.
I should probably go, Professor.
I should go, as well.
What is with you tod Professor?

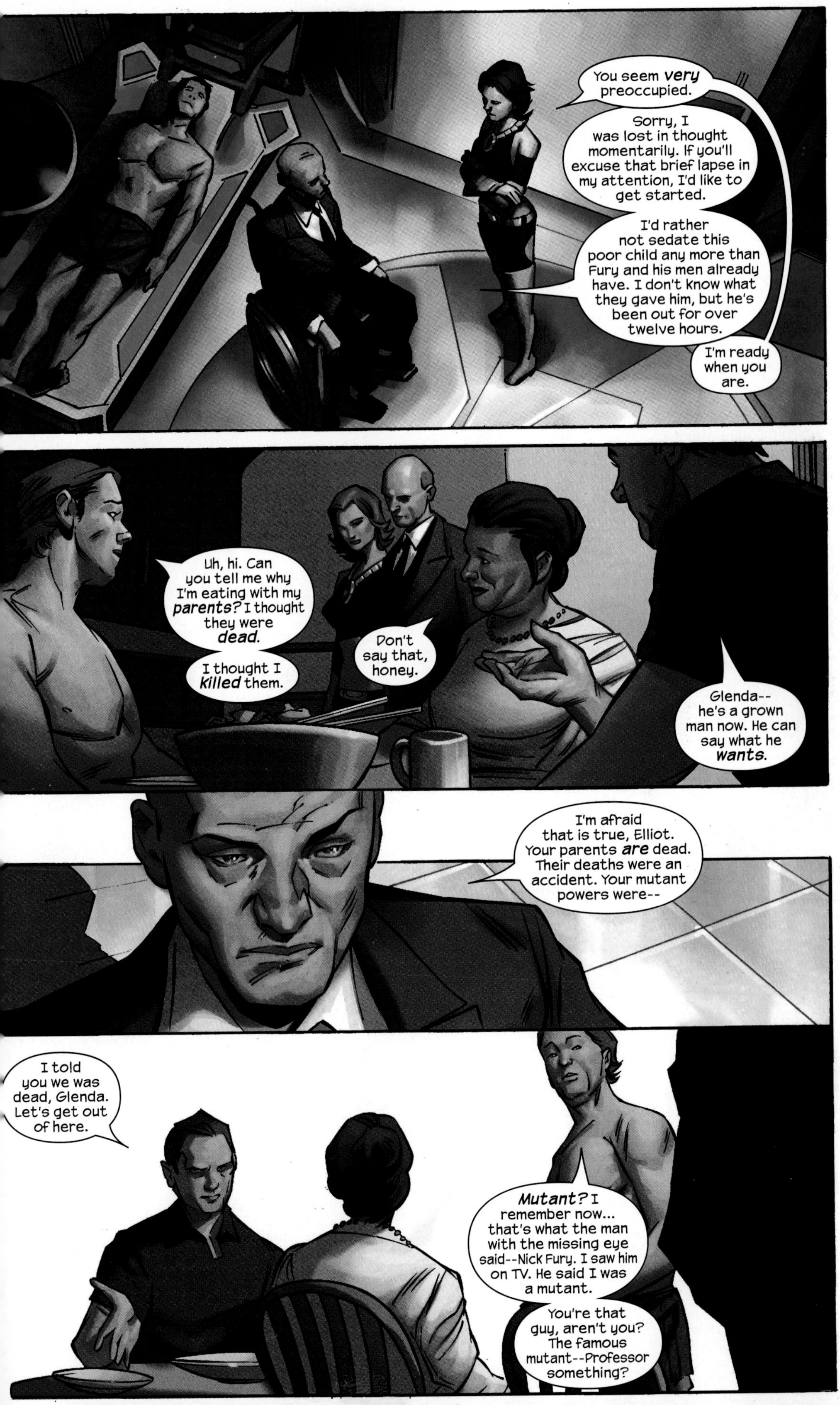
You seem very preoccupied.
Sorry, I was lost in thought momentarily. If you'll excuse that brief lapse in my attention, I'd like to get started.
I'd rather not sedate this poor child any more than Fury and his men already have. I don't know what they gave him, but he's been out for over twelve hours.
I'm ready when you are.
Uh, hi. Can you tell me why I'm eating with my parents? I thought they were dead.
I thought I killed them.
Don't say that, honey.
Glenda-- he's a grown man now. He can say what he wants.
I'm afraid that is true, Elliot. Your parents are dead. Their deaths were an accident. Your mutant powers were--
I told you we was dead, Glenda. Let's get out of here.
Mutant? I remember now... that's what the man with the missing eye said--Nick Fury. I saw him on TV. He said I was a mutant.
You're that guy, aren't you? The famous mutant--Professor something?

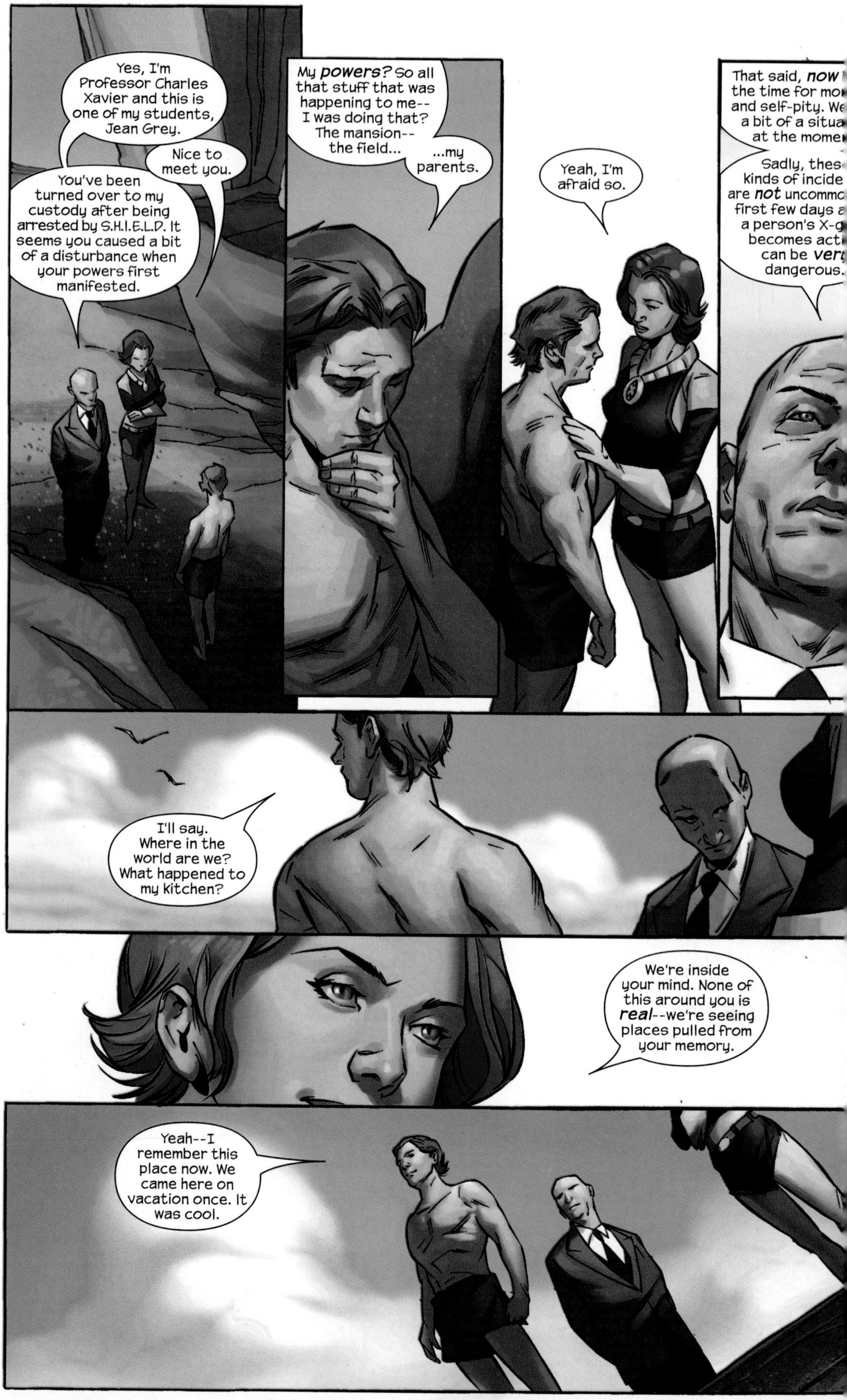

Yes, I'm Professor Charles Xavier and this is one of my students, Jean Grey.
Nice to meet you.
You've been turned over to my custody after being arrested by S.H.I.E.L.D. It seems you caused a bit of a disturbance when your powers first manifested.
My powers? So all that stuff that was happening to me-- I was doing that? The mansion-- the field...
...my parents.
Yeah, I'm afraid so.
That said, now
the time for mo
and self-pity. We
a bit of a situa
at the mome
Sadly, thes
kinds of incide
are not uncommo
first few days a
a person's X-g
becomes acti
can be ver
dangerous.
I'll say. Where in the world are we? What happened to my kitchen?
We're inside your mind. None of this around you is real--we're seeing places pulled from your memory.
Yeah--I remember this place now. We came here on vacation once. It was cool.

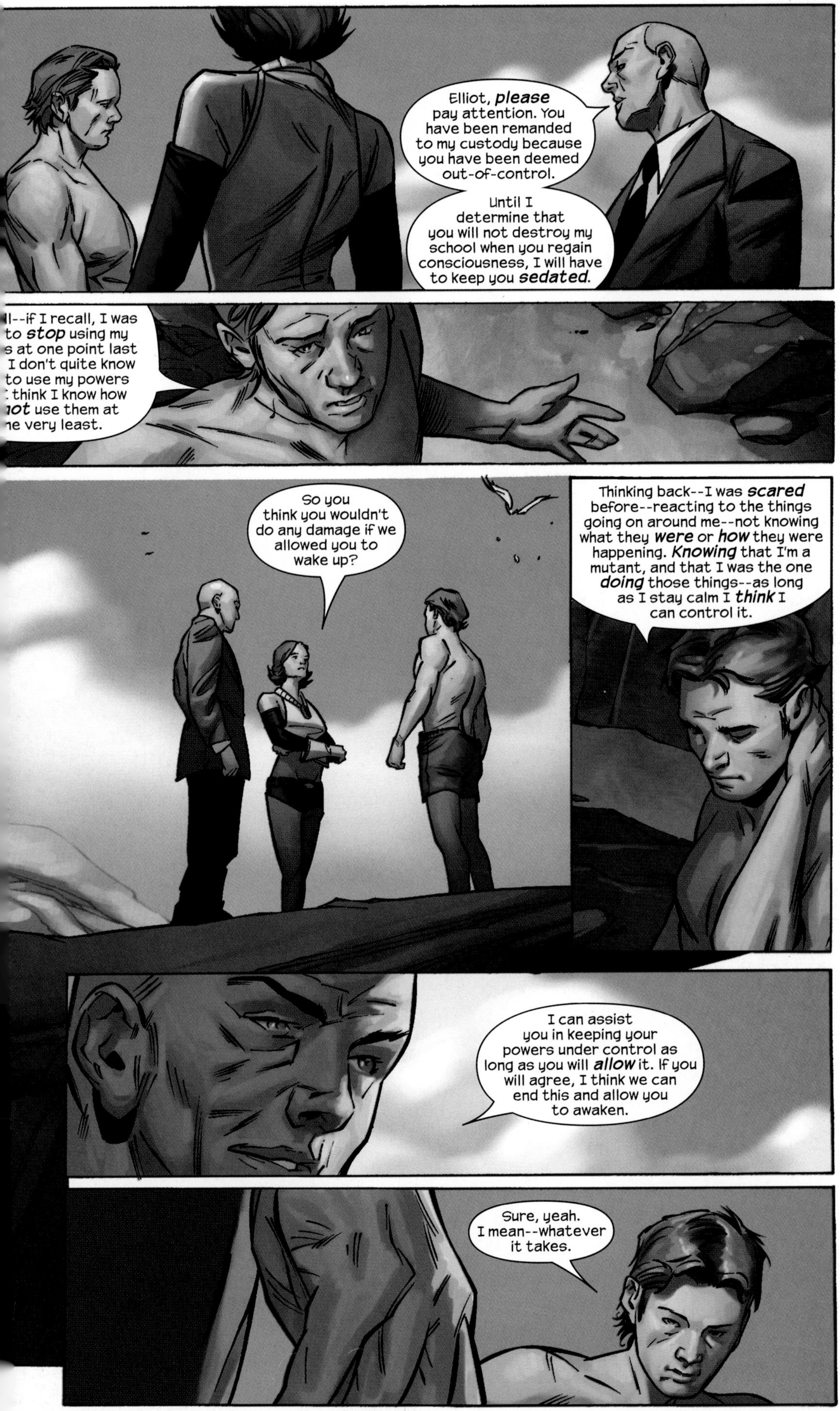
Elliot, please pay attention. You have been remanded to my custody because you have been deemed out-of-control.
Until I determine that you will not destroy my school when you regain consciousness, I will have to keep you sedated.
l--if I recall, I was to stop using my s at one point last I don't quite know to use my powers think I know how ot use them at e very least.
So you think you wouldn't do any damage if we allowed you to wake up?
Thinking back--I was scared before--reacting to the things going on around me--not knowing what they were or how they were happening. Knowing that I'm a mutant, and that I was the one doing those things--as long as I stay calm I think I can control it.
I can assist you in keeping your powers under control as long as you will allow it. If you will agree, I think we can end this and allow you to awaken.
Sure, yeah. I mean--whatever it takes.

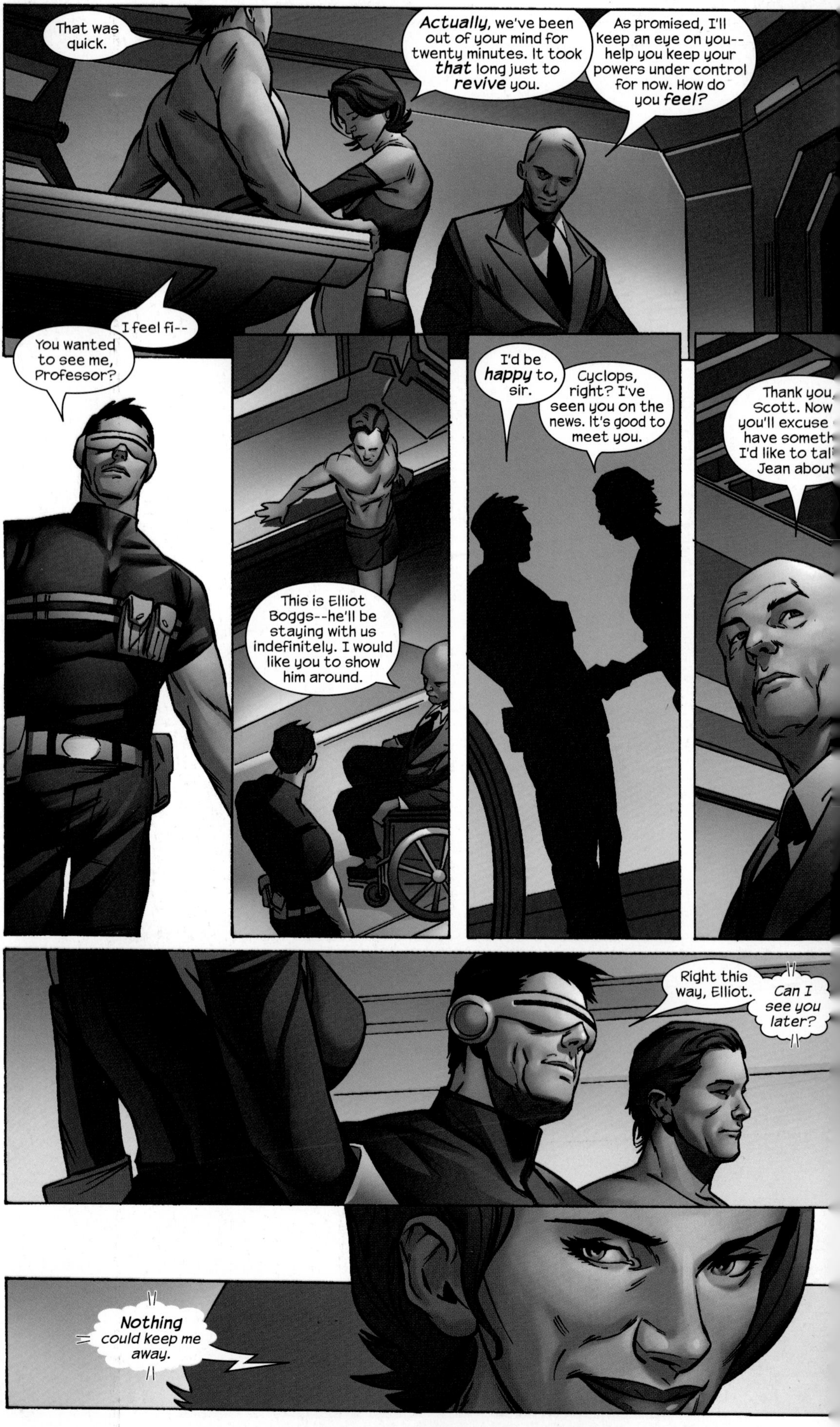
That was quick.
Actually, we've been out of your mind for twenty minutes. It took *that* long just to *revive* you.
As promised, I'll keep an eye on you--help you keep your powers under control for now. How do you *feel*?
I feel fi--
You wanted to see me, Professor?
This is Elliot Boggs--he'll be staying with us indefinitely. I would like you to show him around.
I'd be *happy* to, sir.
Cyclops, right? I've seen you on the news. It's good to meet you.
Thank you, Scott. Now you'll excuse have someth I'd like to tal Jean about
Right this way, Elliot.
Can I see you later?
Nothing could keep me away.

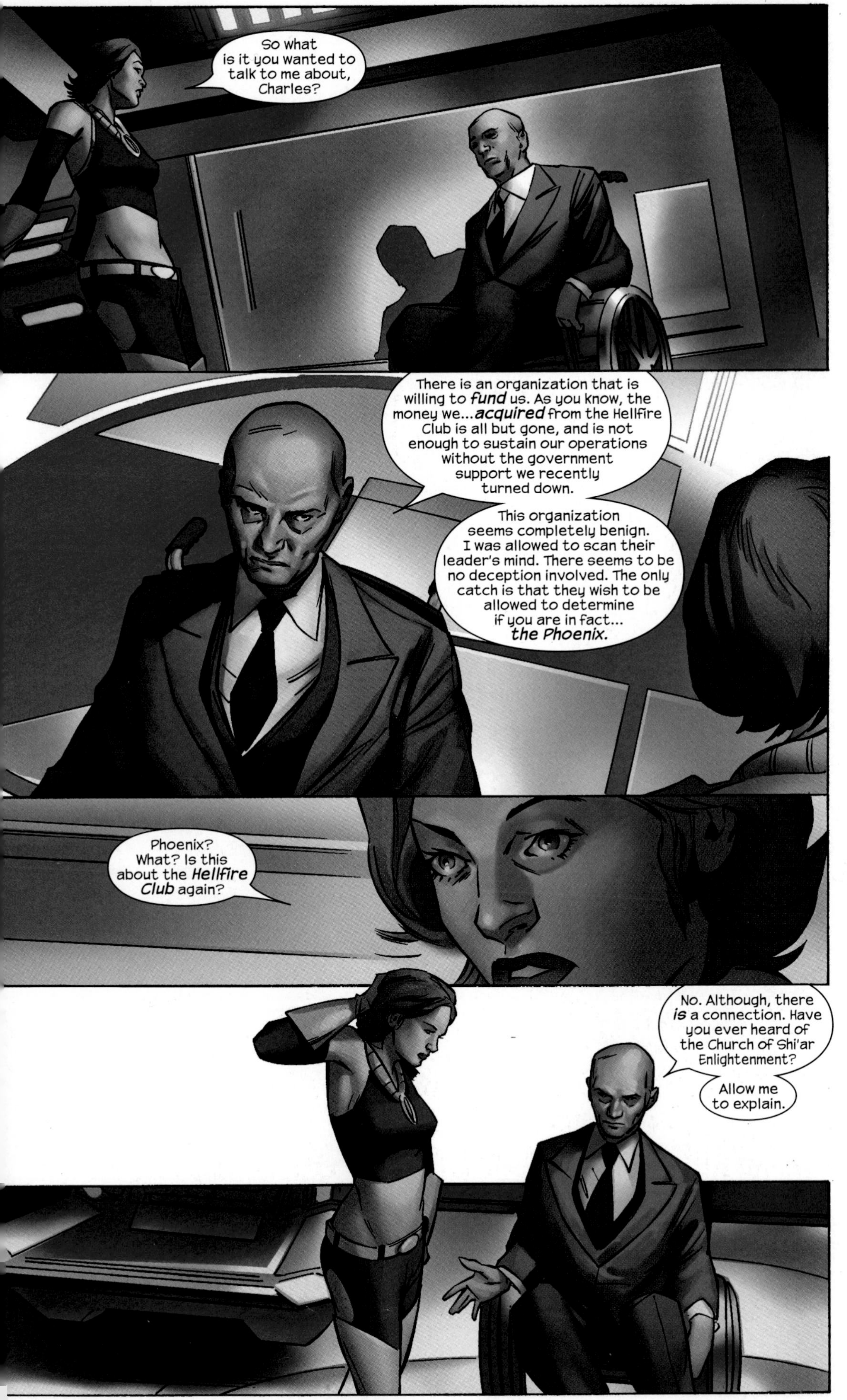
So what is it you wanted to talk to me about, Charles?
There is an organization that is willing to *fund* us. As you know, the money we...*acquired* from the Hellfire Club is all but gone, and is not enough to sustain our operations without the government support we recently turned down.
This organization seems completely benign. I was allowed to scan their leader's mind. There seems to be no deception involved. The only catch is that they wish to be allowed to determine if you are in fact... *the Phoenix.*
Phoenix? What? Is this about the *Hellfire Club* again?
No. Although, there *is* a connection. Have you ever heard of the Church of Shi'ar Enlightenment?
Allow me to explain.

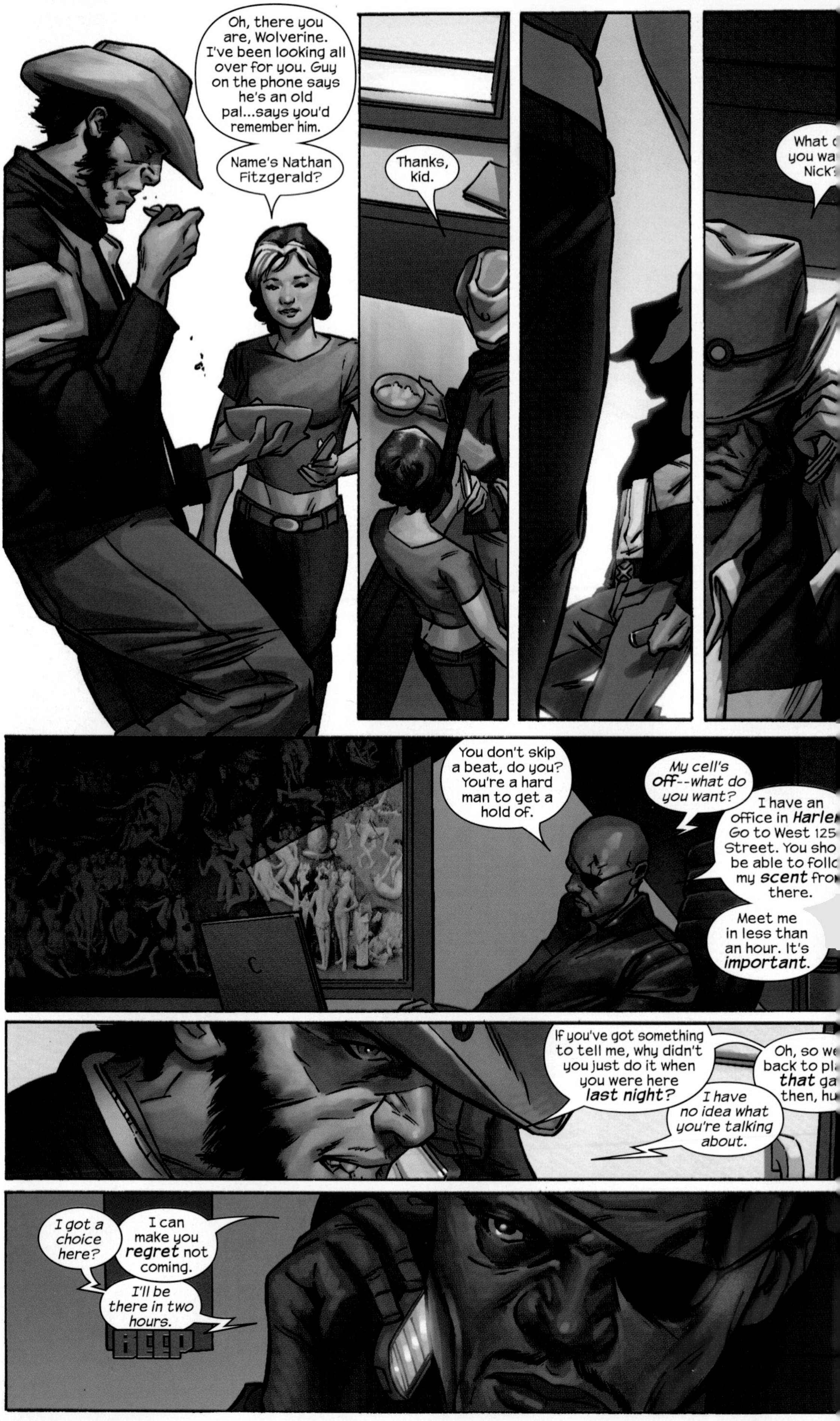

Oh, there you are, Wolverine. I've been looking all over for you. Guy on the phone says he's an old pal...says you'd remember him.
Name's Nathan Fitzgerald?
Thanks, kid.
What d
you wa
Nick's
You don't skip a beat, do you? You're a hard man to get a hold of.
My cell's off--what do you want?
I have an office in Harle
Go to West 125
Street. You sho
be able to follo
my scent fro
there.
Meet me in less than an hour. It's important.
If you've got something to tell me, why didn't you just do it when you were here last night?
I have no idea what you're talking about.
Oh, so we
back to pl
that ga
then, hu
I got a choice here?
I can make you regret not coming.
I'll be there in two hours.
BEEP

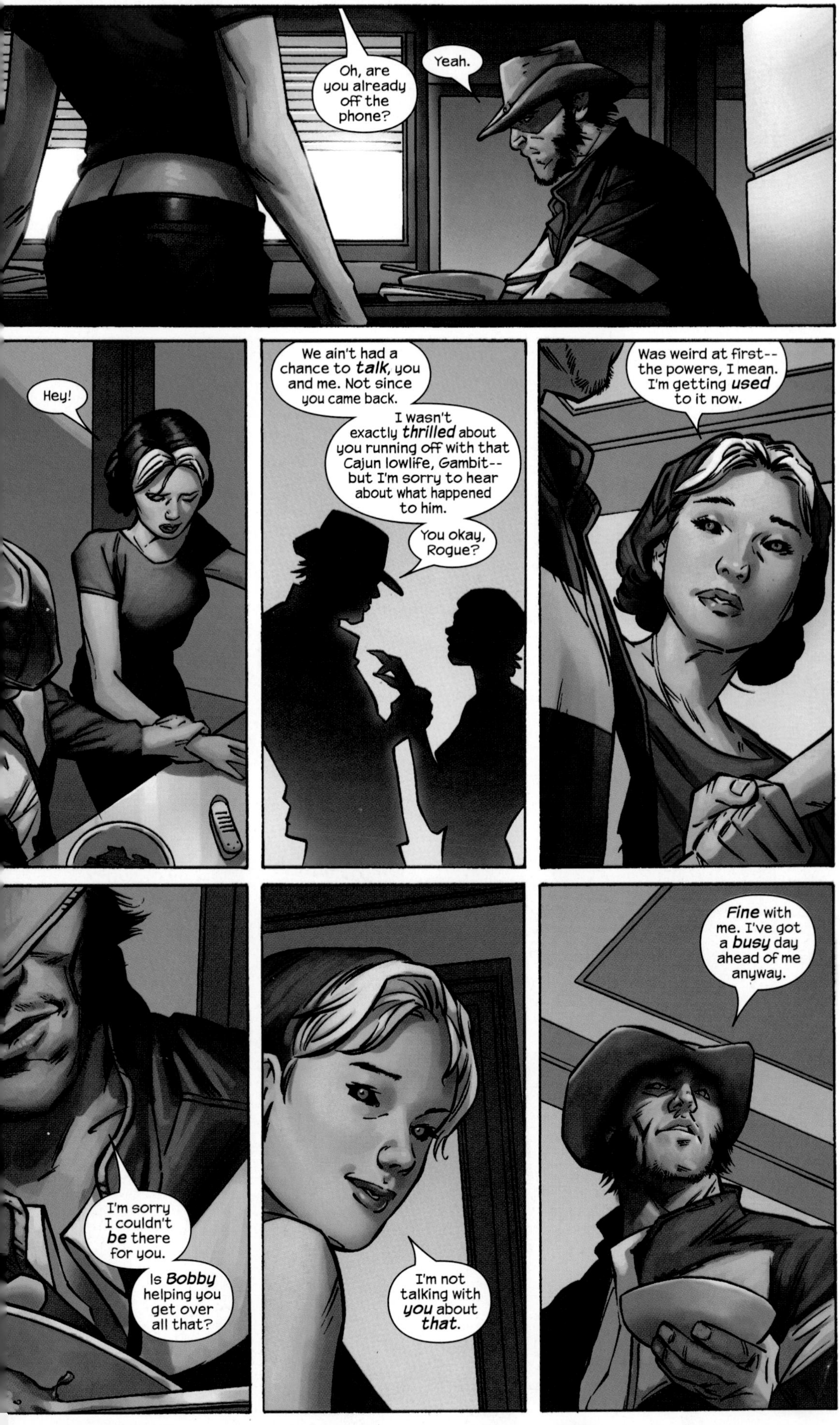
Oh, are you already off the phone?
Yeah.
Hey!
We ain't had a chance to *talk*, you and me. Not since you came back.
I wasn't exactly *thrilled* about you running off with that Cajun lowlife, Gambit-- but I'm sorry to hear about what happened to him.
You okay, Rogue?
Was weird at first-- the powers, I mean. I'm getting *used* to it now.
I'm sorry I couldn't *be* there for you.
Is *Bobby* helping you get over all that?
I'm not talking with *you* about *that*.
Fine with me. I've got a *busy* day ahead of me anyway.

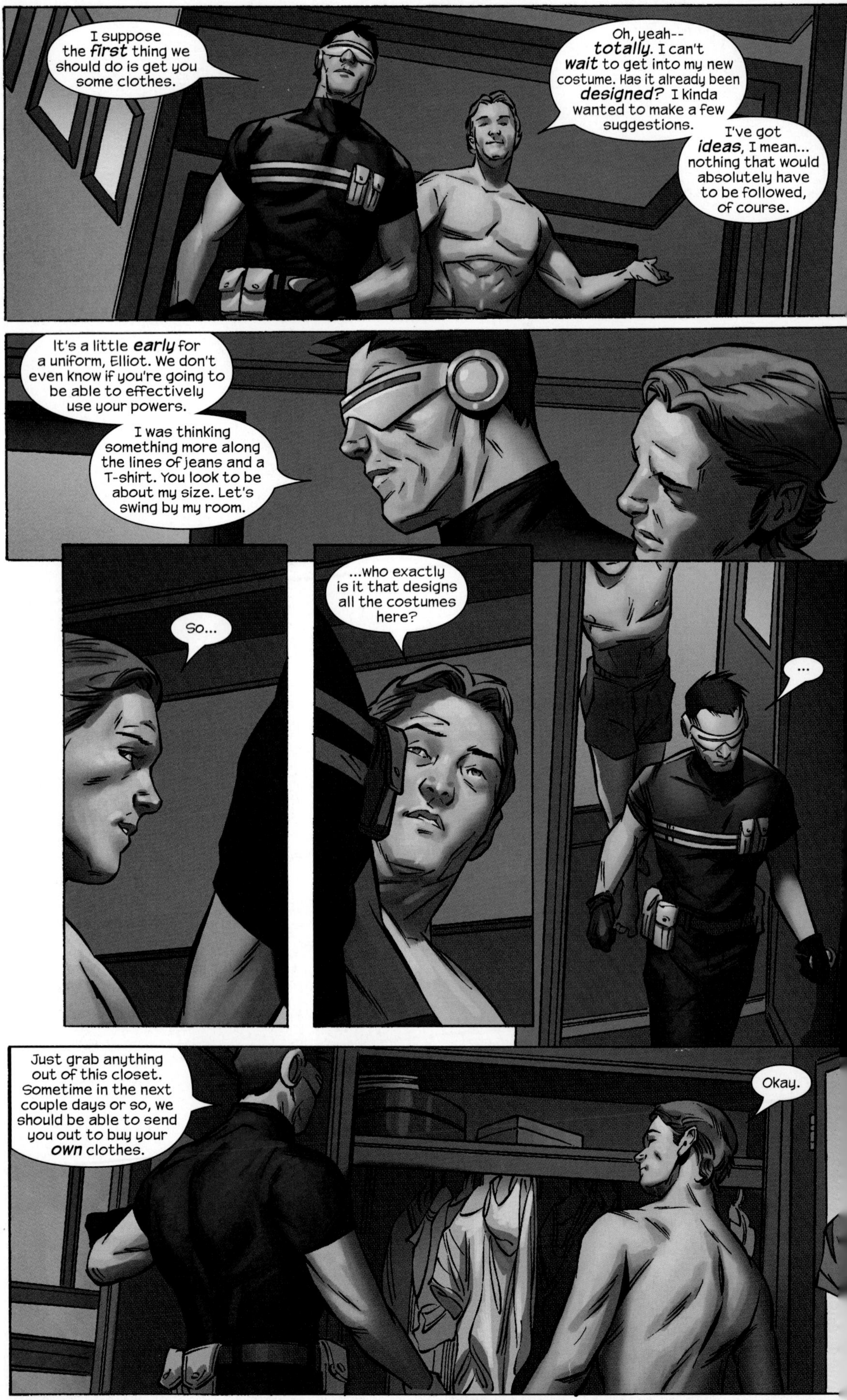
I suppose the *first* thing we should do is get you some clothes.
Oh, yeah-- *totally*. I can't *wait* to get into my new costume. Has it already been *designed?* I kinda wanted to make a few suggestions.
I've got *ideas*, I mean... nothing that would absolutely have to be followed, of course.
It's a little *early* for a uniform, Elliot. We don't even know if you're going to be able to effectively use your powers.
I was thinking something more along the lines of jeans and a T-shirt. You look to be about my size. Let's swing by my room.
So...
...who exactly is it that designs all the costumes here?
...
Just grab anything out of this closet. Sometime in the next couple days or so, we should be able to send you out to buy your *own* clothes.
Okay.

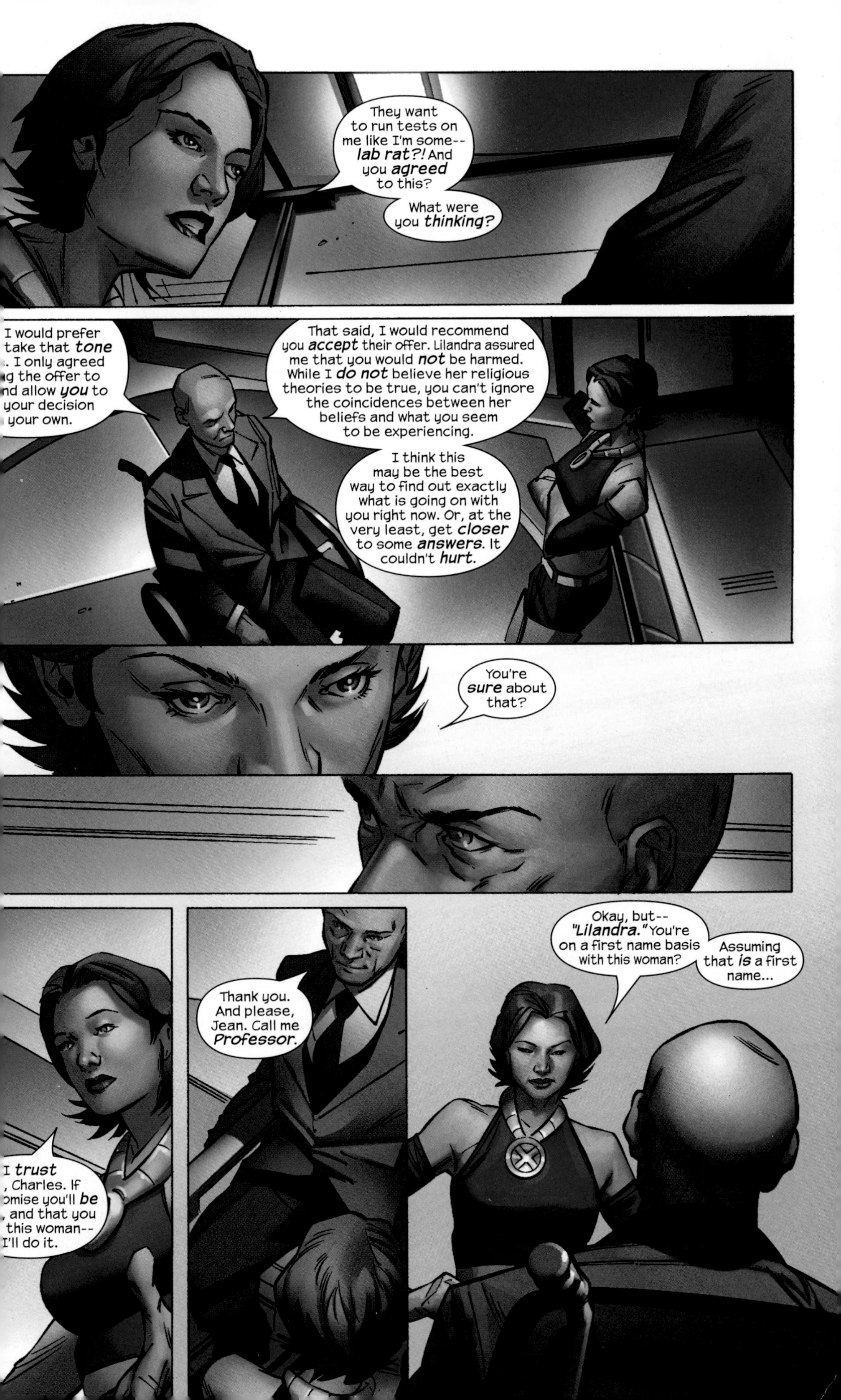

They want to run tests on me like I'm some-- *lab rat?!* And you *agreed* to this?
What were you *thinking?*
I would prefer take that *tone* . I only agreed g the offer to nd allow *you* to your decision your own.
That said, I would recommend you *accept* their offer. Lilandra assured me that you would *not* be harmed. While I *do not* believe her religious theories to be true, you can't ignore the coincidences between her beliefs and what you seem to be experiencing.
I think this may be the best way to find out exactly what is going on with you right now. Or, at the very least, get *closer* to some *answers*. It couldn't *hurt*.
You're *sure* about that?
I *trust* , Charles. If omise you'll *be* , and that you this woman-- I'll do it.
Thank you. And please, Jean. Call me *Professor*.
Okay, but-- *"Lilandra."* You're on a first name basis with this woman?
Assuming that *is* a first name...

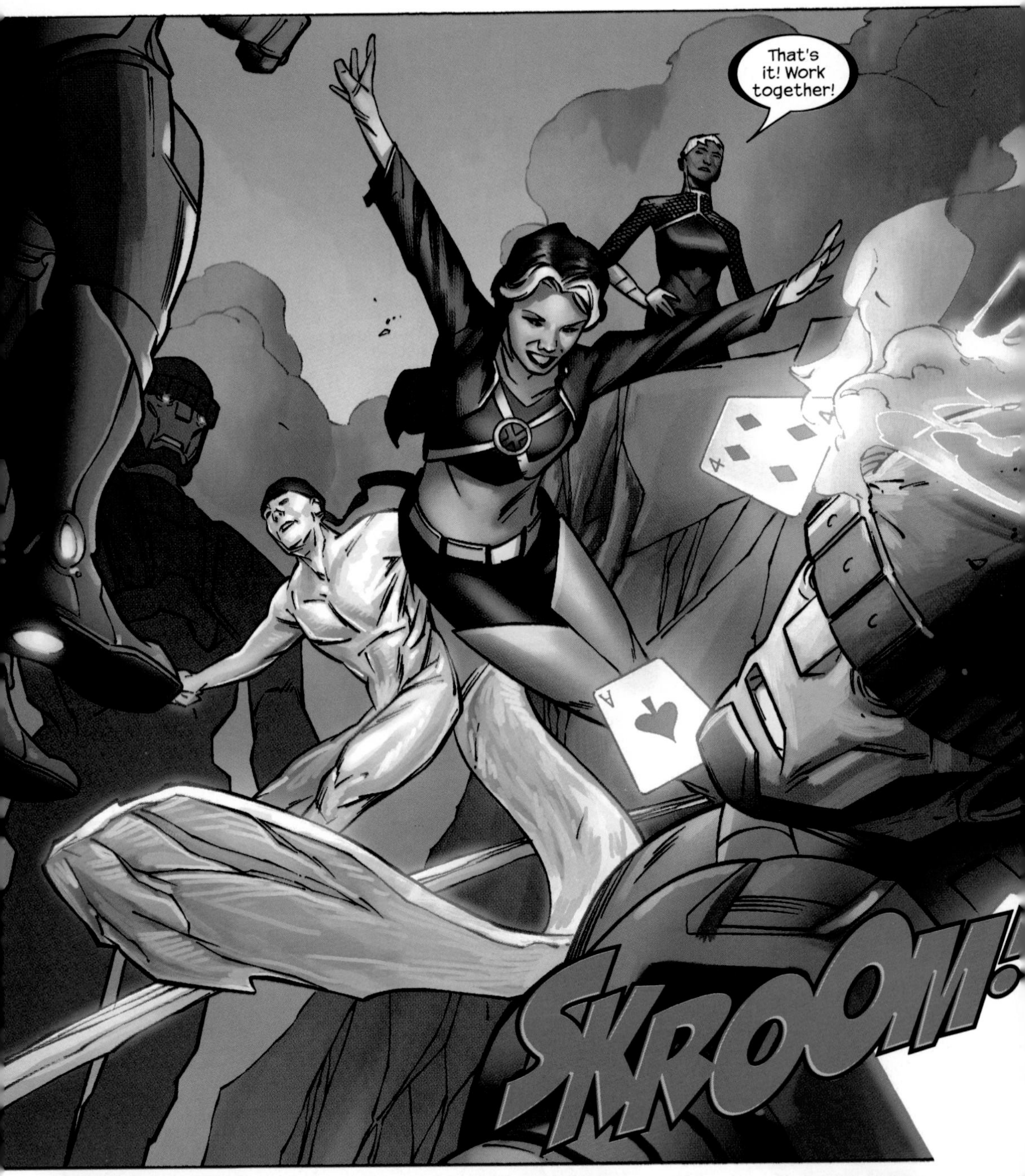
That's it! Work together!
SKROOM!

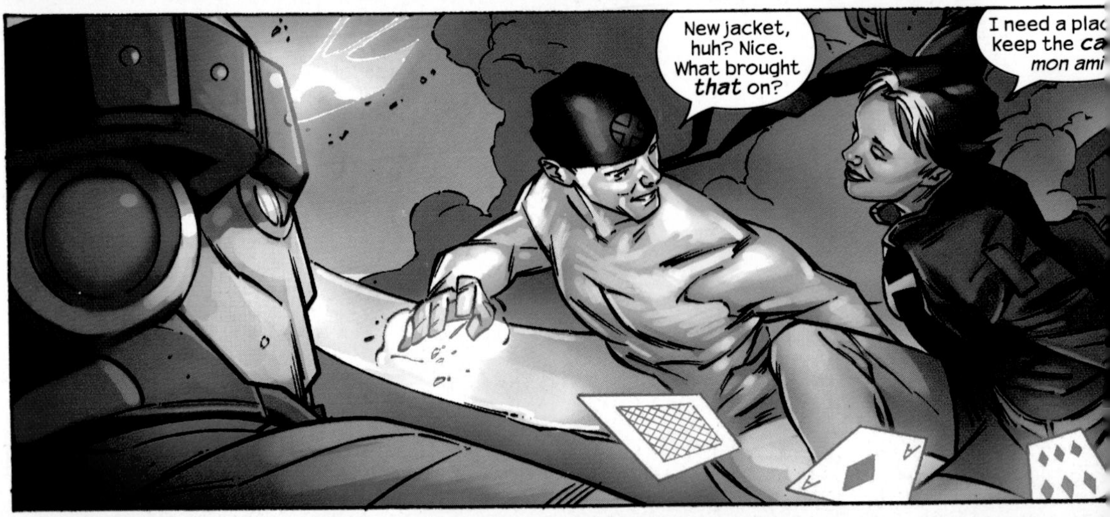
New jacket, huh? Nice. What brought *that* on?
I need a plac keep the ca mon ami

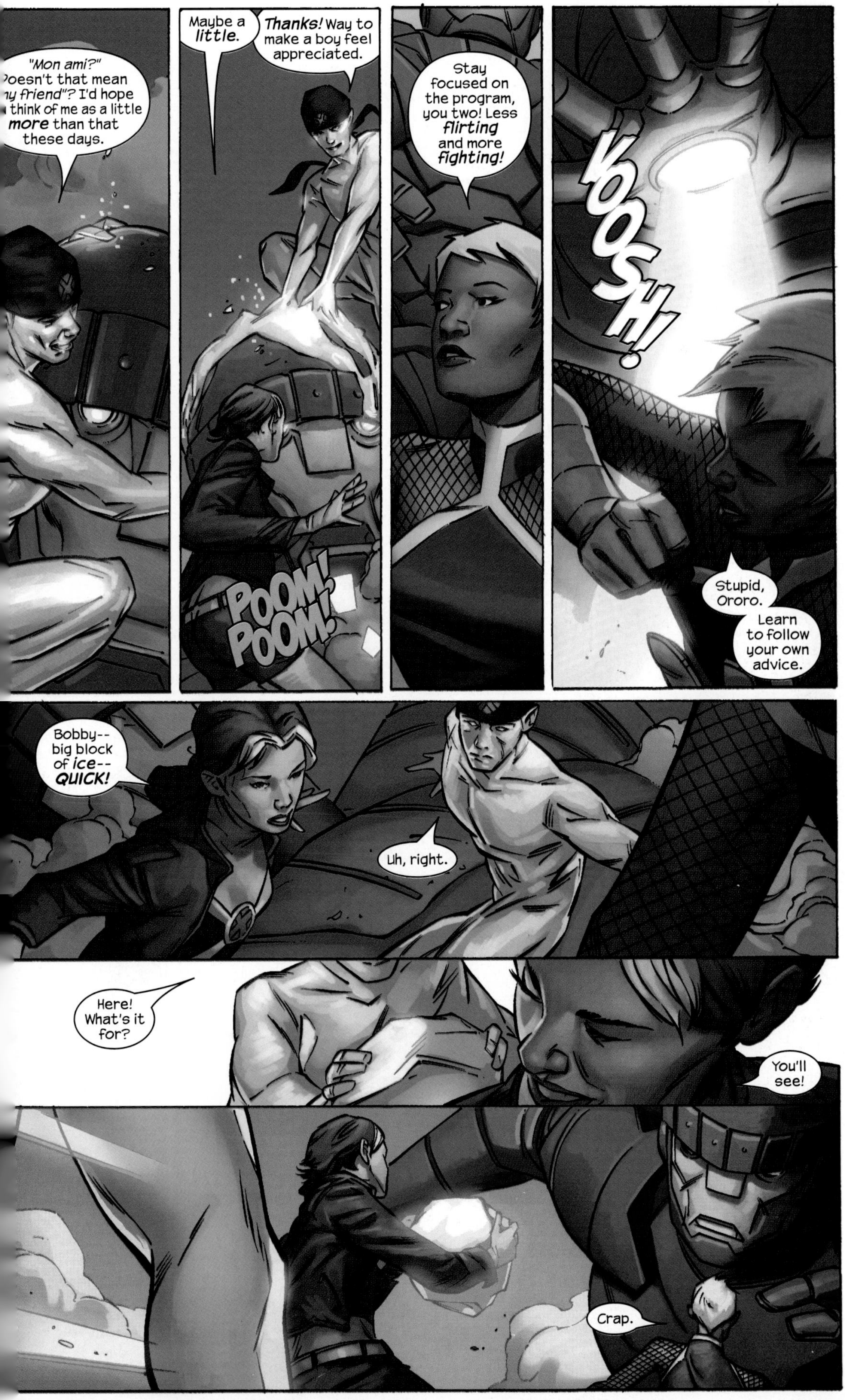
"Mon ami?" Doesn't that mean "my friend"? I'd hope u think of me as a little more than that these days.
Maybe a little.
Thanks! Way to make a boy feel appreciated.
POOM! POOM!
Stay focused on the program, you two! Less flirting and more fighting!
VOOSH!
Stupid, Ororo.
Learn to follow your own advice.
Bobby-- big block of ice-- QUICK!
Uh, right.
Here! What's it for?
You'll see!
Crap.

Storm--take COVER!

What?

FRAGA-BOOM!

Okay, program OFF.

That's not exactly what I had *planned* when I wrote this program--but it works.

Thanks for giving it a run-through with me.

Anytime. Thanks for the workout.

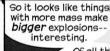

So it looks like things with more mass make *bigger* explosions-- interesting.

Of all th things you carry in ord charge up a as a weapo why *card*

I don't really know...

Easy to carry a bunch? It gives me something to do if I get bored?

One of those.

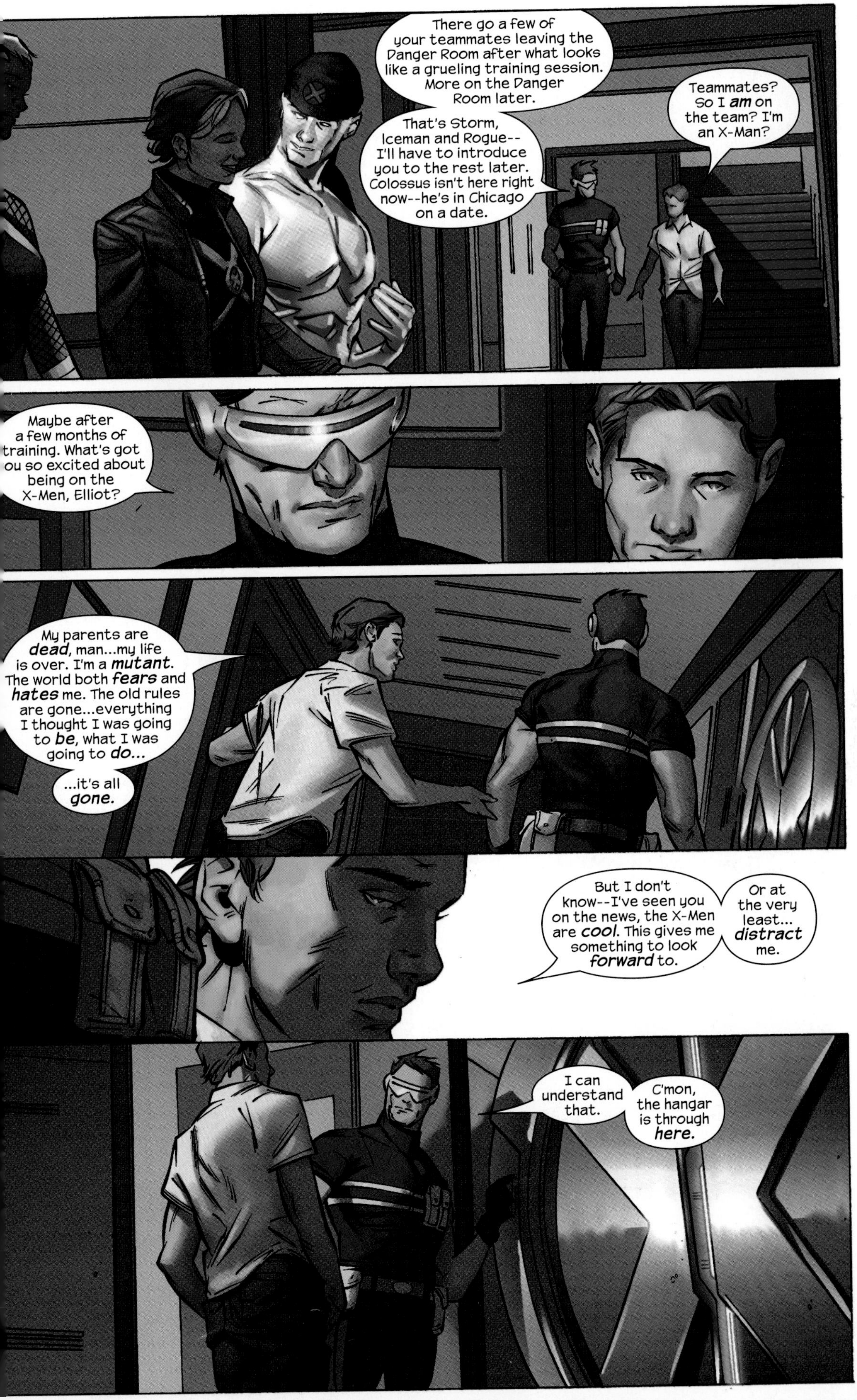
There go a few of your teammates leaving the Danger Room after what looks like a grueling training session. More on the Danger Room later.
That's Storm, Iceman and Rogue-- I'll have to introduce you to the rest later. Colossus isn't here right now--he's in Chicago on a date.
Teammates? So I *am* on the team? I'm an X-Man?
Maybe after a few months of training. What's got ou so excited about being on the X-Men, Elliot?
My parents are *dead*, man...my life is over. I'm a *mutant*. The world both *fears* and *hates* me. The old rules are gone...everything I thought I was going to *be*, what I was going to *do...*
...it's all *gone.*
But I don't know--I've seen you on the news, the X-Men are *cool*. This gives me something to look *forward* to.
Or at the very least... *distract* me.
I can understand that.
C'mon, the hangar is through *here.*

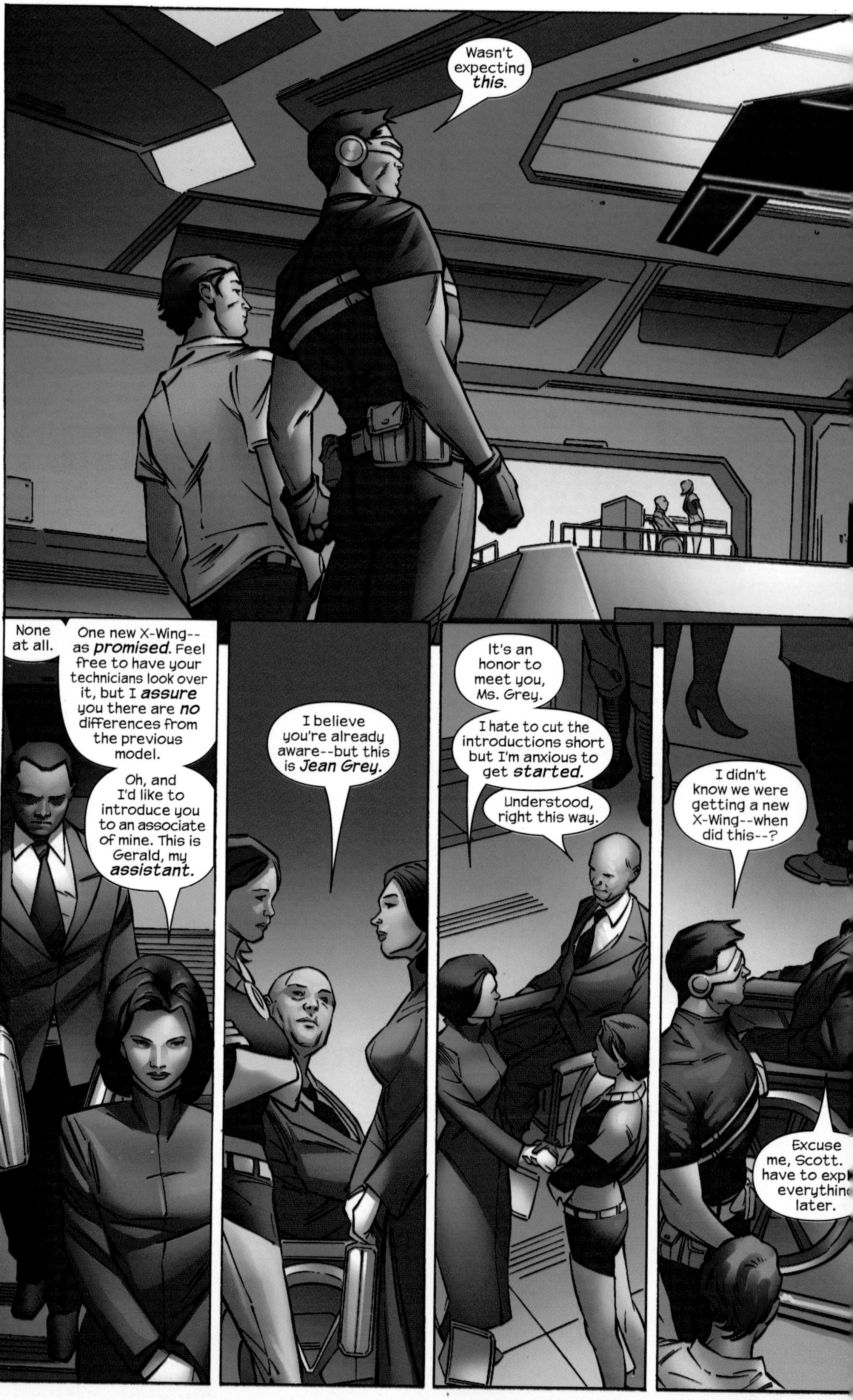

Wasn't expecting *this*.
None at all.
One new X-Wing--as *promised*. Feel free to have your technicians look over it, but I *assure* you there are *no* differences from the previous model.
Oh, and I'd like to introduce you to an associate of mine. This is Gerald, my *assistant*.
I believe you're already aware--but this is *Jean Grey*.
It's an honor to meet you, Ms. Grey.
I hate to cut the introductions short but I'm anxious to get *started*.
Understood, right this way.
I didn't know we were getting a new X-Wing--when did this--?
Excuse me, Scott.

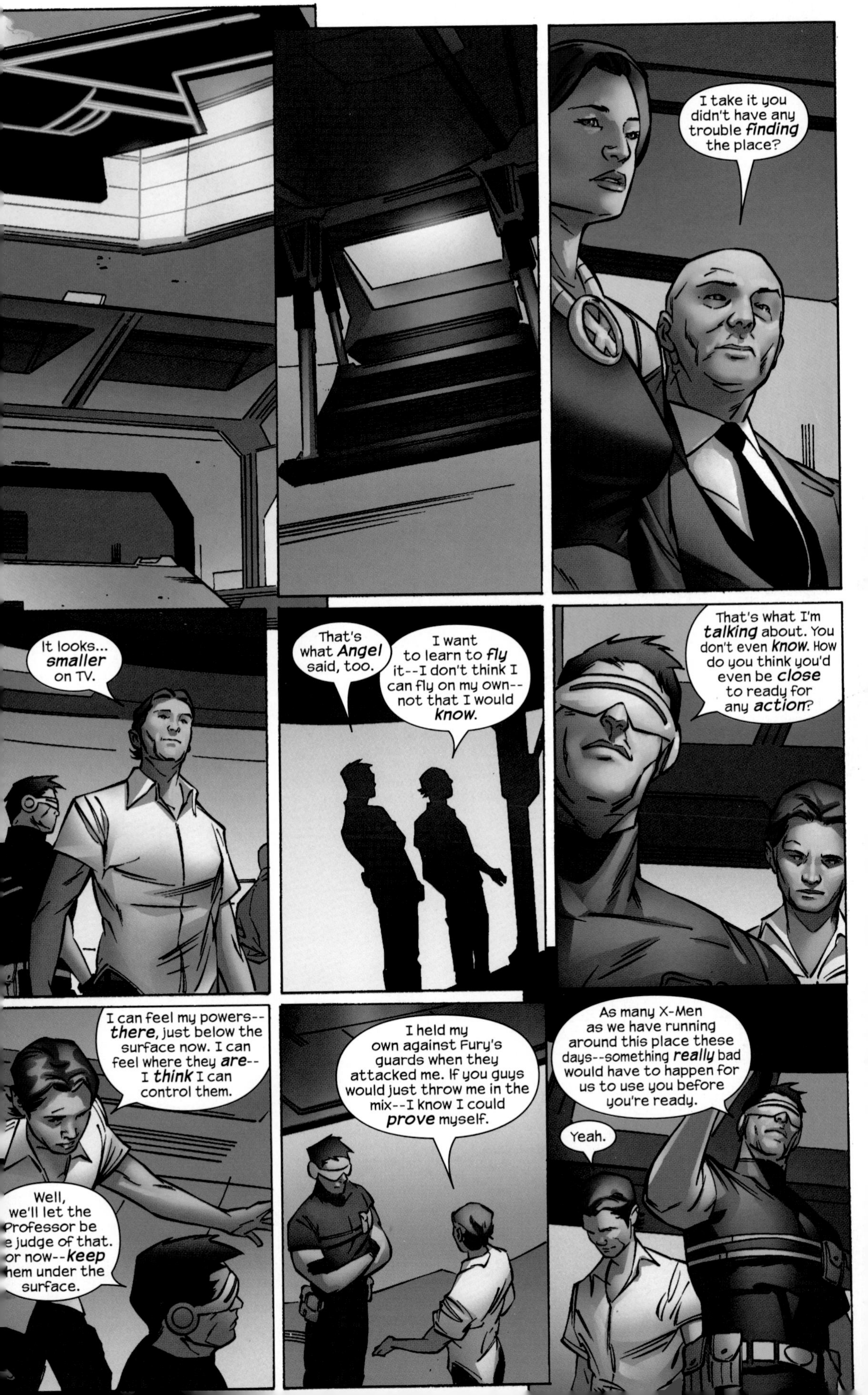
I take it you didn't have any trouble *finding* the place?
It looks... *smaller* on TV.
That's what *Angel* said, too.
I want to learn to *fly* it--I don't think I can fly on my own--not that I would *know*.
That's what I'm *talking* about. You don't even *know*. How do you think you'd even be *close* to ready for any *action*?
I can feel my powers--*there*, just below the surface now. I can feel where they *are*--I *think* I can control them.
Well, we'll let the Professor be e judge of that. or now--*keep* hem under the surface.
I held my own against Fury's guards when they attacked me. If you guys would just throw me in the mix--I know I could *prove* myself.
As many X-Men as we have running around this place these days--something *really* bad would have to happen for us to use you before you're ready.
Yeah.

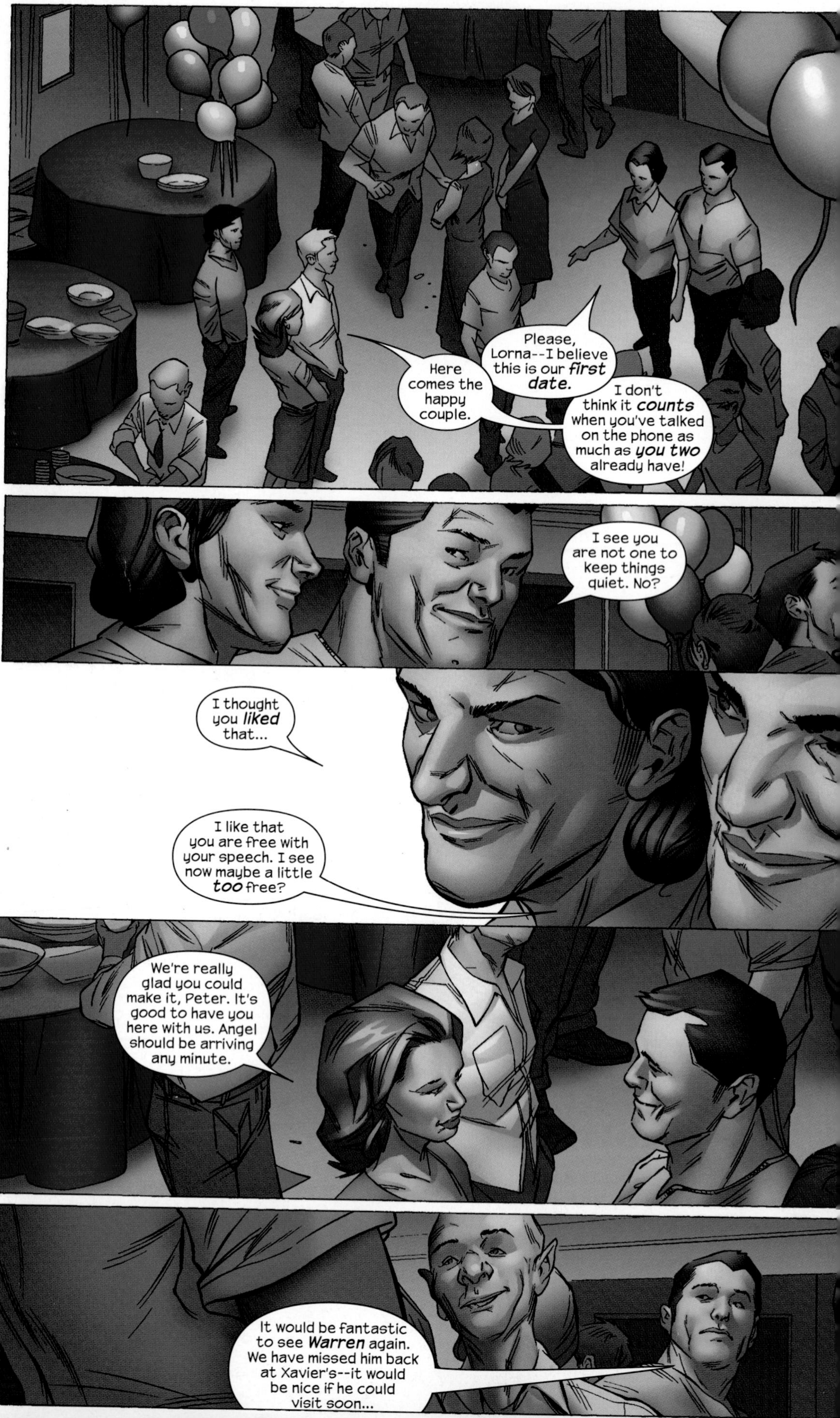

Here comes the happy couple.
Please, Lorna--I believe this is our *first* *date.*
I don't think it *counts* when you've talked on the phone as much as *you two* already have!
I see you are not one to keep things quiet. No?
I thought you *liked* that...
I like that you are free with your speech. I see now maybe a little *too* free?
We're really glad you could make it, Peter. It's good to have you here with us. Angel should be arriving any minute.
It would be fantastic to see *Warren* again. We have missed him back at Xavier's--it would be nice if he could visit soon...

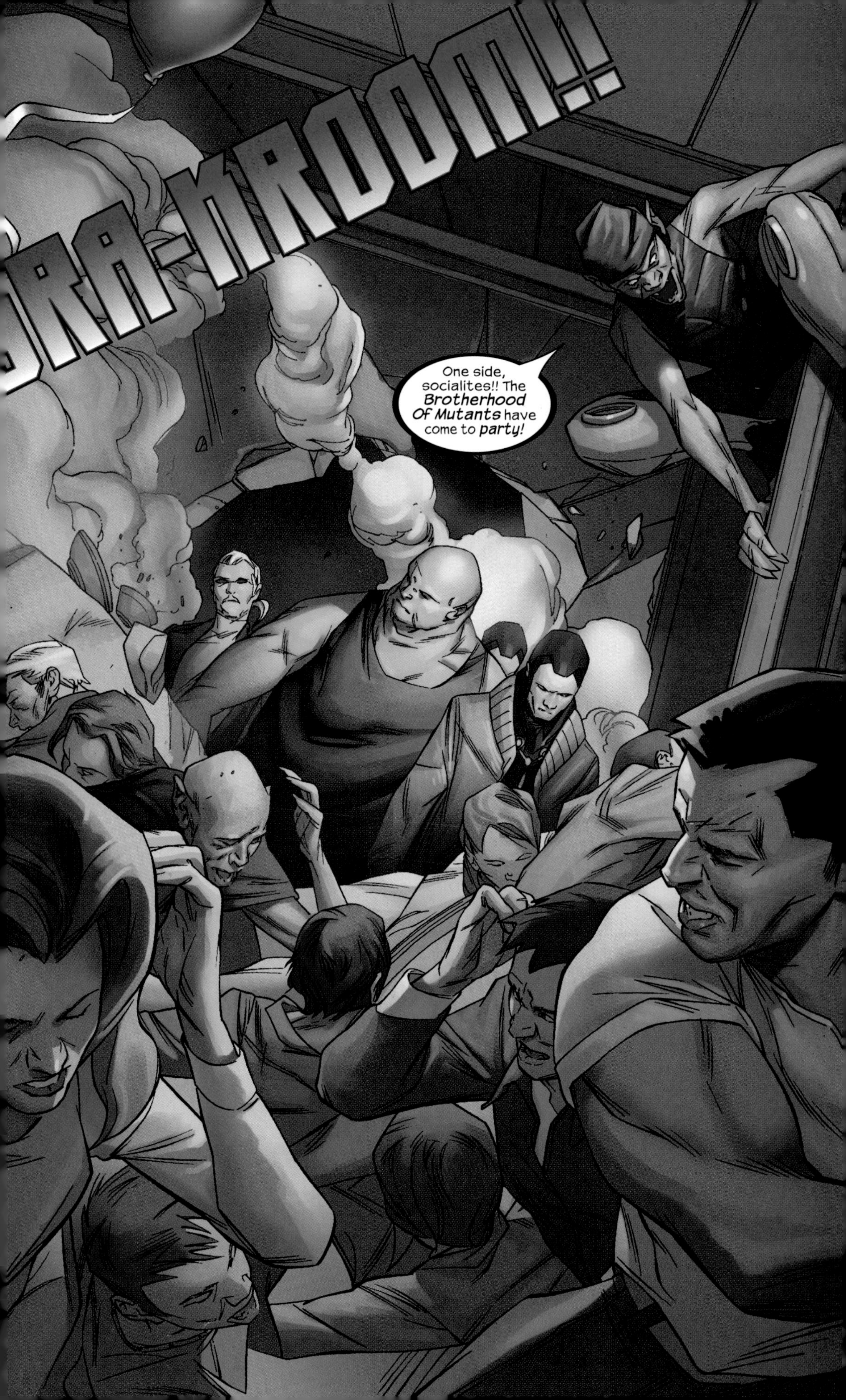
KRA-KROOM!!
One side, socialites!! The *Brotherhood Of Mutants* have come to *party!*

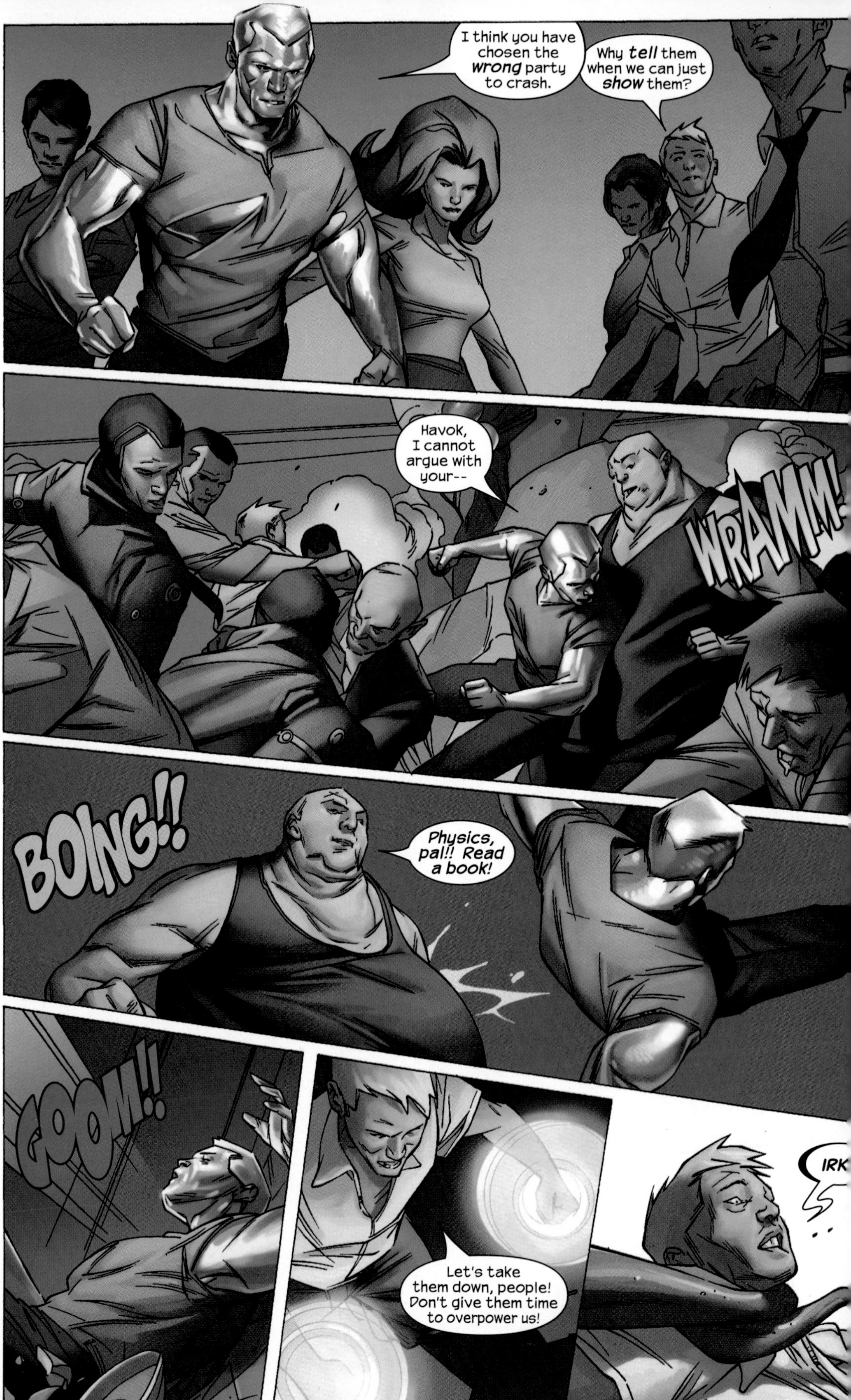
I think you have chosen the *wrong* party to crash.
Why *tell* them when we can just *show* them?
Havok, I cannot argue with your--
WRAMM!
BOING!!
Physics, pal!! Read a book!
GOOM!!
Let's take them down, people! Don't give them time to overpower us!
IRK

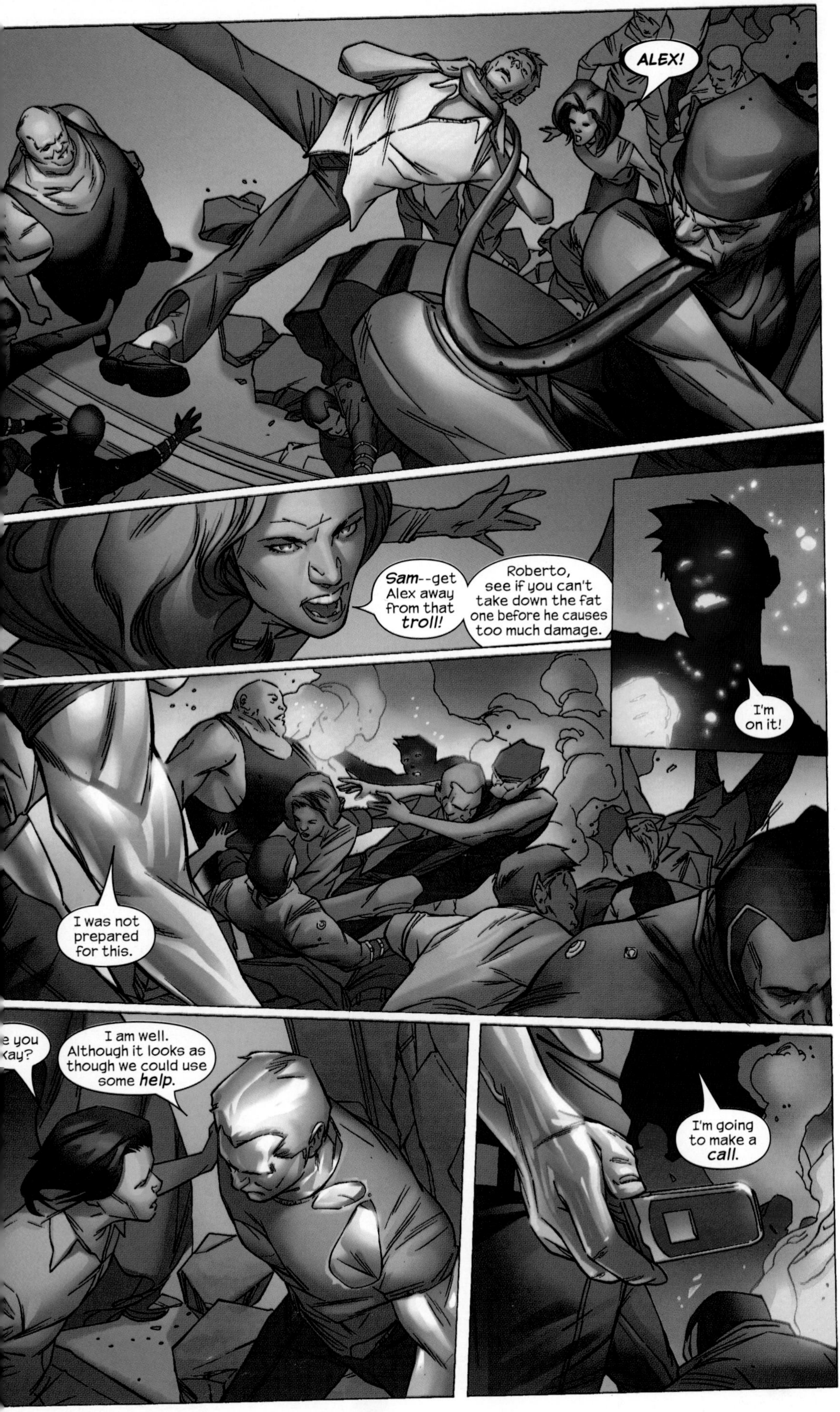
ALEX!
Sam--get Alex away from that troll!
Roberto, see if you can't take down the fat one before he causes too much damage.
I'm on it!
I was not prepared for this.
e you kay?
I am well. Although it looks as though we could use some help.
I'm going to make a call.

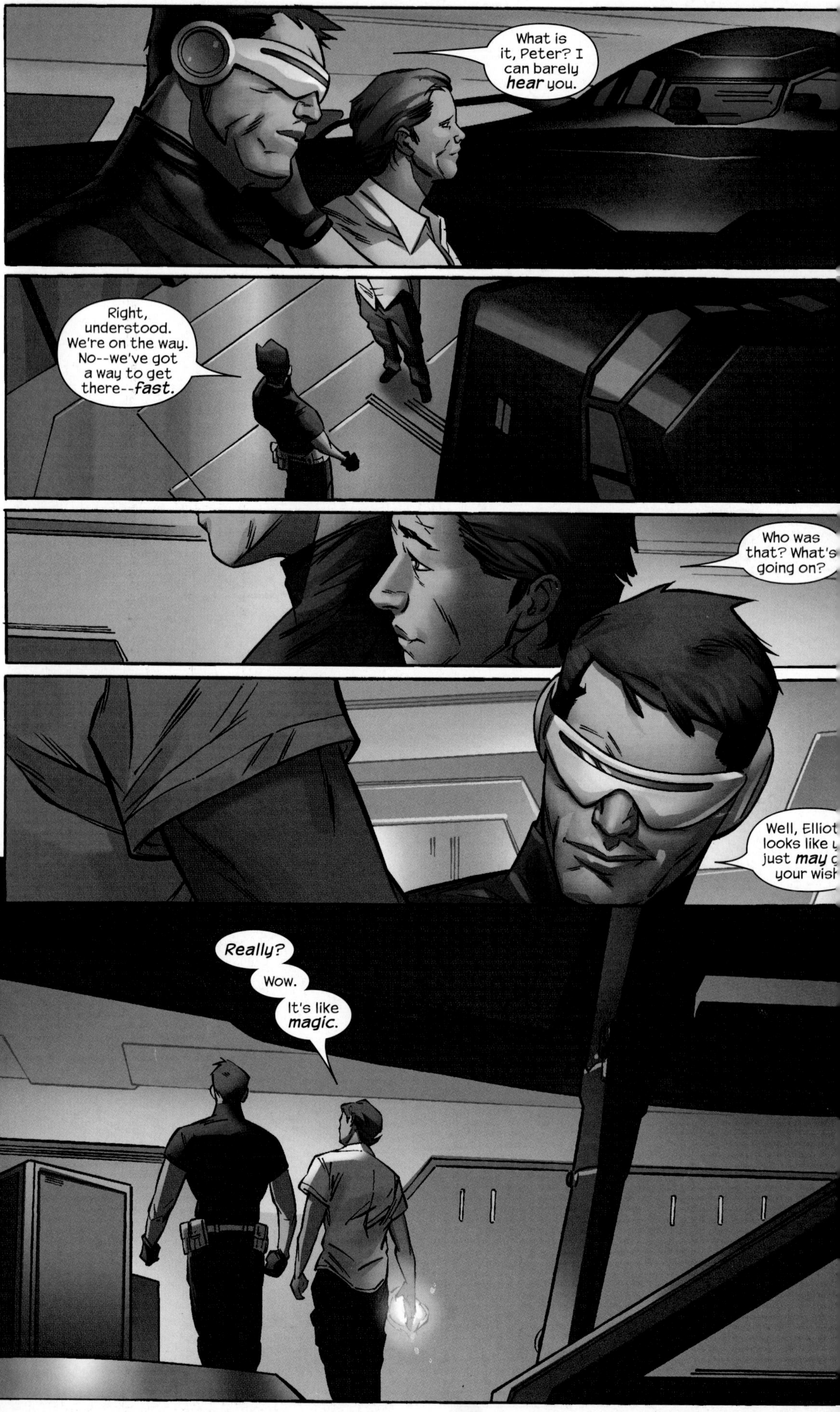
What is it, Peter? I can barely *hear* you.
Right, understood. We're on the way. No--we've got a way to get there--*fast.*
Who was that? What's going on?
Well, Elliot looks like y just *may* g your wish
Really?
Wow.
It's like *magic*.

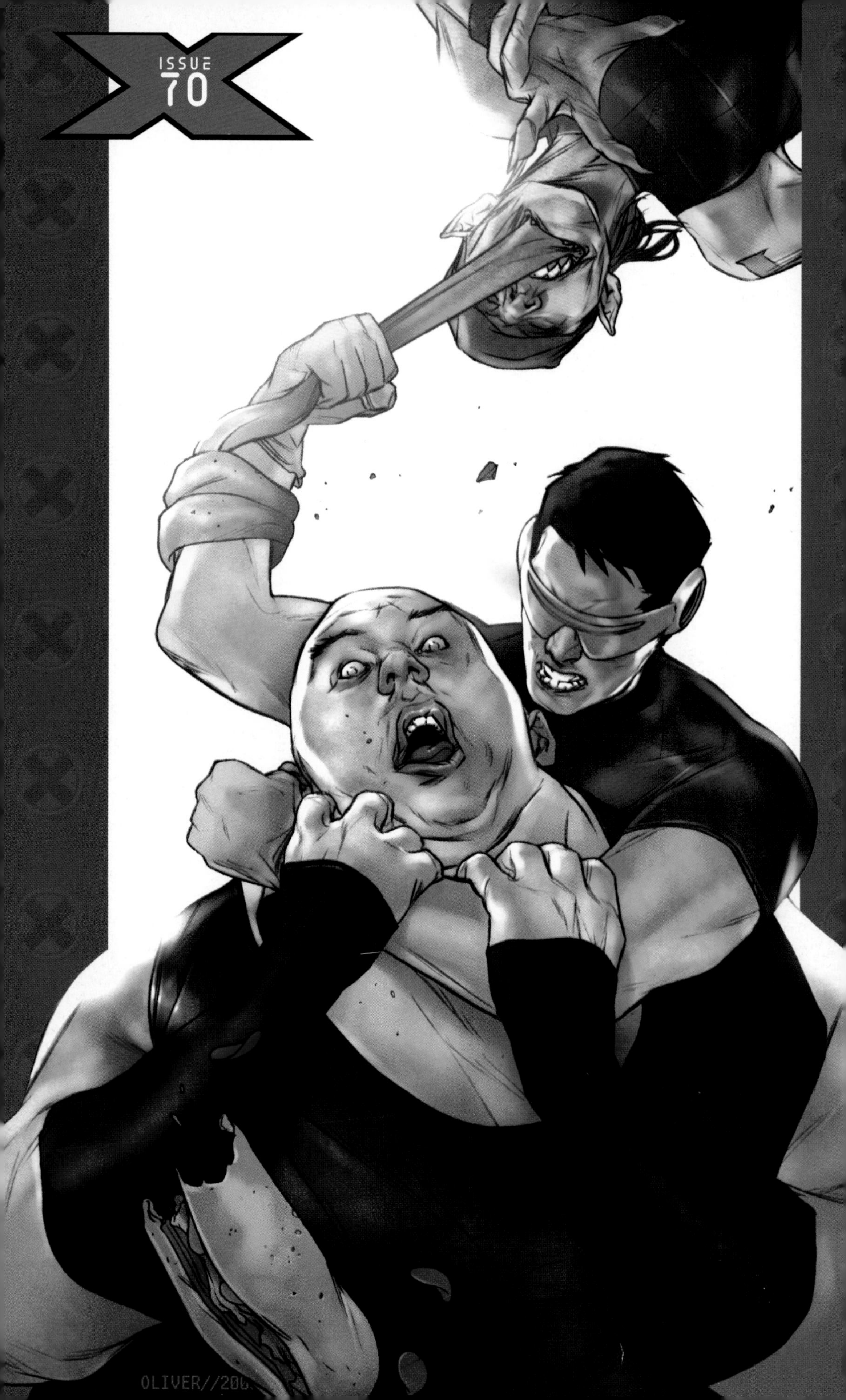
ISSUE
70

PHOENIX?

PART 2 OF 3

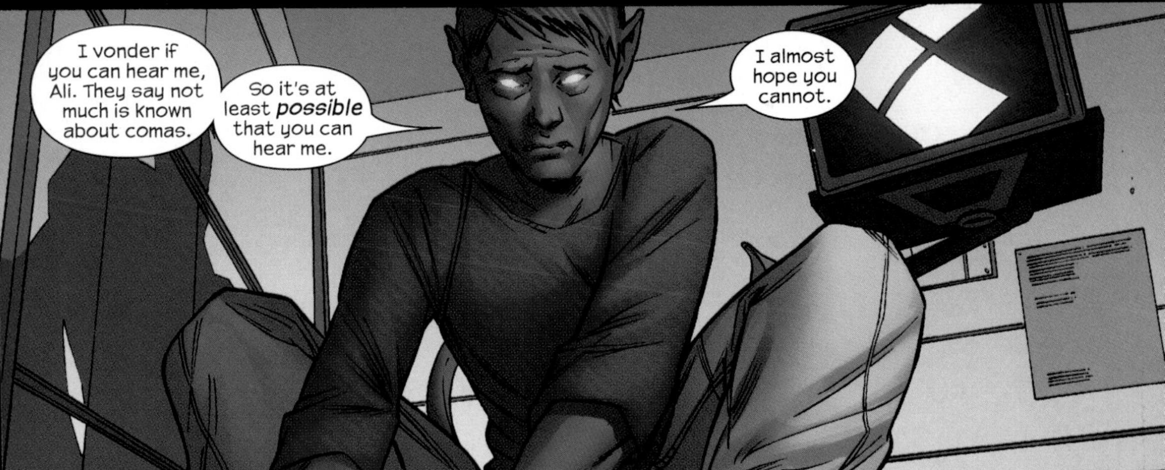
I vonder if you can hear me, Ali. They say not much is known about comas.
So it's at least *possible* that you can hear me.
I almost hope you cannot.

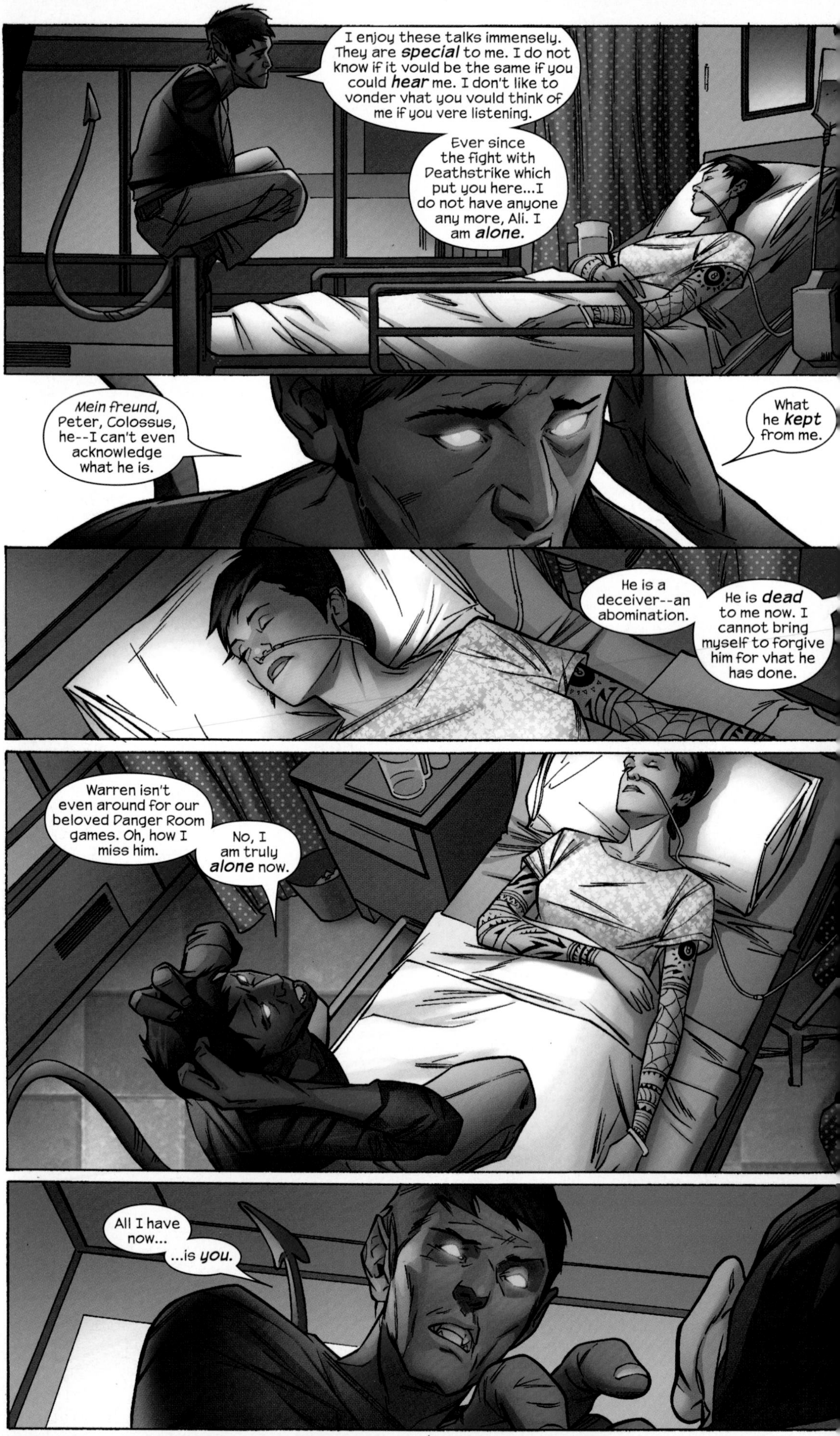
I enjoy these talks immensely. They are *special* to me. I do not know if it vould be the same if you could *hear* me. I don't like to vonder vhat you vould think of me if you vere listening.
Ever since the fight with Deathstrike which put you here...I do not have anyone any more, Ali. I am *alone.*
Mein freund, Peter, Colossus, he--I can't even acknowledge what he is.
What he *kept* from me.
He is a deceiver--an abomination.
He is *dead* to me now. I cannot bring myself to forgive him for vhat he has done.
Warren isn't even around for our beloved Danger Room games. Oh, how I miss him.
No, I am truly *alone* now.
All I have now...
...is *you.*

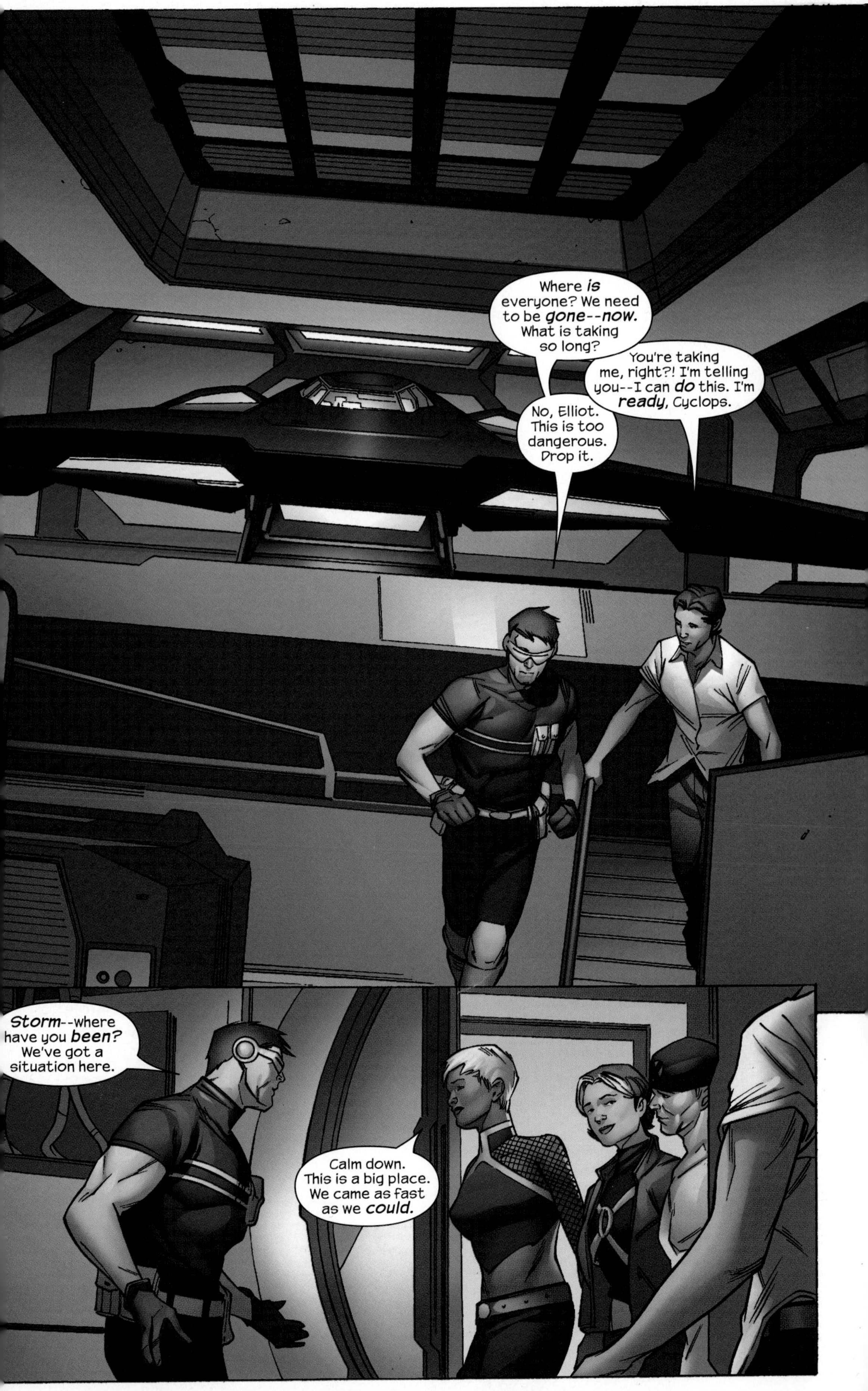

Where *is* everyone? We need to be *gone*--*now.* What is taking so long?
You're taking me, right?! I'm telling you--I can *do* this. I'm *ready*, Cyclops.
No, Elliot. This is too dangerous. Drop it.
Storm--where have you *been?* We've got a situation here.
Calm down. This is a big place. We came as fast as we *could.*

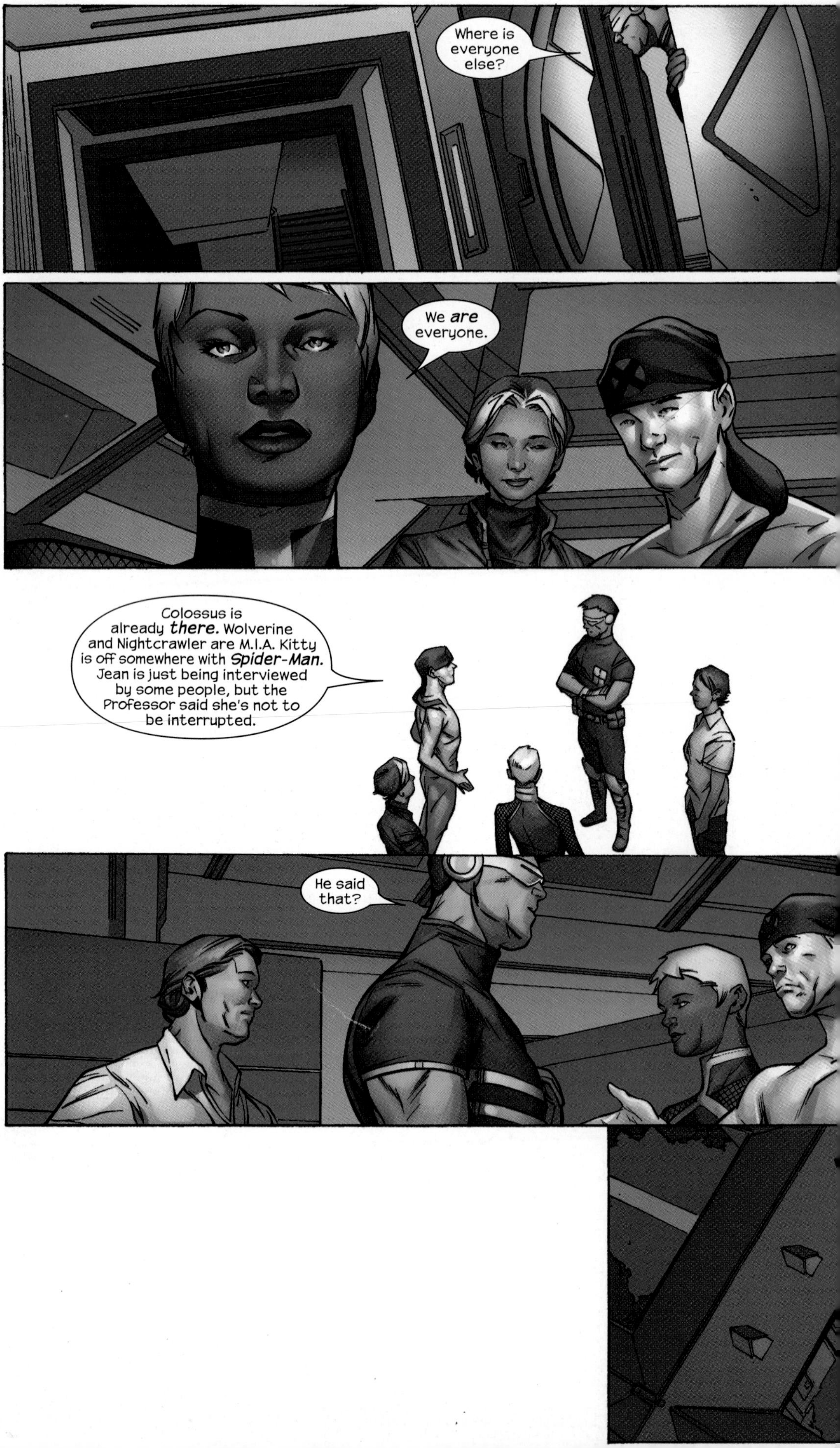

Where is everyone else?
We *are* everyone.
Colossus is already *there.* Wolverine and Nightcrawler are M.I.A. Kitty is off somewhere with *Spider-Man.* Jean is just being interviewed by some people, but the Professor said she's not to be interrupted.
He said that?

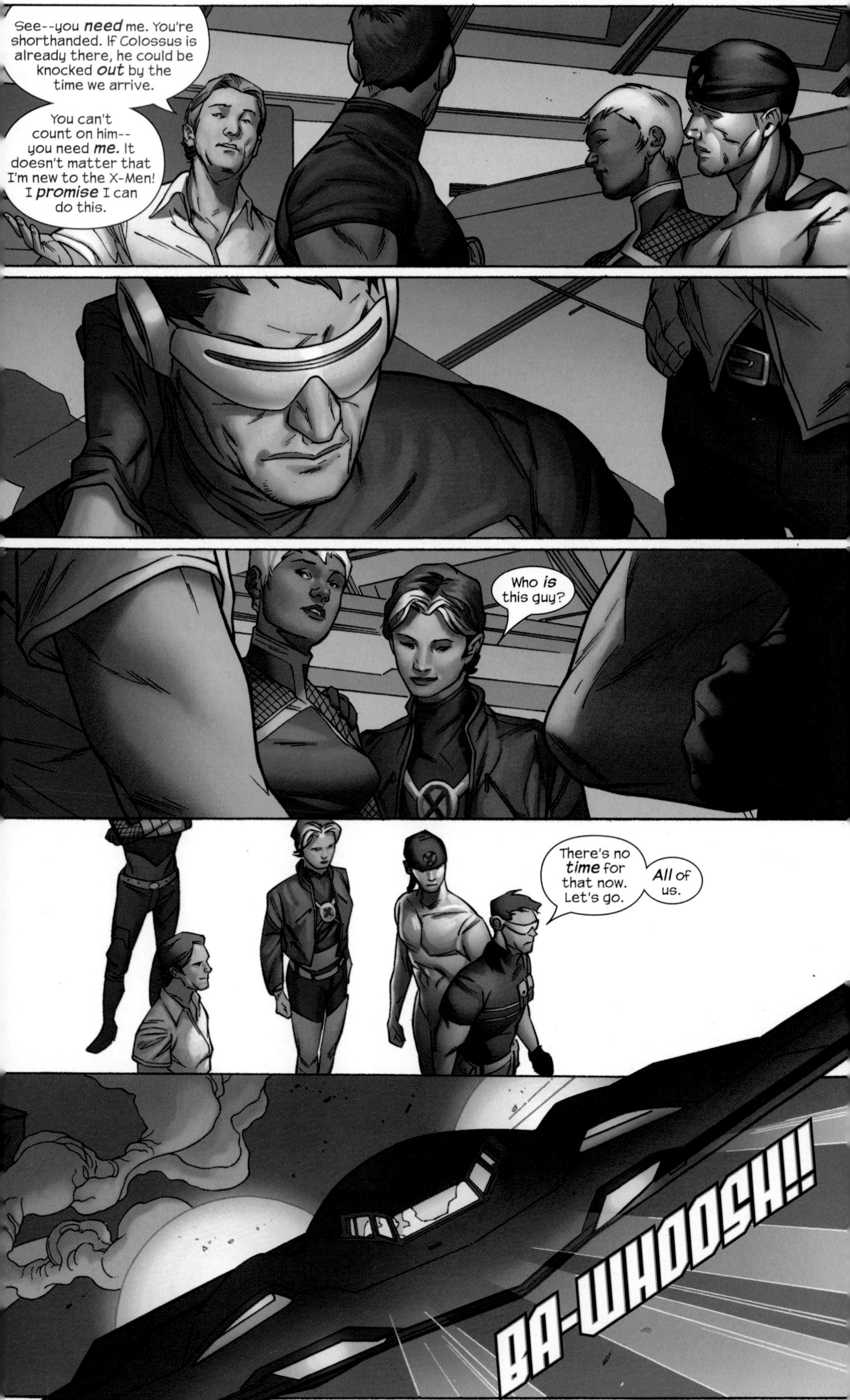
See--you *need* me. You're shorthanded. If Colossus is already there, he could be knocked *out* by the time we arrive.
You can't count on him--you need *me.* It doesn't matter that I'm new to the X-Men! I *promise* I can do this.
Who *is* this guy?
There's no *time* for that now. Let's go.
All of us.
BA-WHOOSH!!

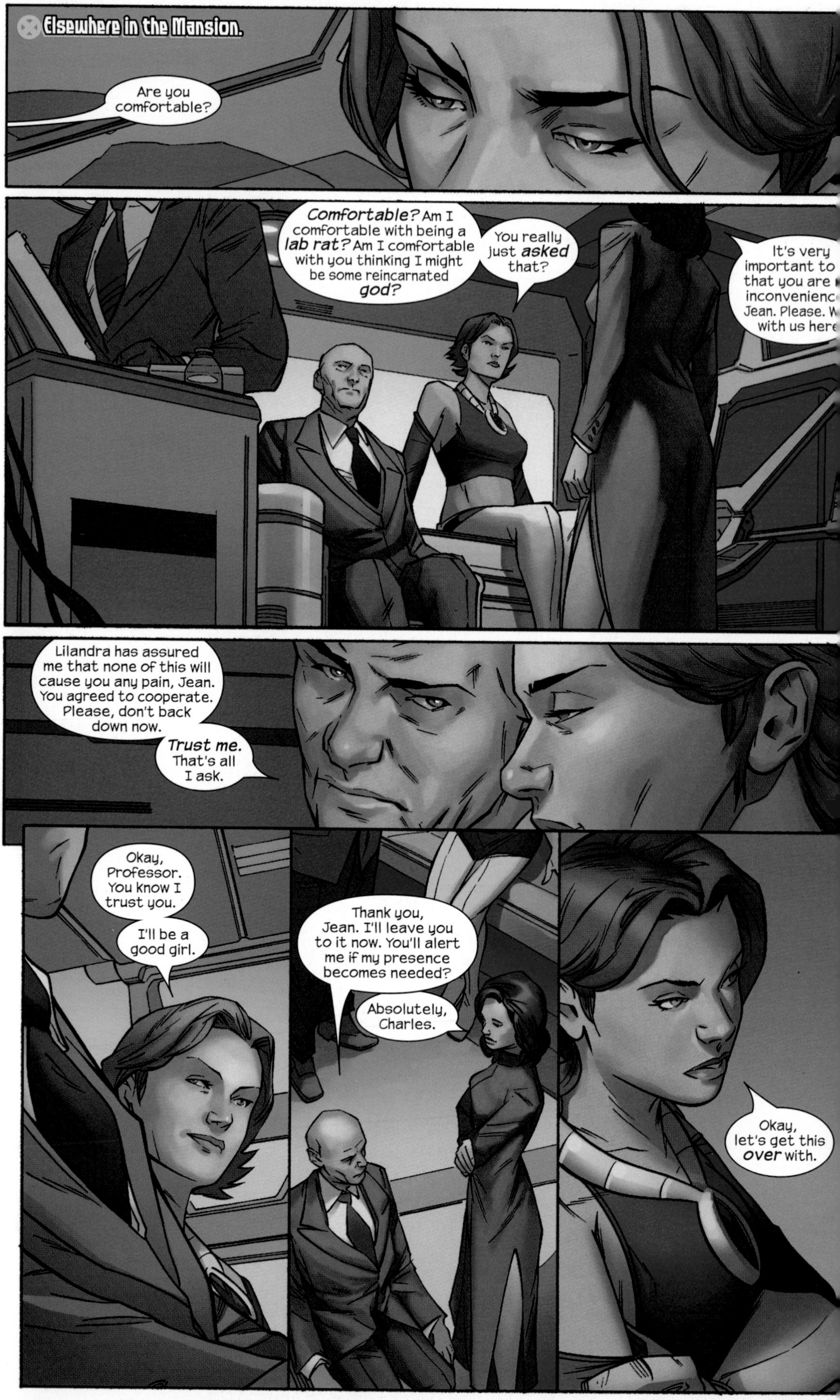
Elsewhere in the Mansion.
Are you comfortable?
Comfortable? Am I comfortable with being a lab rat? Am I comfortable with you thinking I might be some reincarnated god?
You really just asked that?
It's very important to that you are inconvenienc Jean. Please. W with us here
Lilandra has assured me that none of this will cause you any pain, Jean. You agreed to cooperate. Please, don't back down now.
Trust me. That's all I ask.
Okay, Professor. You know I trust you.
I'll be a good girl.
Thank you, Jean. I'll leave you to it now. You'll alert me if my presence becomes needed?
Absolutely, Charles.
Okay, let's get this over with.

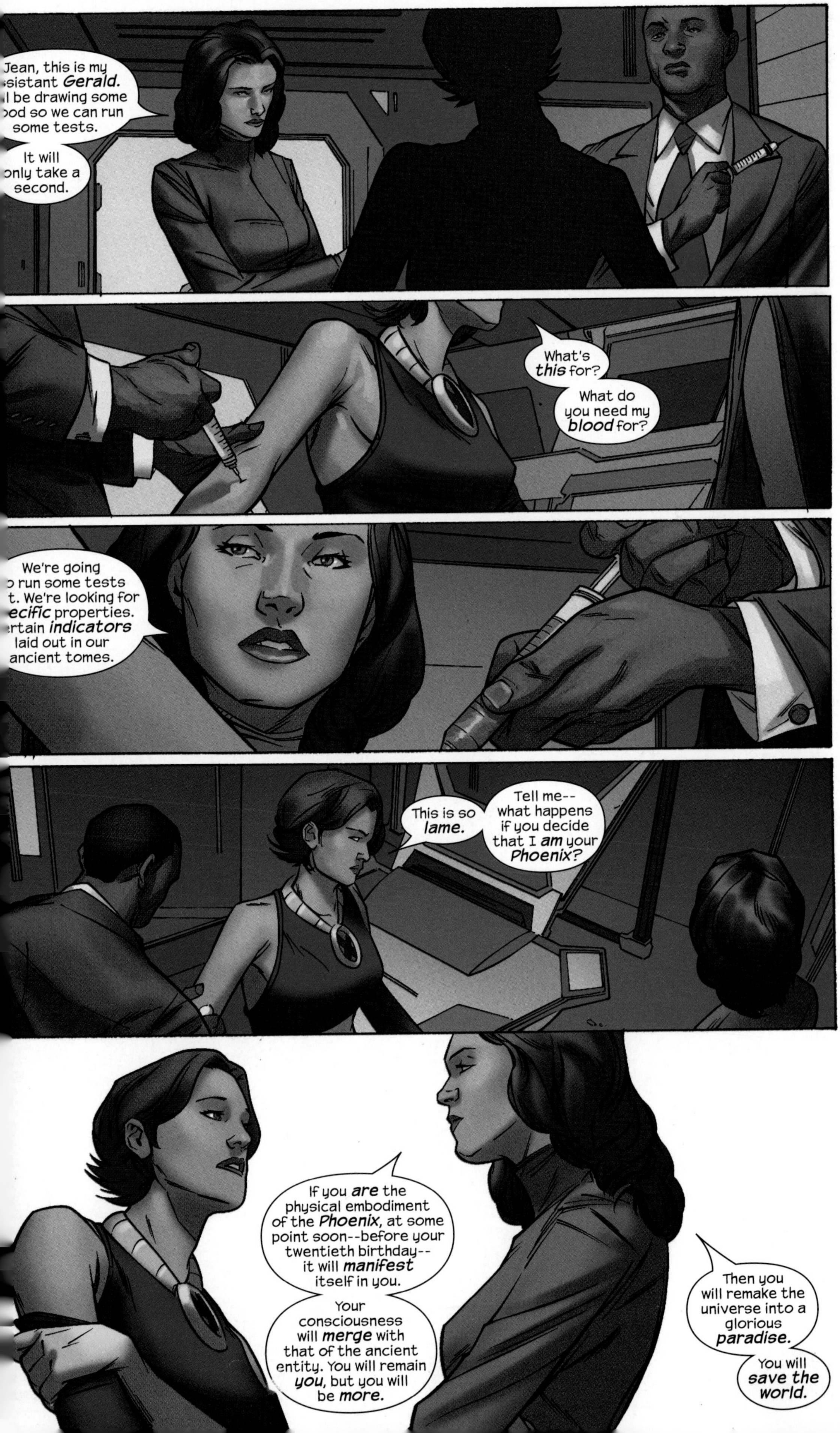

Jean, this is my
ssistant Gerald.
l be drawing some
ood so we can run
some tests.
It will
only take a
second.
What's
this for?
What do
you need my
blood for?
We're going
o run some tests
t. We're looking for
ecific properties.
rtain indicators
laid out in our
ancient tomes.
This is so
lame.
Tell me--
what happens
if you decide
that I am your
Phoenix?
If you are the
physical embodiment
of the Phoenix, at some
point soon--before your
twentieth birthday--
it will manifest
itself in you.
Your
consciousness
will merge with
that of the ancient
entity. You will remain
you, but you will
be more.
Then you
will remake the
universe into a
glorious
paradise.
You will
save the
world.

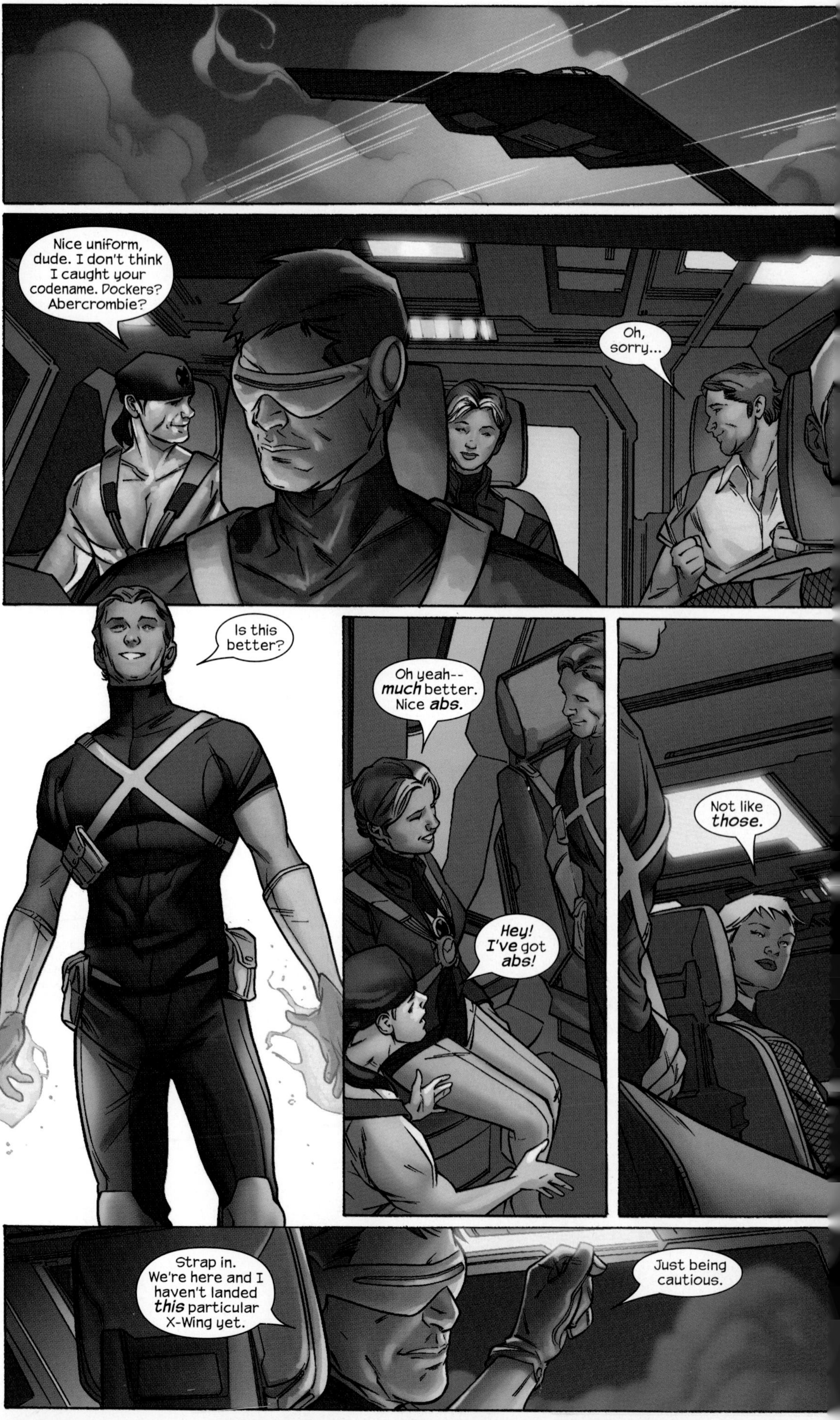
Nice uniform, dude. I don't think I caught your codename. Dockers? Abercrombie?
Oh, sorry...
Is this better?
Oh yeah-- *much* better. Nice *abs.*
Hey! I've got abs!
Not like *those.*
Strap in. We're here and I haven't landed *this* particular X-Wing yet.
Just being cautious.

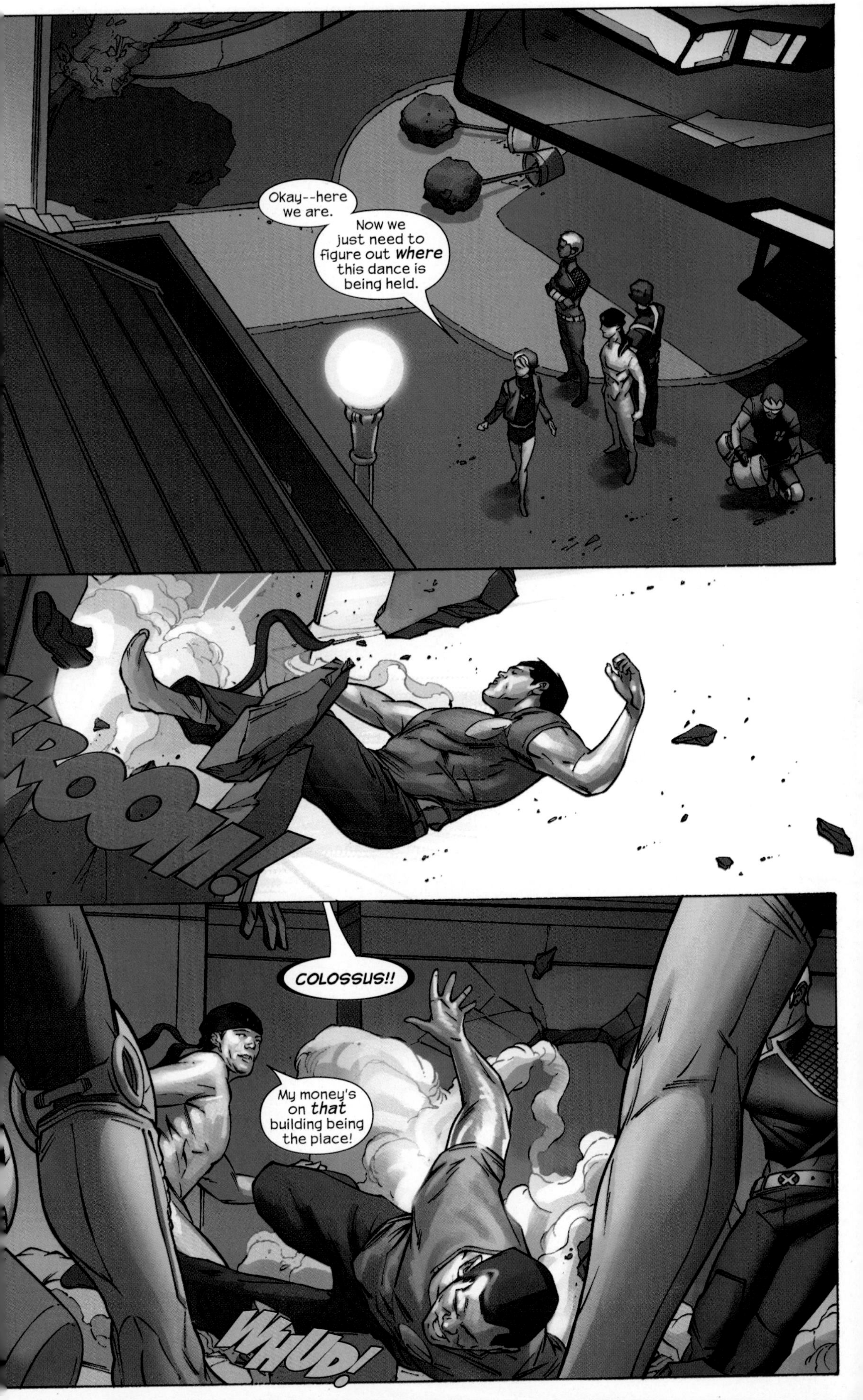
Okay--here we are.
Now we just need to figure out *where* this dance is being held.
WHOOM!
COLOSSUS!!
My money's on *that* building being the place!
WHUD!

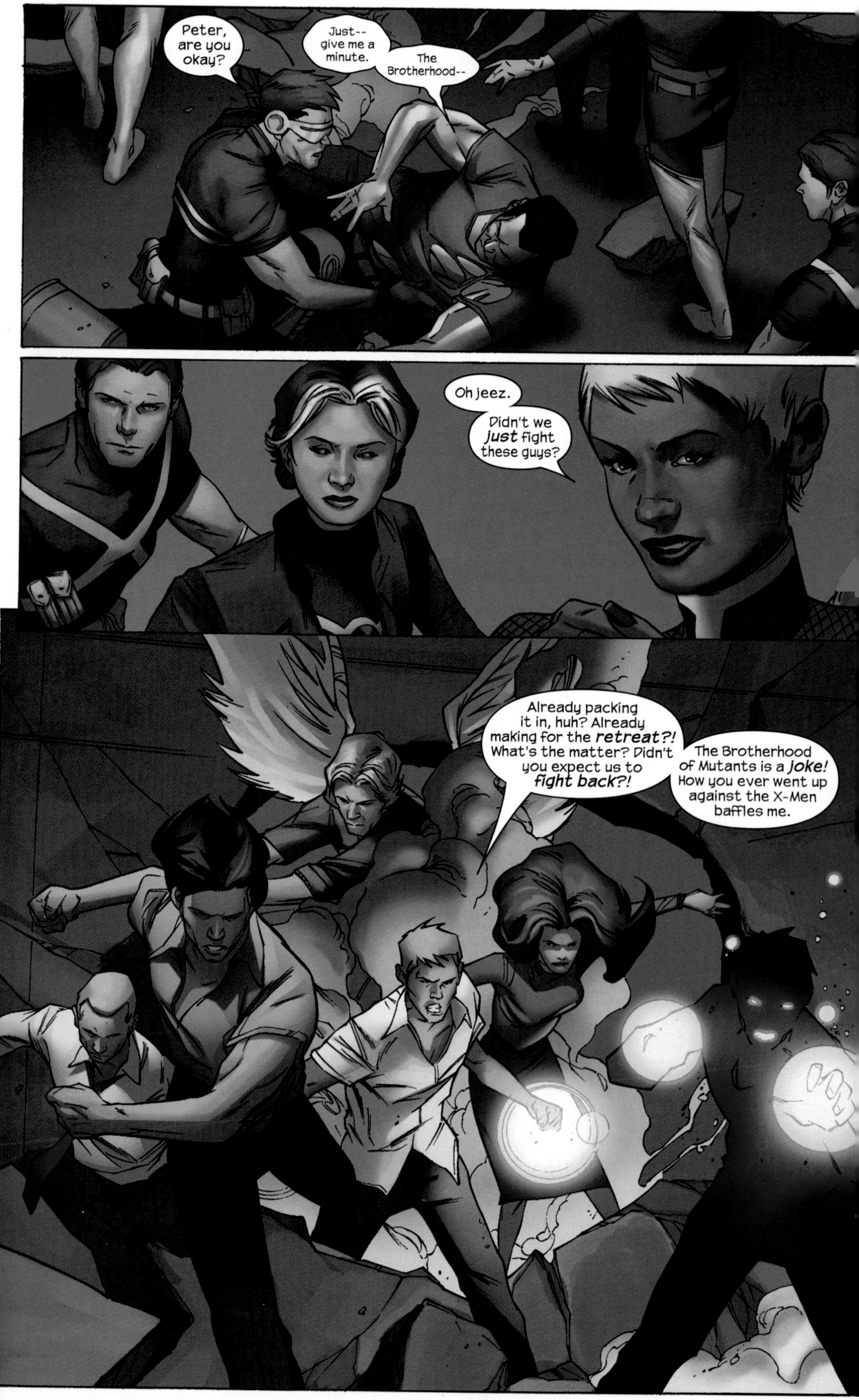
Peter, are you okay?
Just-- give me a minute.
The Brotherhood--
Oh jeez.
Didn't we *just* fight these guys?
Already packing it in, huh? Already making for the ***retreat?!*** What's the matter? Didn't you expect us to ***fight back?!***
The Brotherhood of Mutants is a ***joke!*** How you ever went up against the X-Men baffles me.

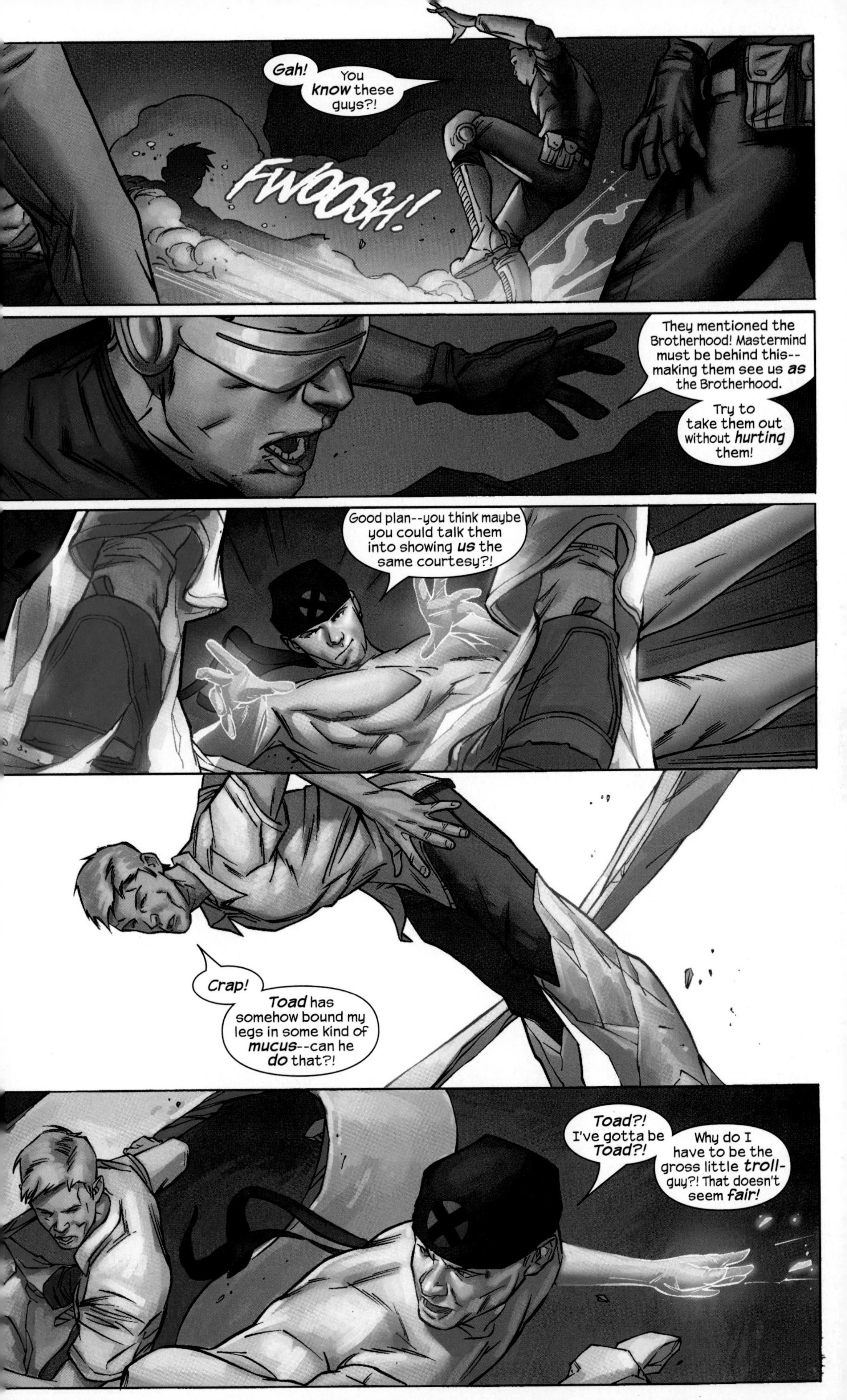
Gah!
You know these guys?!
FWOOSH!
They mentioned the Brotherhood! Mastermind must be behind this-- making them see us as the Brotherhood.
Try to take them out without hurting them!
Good plan--you think maybe you could talk them into showing us the same courtesy?!
Crap!
Toad has somehow bound my legs in some kind of mucus--can he do that?!
Toad?! I've gotta be Toad?!
Why do I have to be the gross little troll-guy?! That doesn't seem fair!

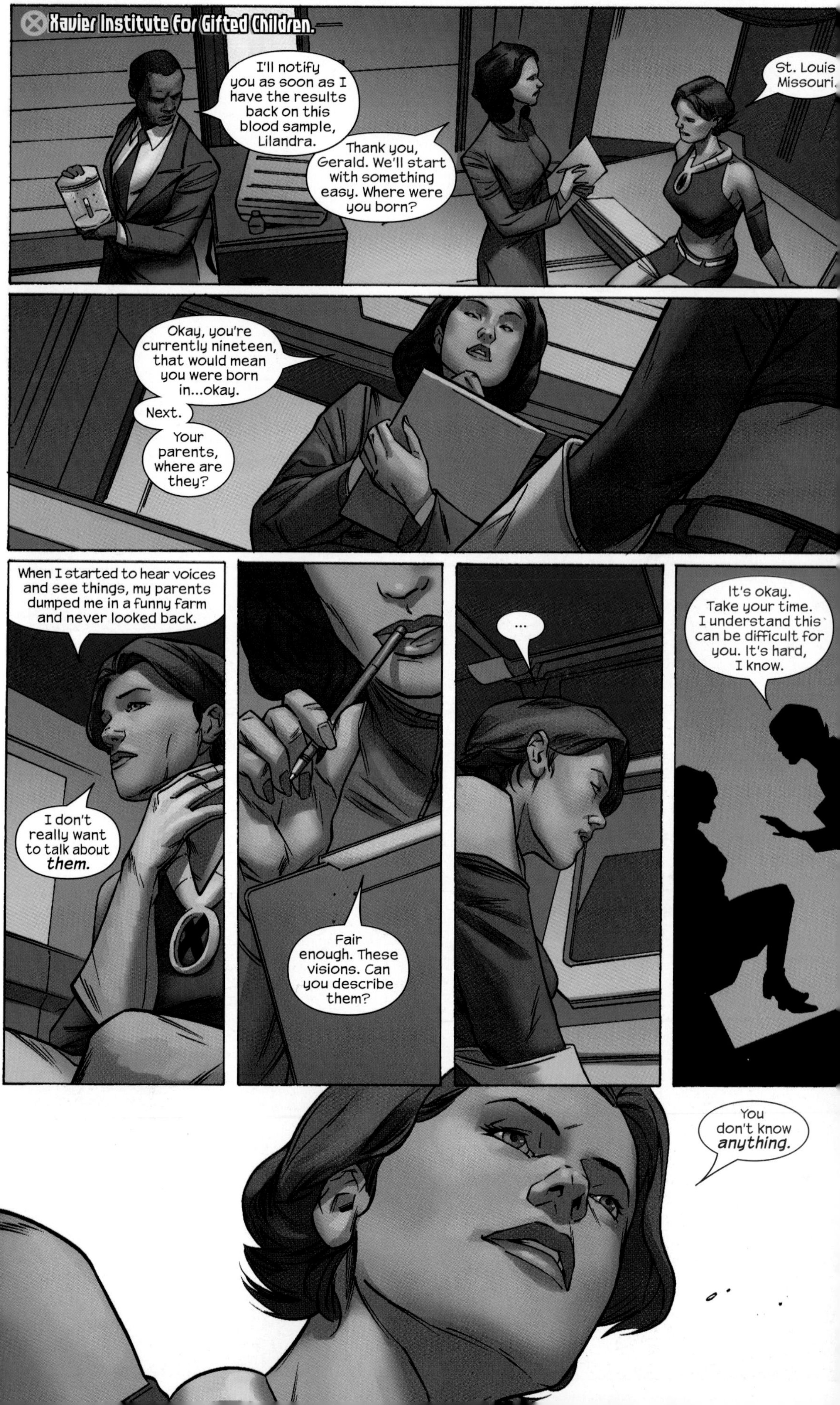

Xavier Institute for Gifted Children.
I'll notify you as soon as I have the results back on this blood sample, Lilandra.
Thank you, Gerald. We'll start with something easy. Where were you born?
St. Louis Missouri.
Okay, you're currently nineteen, that would mean you were born in...okay.
Next.
Your parents, where are they?
When I started to hear voices and see things, my parents dumped me in a funny farm and never looked back.
I don't really want to talk about *them.*
Fair enough. These visions. Can you describe them?
...
It's okay. Take your time. I understand this can be difficult for you. It's hard, I know.
You don't know *anything.*

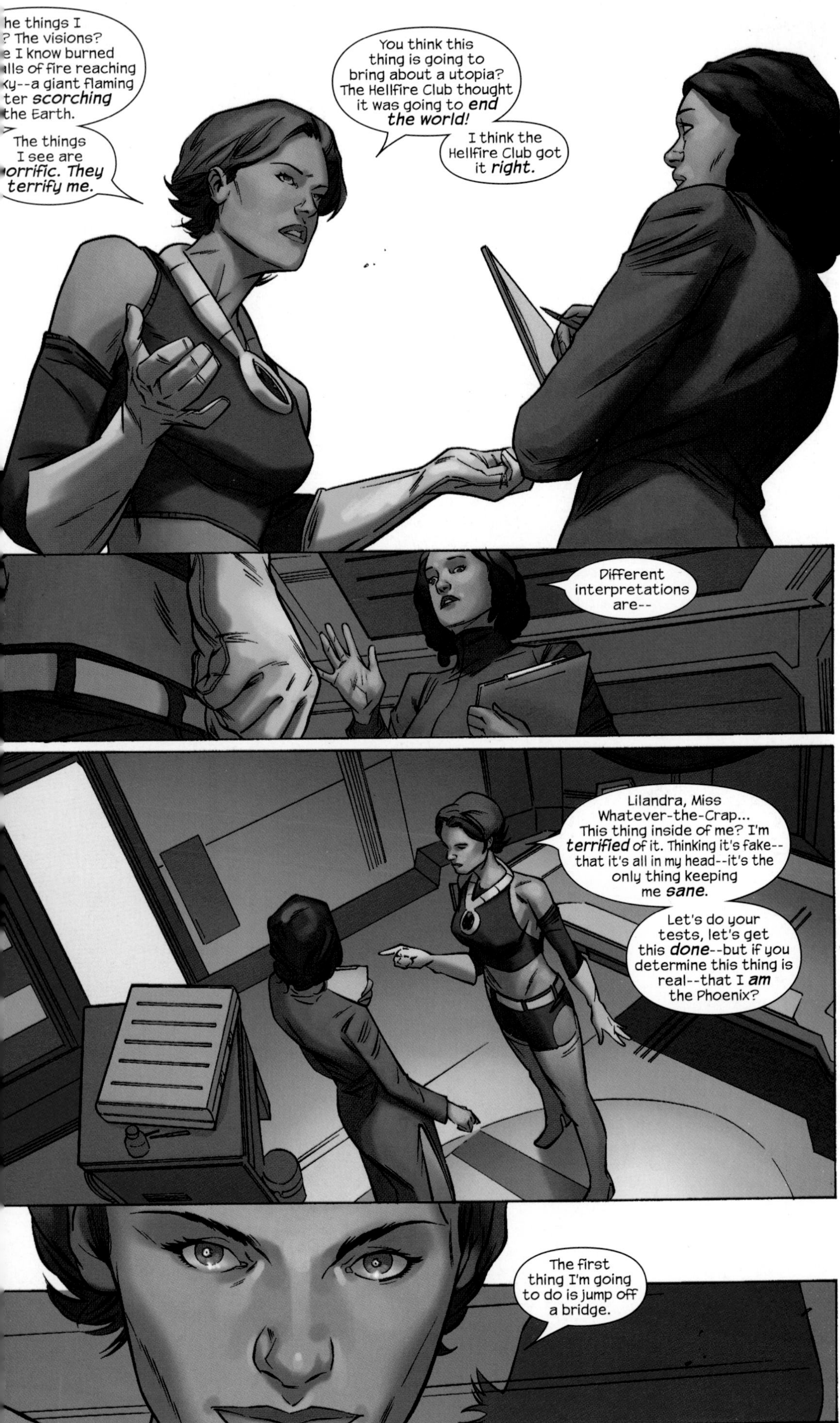

he things I ? The visions? e I know burned alls of fire reaching ky--a giant flaming ter *scorching* the Earth.
The things I see are *orrific. They terrify me.*
You think this thing is going to bring about a utopia? The Hellfire Club thought it was going to *end the world!*
I think the Hellfire Club got it *right.*
Different interpretations are--
Lilandra, Miss Whatever-the-Crap... This thing inside of me? I'm *terrified* of it. Thinking it's fake--that it's all in my head--it's the only thing keeping me *sane*.
Let's do your tests, let's get this *done*--but if you determine this thing is real--that I *am* the Phoenix?
The first thing I'm going to do is jump off a bridge.

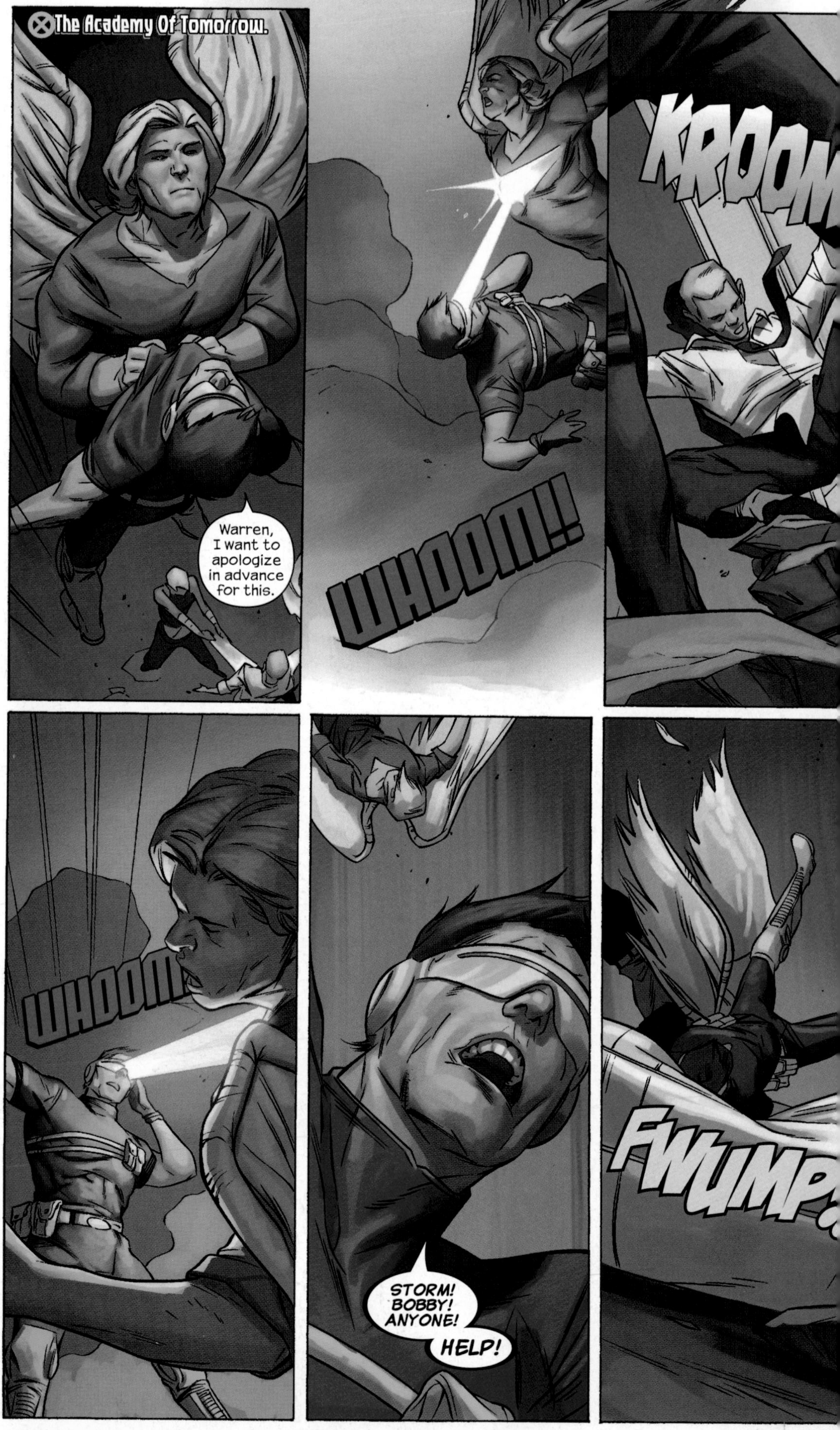
The Academy Of Tomorrow.
Warren, I want to apologize in advance for this.
WHOOM!!
KROOM
WHOOM
STORM! BOBBY! ANYONE!
HELP!
FWUMP

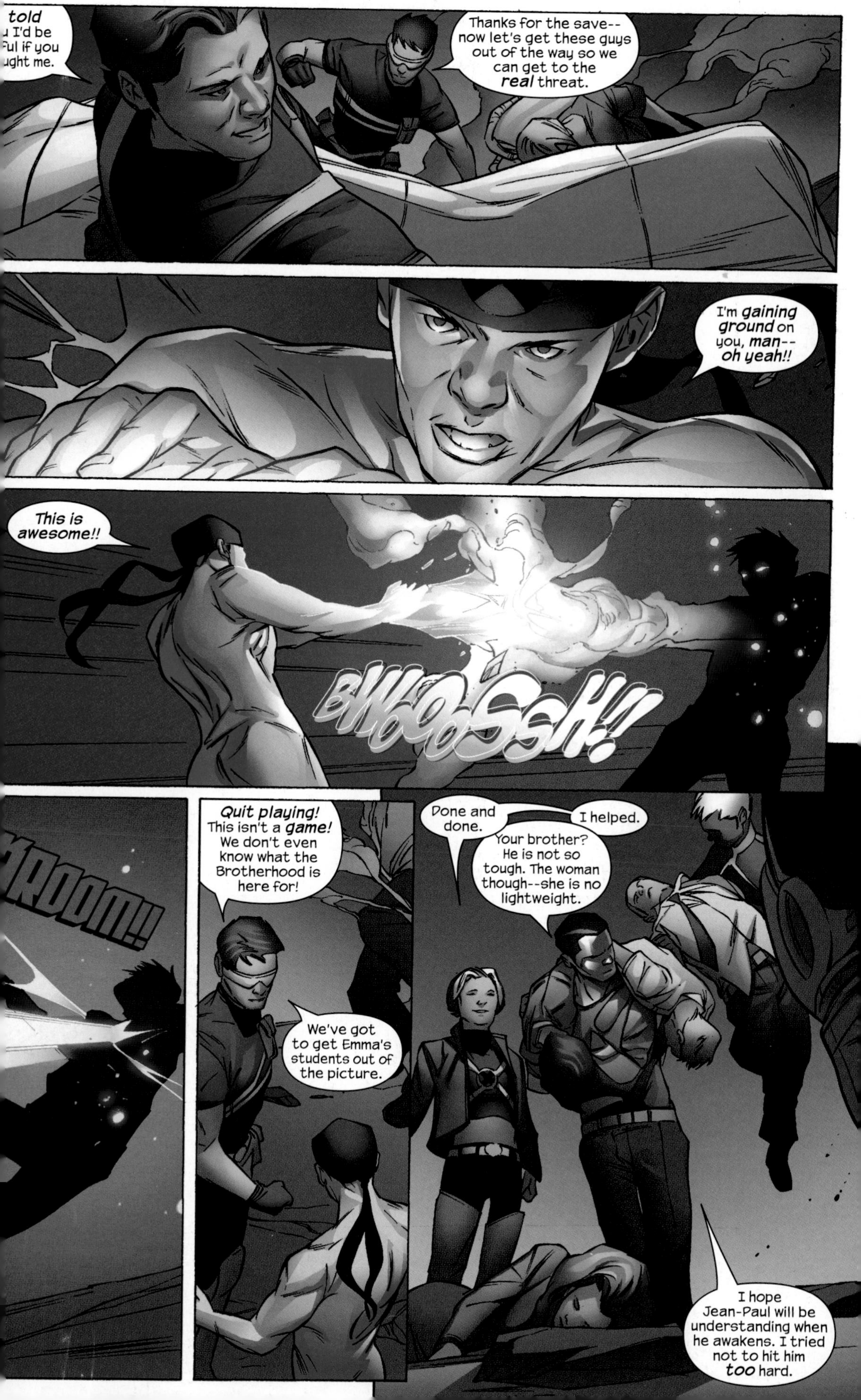

told
u I'd be
ful if you
ught me.
Thanks for the save--now let's get these guys out of the way so we can get to the *real* threat.
I'm *gaining ground* on you, *man--oh yeah!!*
This is awesome!!
BWOOSSH!!
RDOOM!!
Quit playing! This isn't a *game!* We don't even know what the Brotherhood is here for!
We've got to get Emma's students out of the picture.
Done and done.
I helped.
Your brother? He is not so tough. The woman though--she is no lightweight.
I hope Jean-Paul will be understanding when he awakens. I tried not to hit him *too* hard.

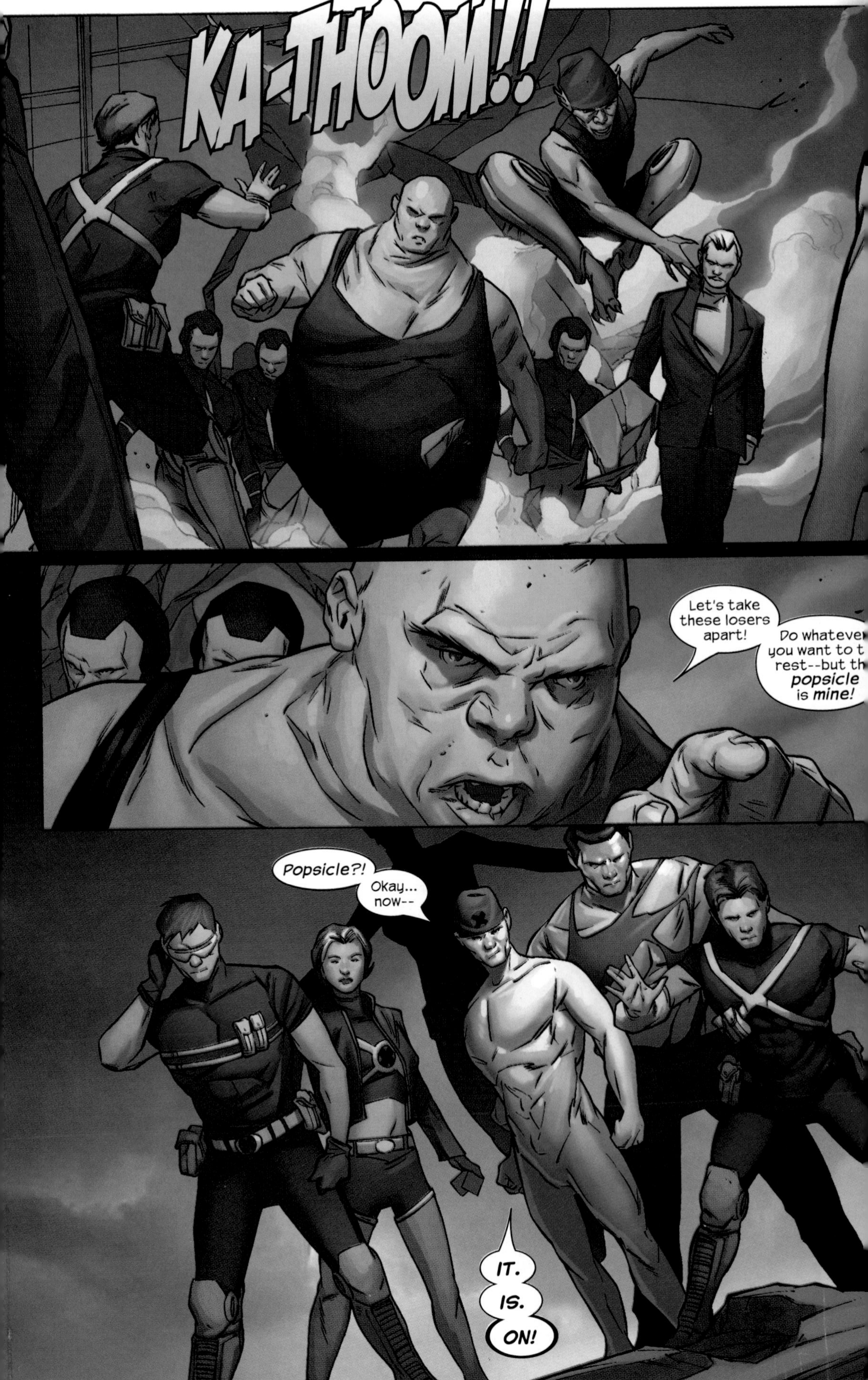
KA-THOOM!!
Let's take these losers apart!
Do whateve you want to t rest--but th popsicle is mine!
Popsicle?!
Okay... now--
IT. IS. ON!

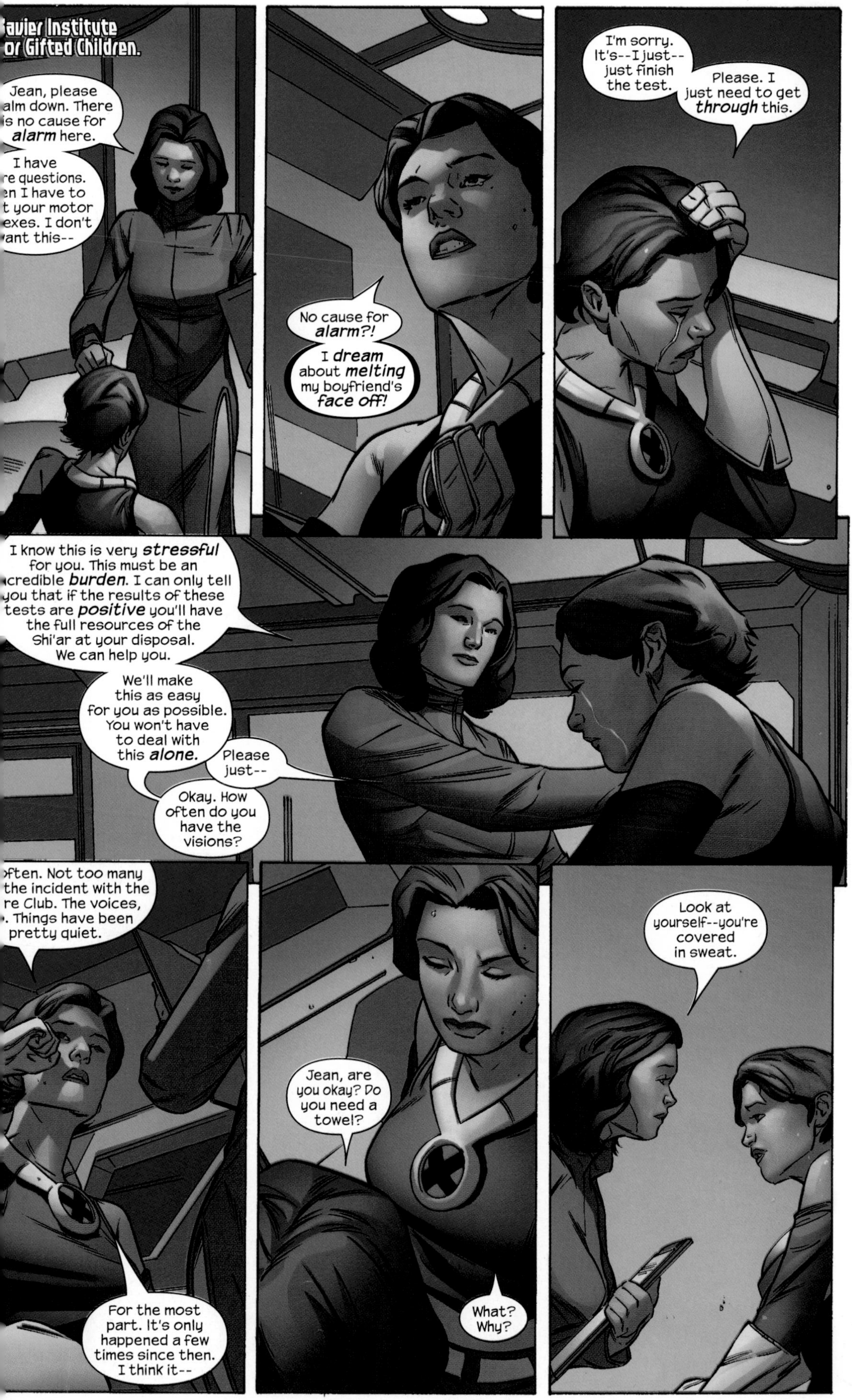

avier Institute
or Gifted Children.
Jean, please alm down. There is no cause for alarm here.
I have re questions. en I have to t your motor exes. I don't ant this--
No cause for alarm?!
I dream about melting my boyfriend's face off!
I'm sorry. It's--I just--just finish the test.
Please. I just need to get through this.
I know this is very stressful for you. This must be an credible burden. I can only tell you that if the results of these tests are positive you'll have the full resources of the Shi'ar at your disposal. We can help you.
We'll make this as easy for you as possible. You won't have to deal with this alone.
Please just--
Okay. How often do you have the visions?
ften. Not too many the incident with the re Club. The voices, . Things have been pretty quiet.
For the most part. It's only happened a few times since then. I think it--
Jean, are you okay? Do you need a towel?
What? Why?
Look at yourself--you're covered in sweat.

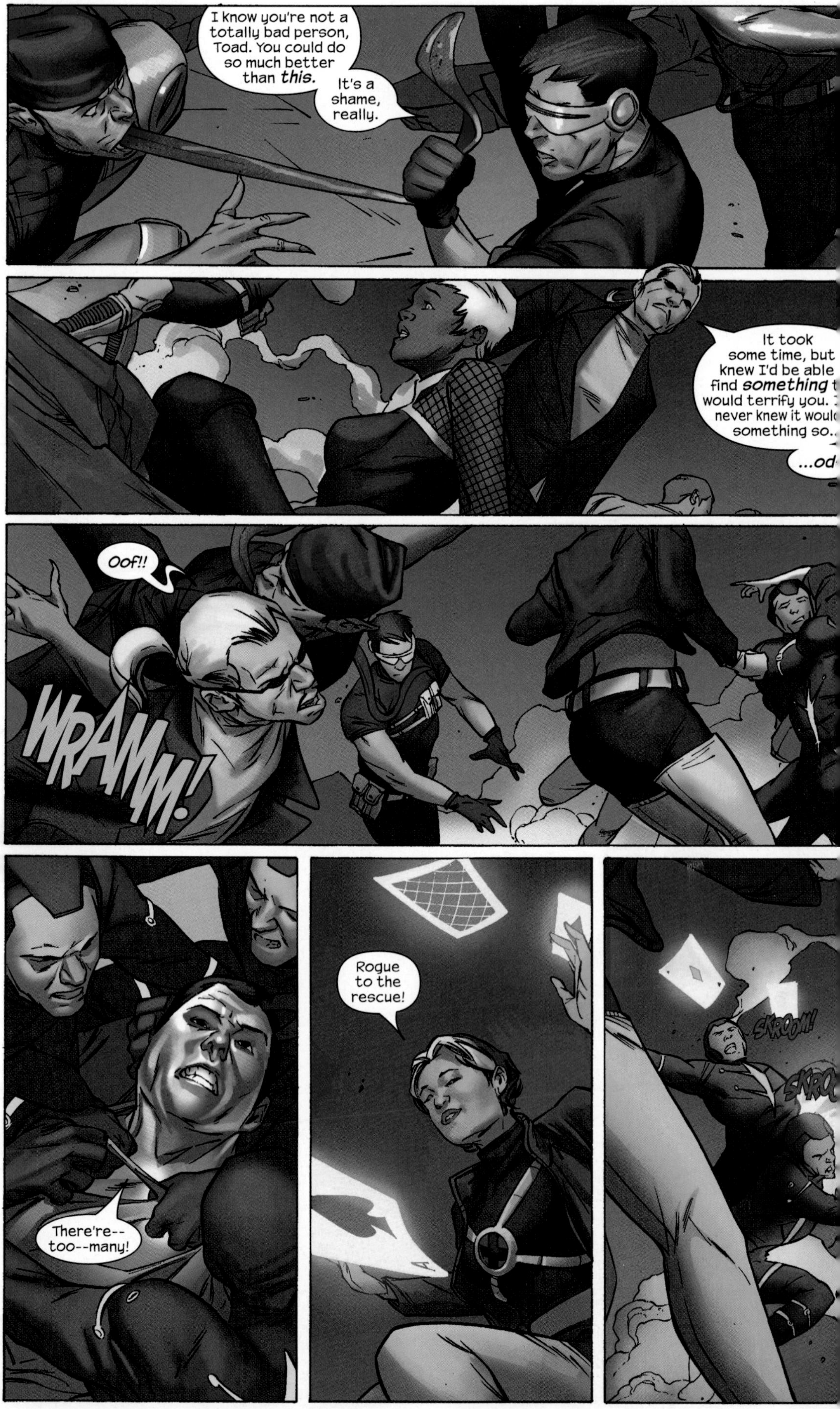

I know you're not a totally bad person, Toad. You could do so much better than *this.*
It's a shame, really.
It took some time, but knew I'd be able find *something* would terrify you. never knew it would something so..
...od
Oof!!
WRAMM!
There're-- too--many!
Rogue to the rescue!
SKROOM!

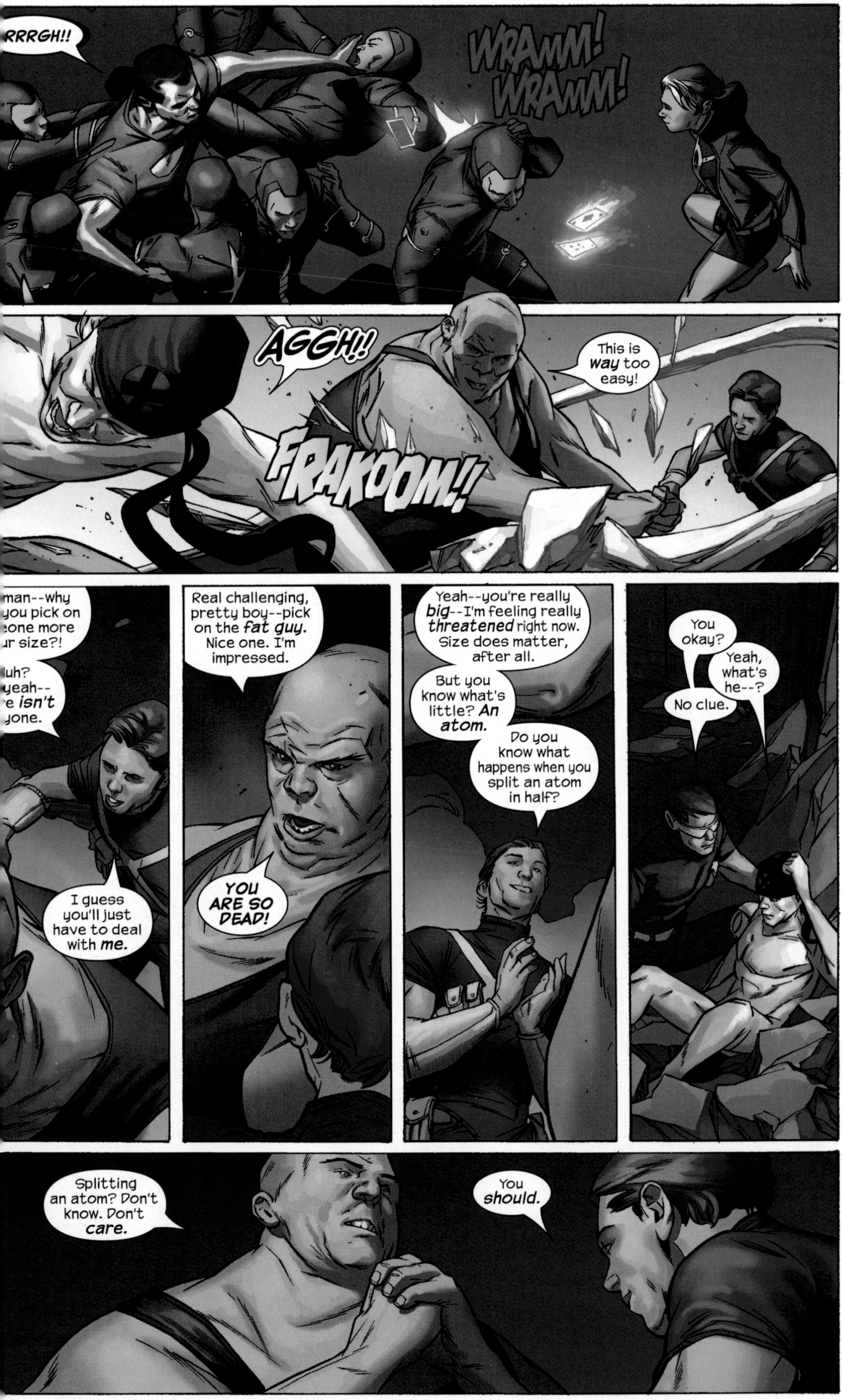

RRRGH!!
WRAMM! WRAMM!
AGGH!!
This is way too easy!
FRAKOOM!!
man--why you pick on one more ur size?!
Huh? yeah-- e isn't gone.
I guess you'll just have to deal with me.
Real challenging, pretty boy--pick on the fat guy. Nice one. I'm impressed.
YOU ARE SO DEAD!
Yeah--you're really big--I'm feeling really threatened right now. Size does matter, after all.
But you know what's little? An atom.
Do you know what happens when you split an atom in half?
You okay?
Yeah, what's he--?
No clue.
Splitting an atom? Don't know. Don't care.
You should.

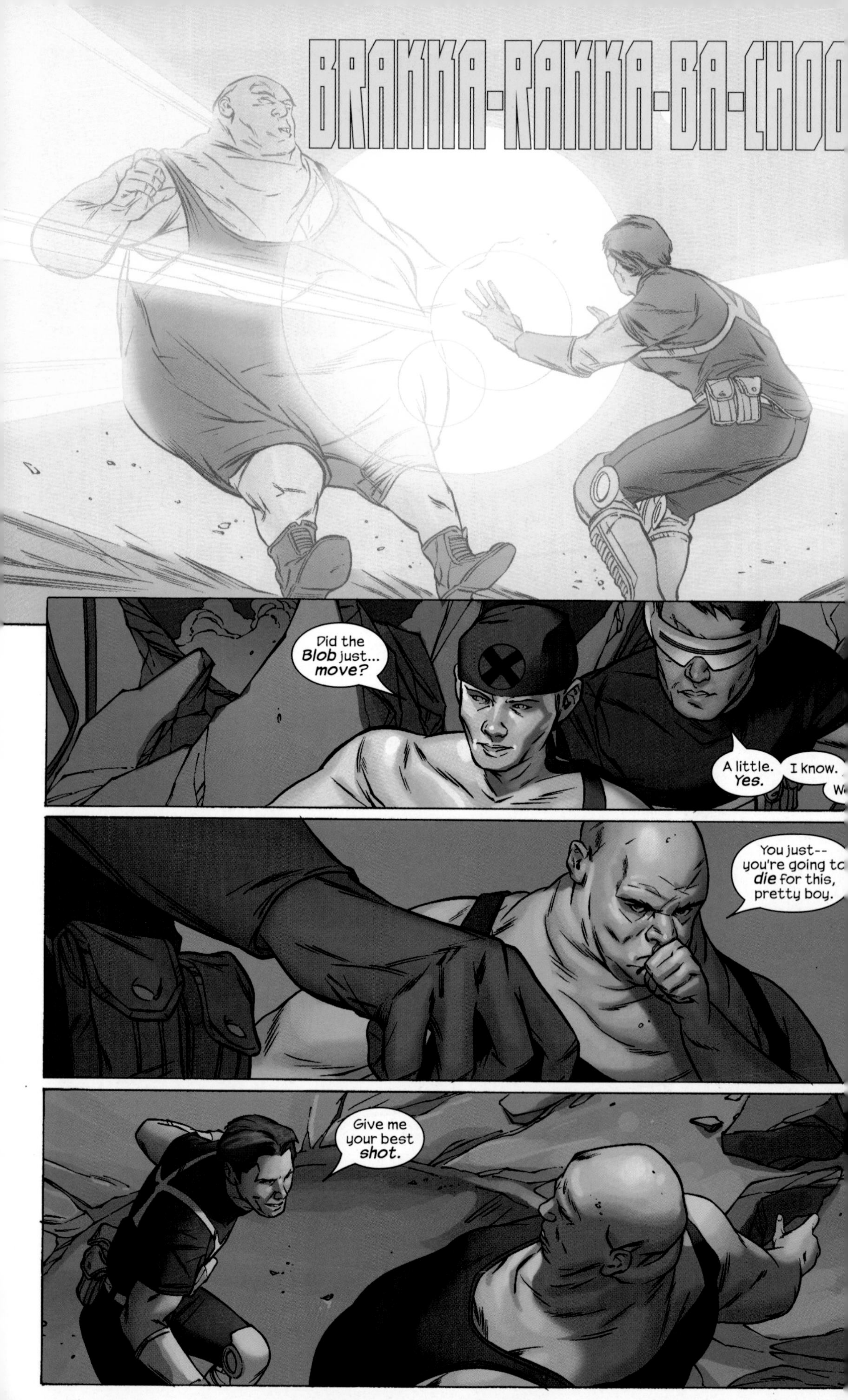
BRAKKA-RAKKA-BA-CHOO
Did the Blob just... move?
A little. Yes.
I know.
You just-- you're going to die for this, pretty boy.
Give me your best shot.

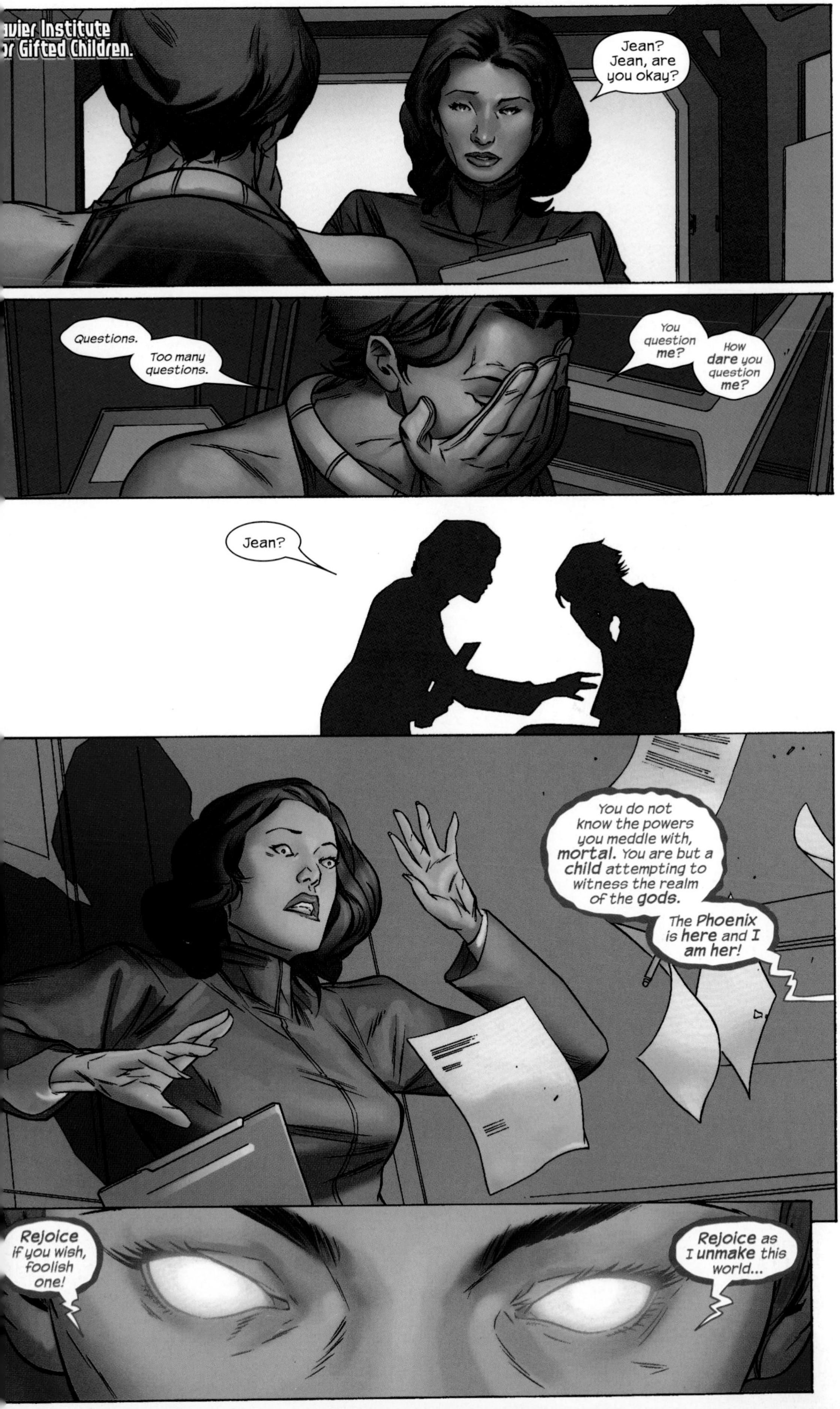

avier Institute
or Gifted Children.
Jean? Jean, are you okay?
Questions.
Too many questions.
You question me?
How dare you question me?
Jean?
You do not know the powers you meddle with, mortal. You are but a child attempting to witness the realm of the gods.
The Phoenix is here and I am her!
Rejoice if you wish, foolish one!
Rejoice as I unmake this world...

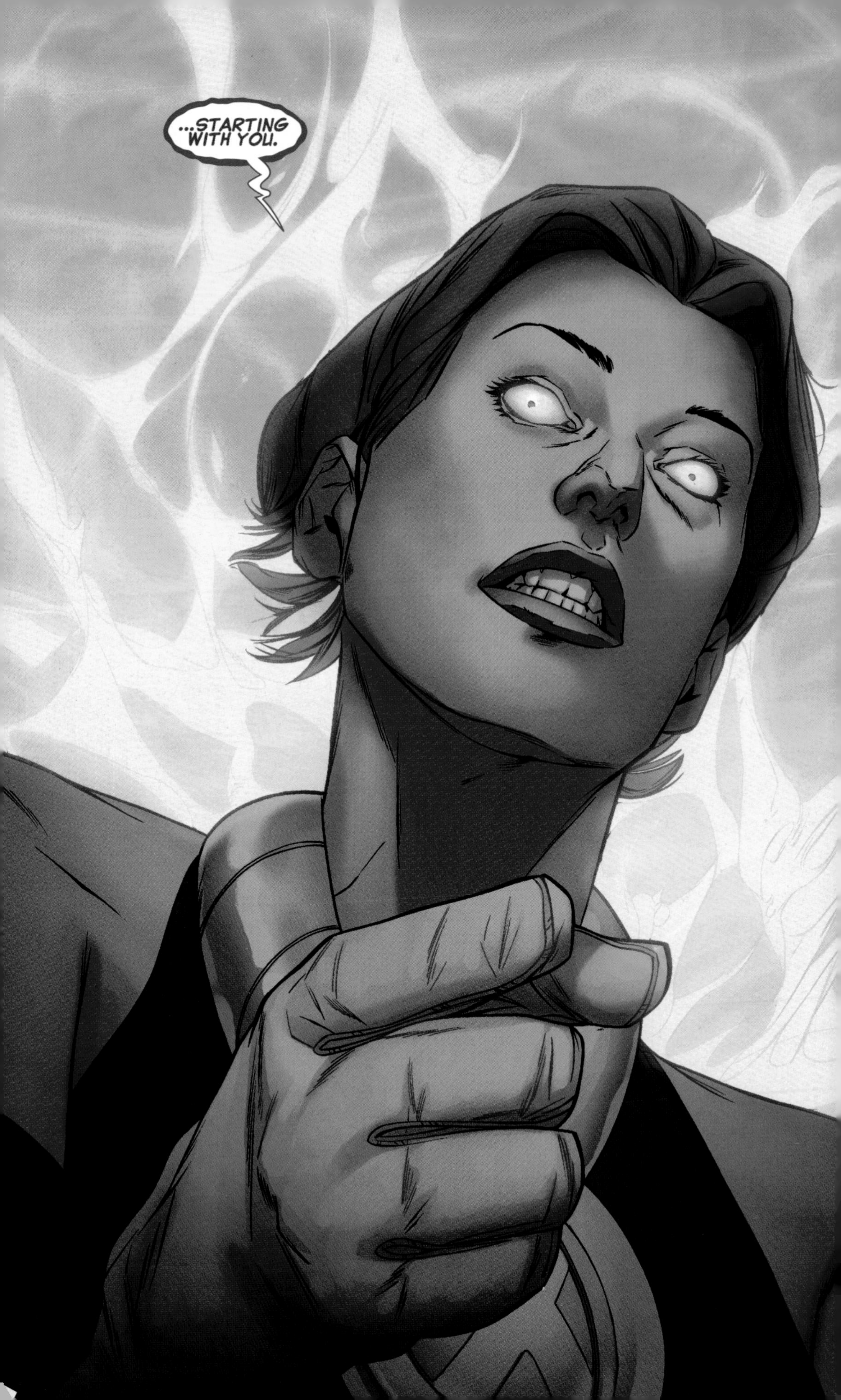
...STARTING WITH YOU.

ISSUE 71

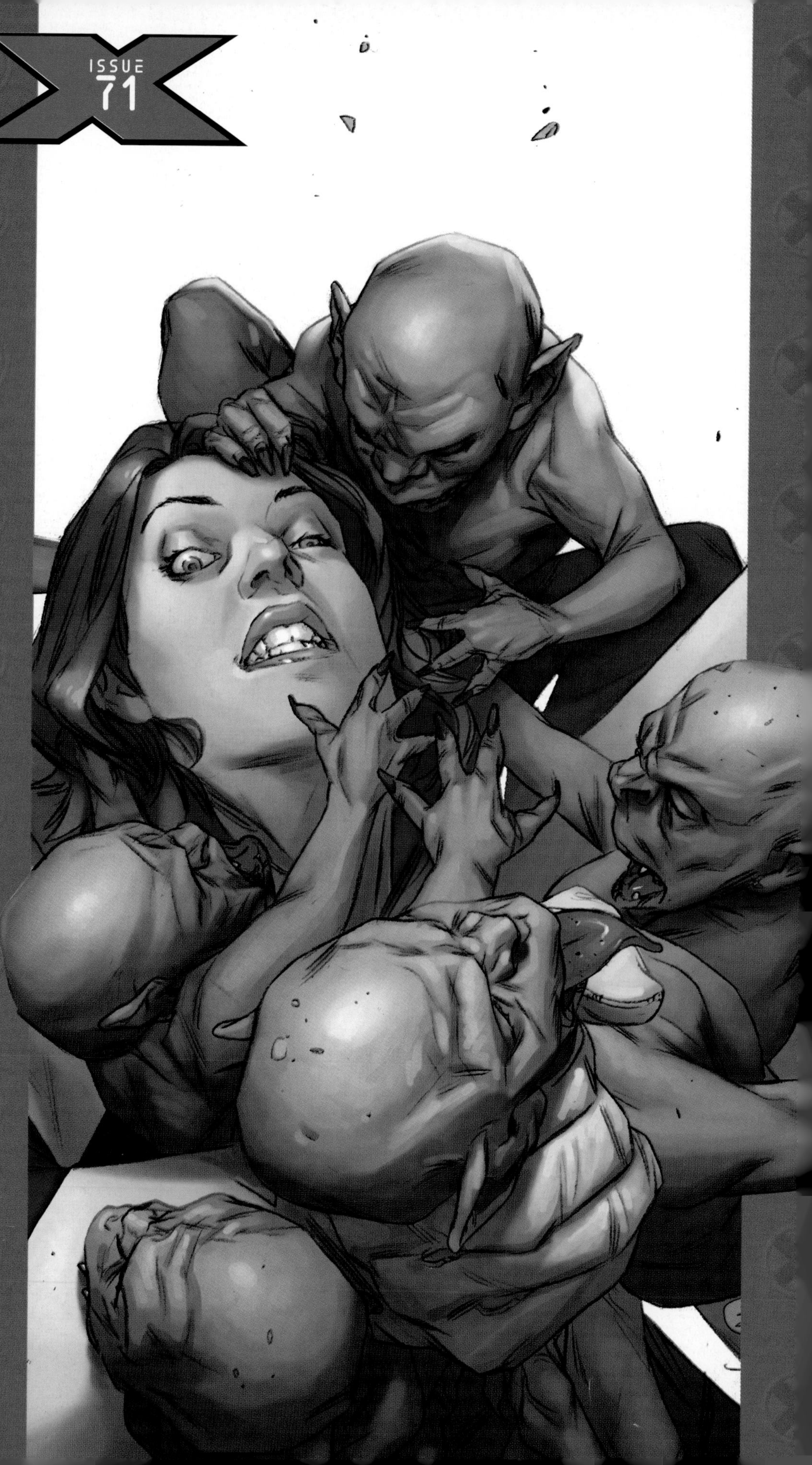

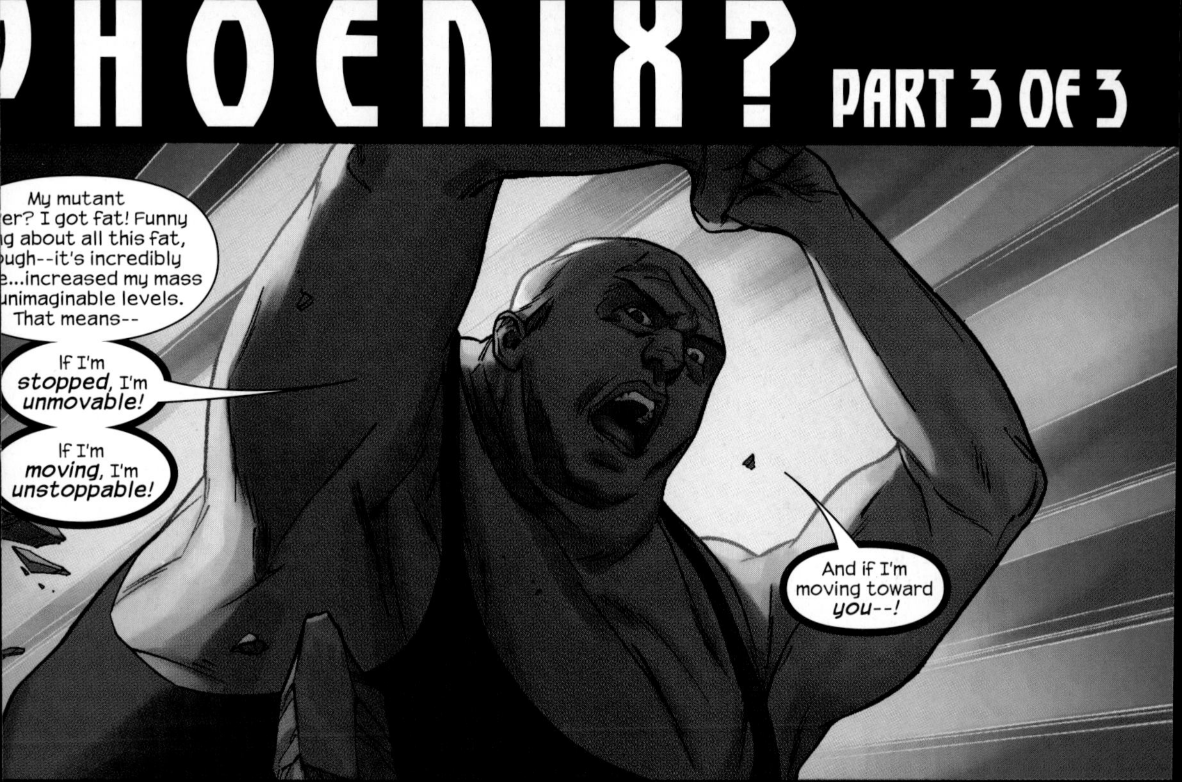
PHOENIX? PART 3 OF 3
My mutant er? I got fat! Funny g about all this fat, ugh--it's incredibly e...increased my mass unimaginable levels. That means--
If I'm stopped, I'm unmovable!
If I'm moving, I'm unstoppable!
And if I'm moving toward you--!

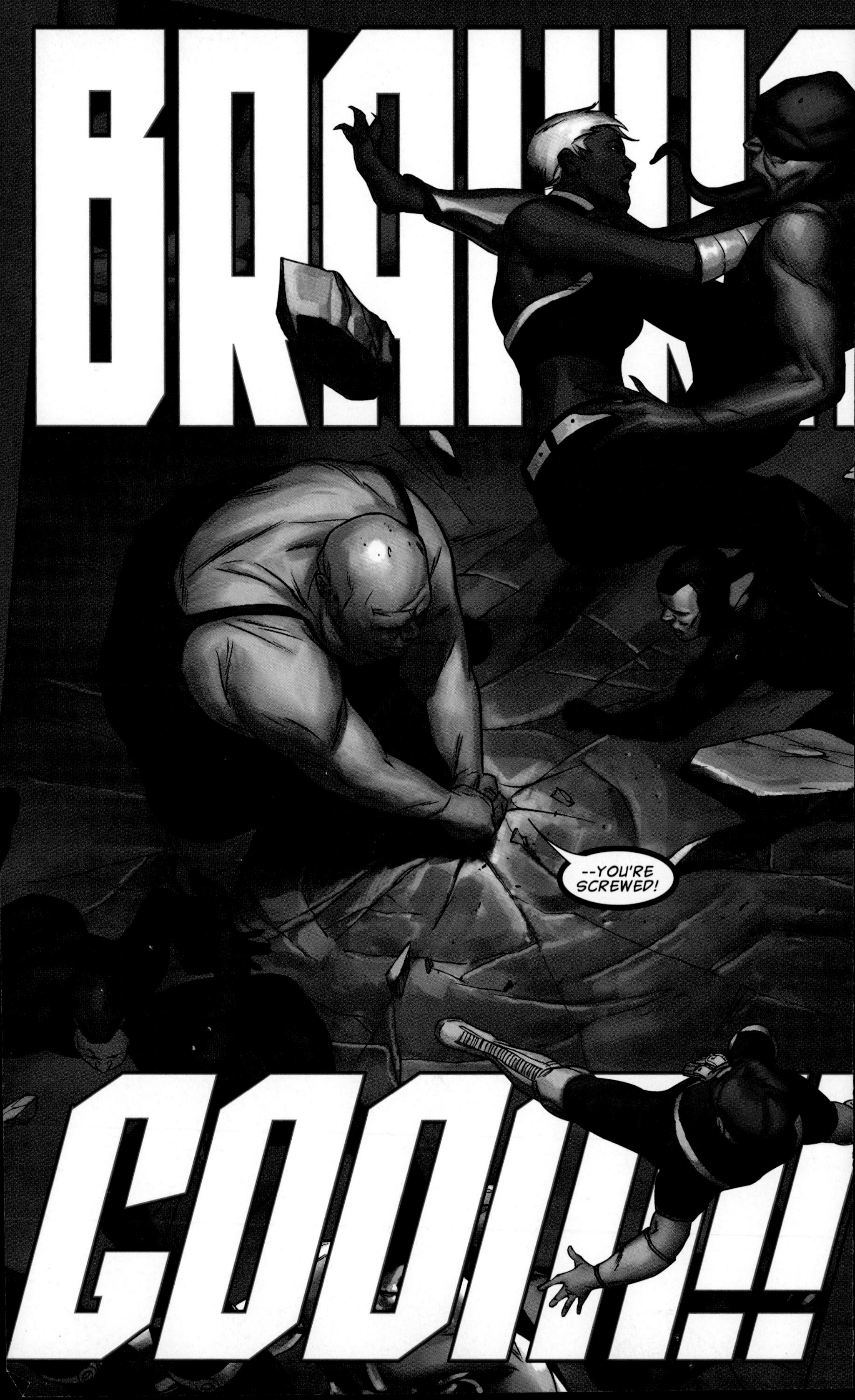
--YOU'RE SCREWED!

If I can't move you--I'll just move things around you!
Or--below you!
SKROOM!!
Oh, great--who alerted the media!?
I can see the spin now--mutant picnic puts reporters in danger!
You okay down there, fatty? Not a lot of oxygen, huh?
I bet you can't even hear me. When you're underground are you unhearable?
SCREECH!

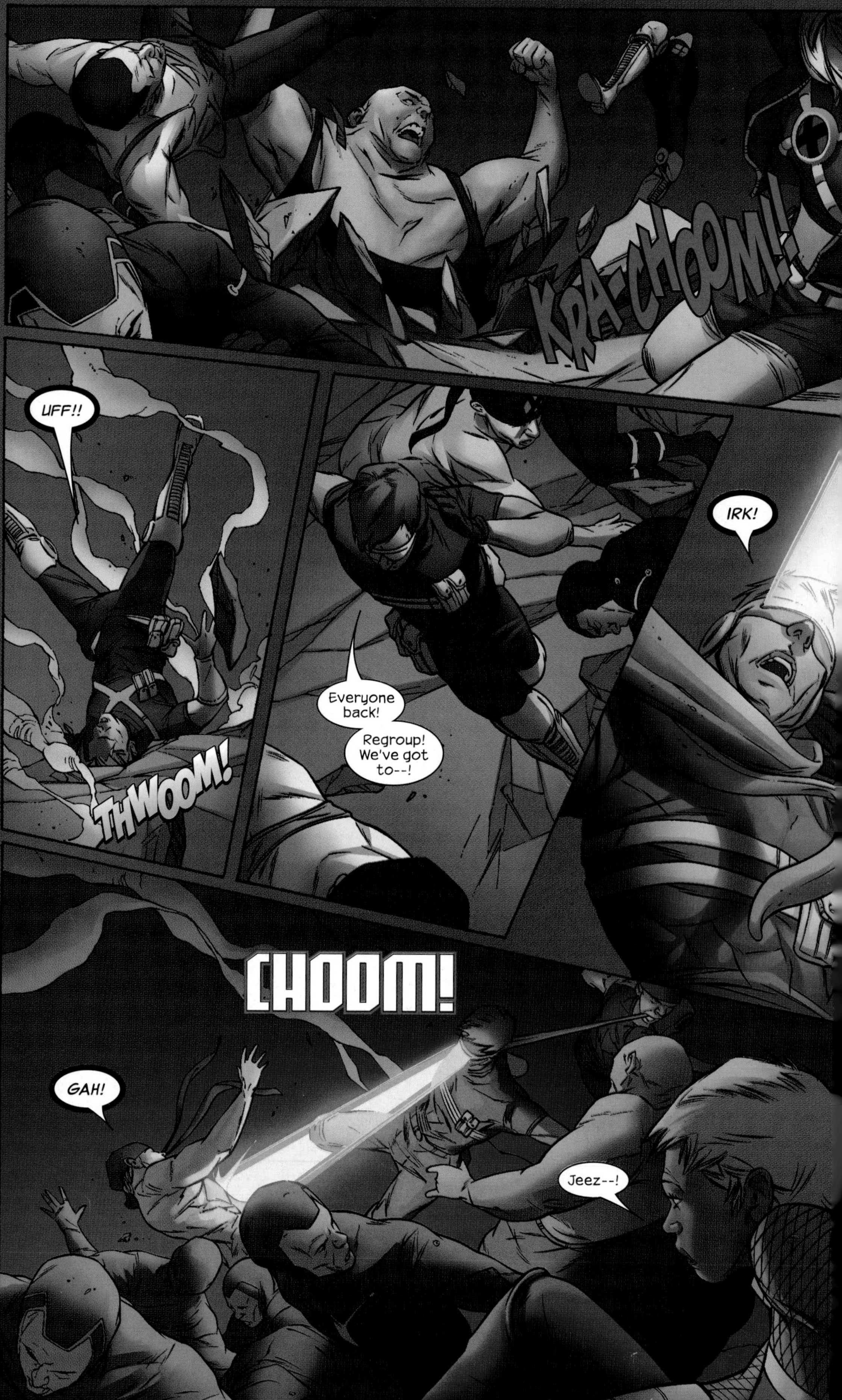
KRA-CHOOM!!
UFF!!
THWOOM!
Everyone back!
Regroup! We've got to--!
IRK!
CHOOM!
GAH!
Jeez--!

Everyone with an "X" on their costume--
--HOLD ON TO SOMETHING!
WHOOSH!!
SKROOM!
Ungh.
Take a *nap.*
ROOM!!
C'mon, boys! Don't start slacking off! The party's just *starting!!*

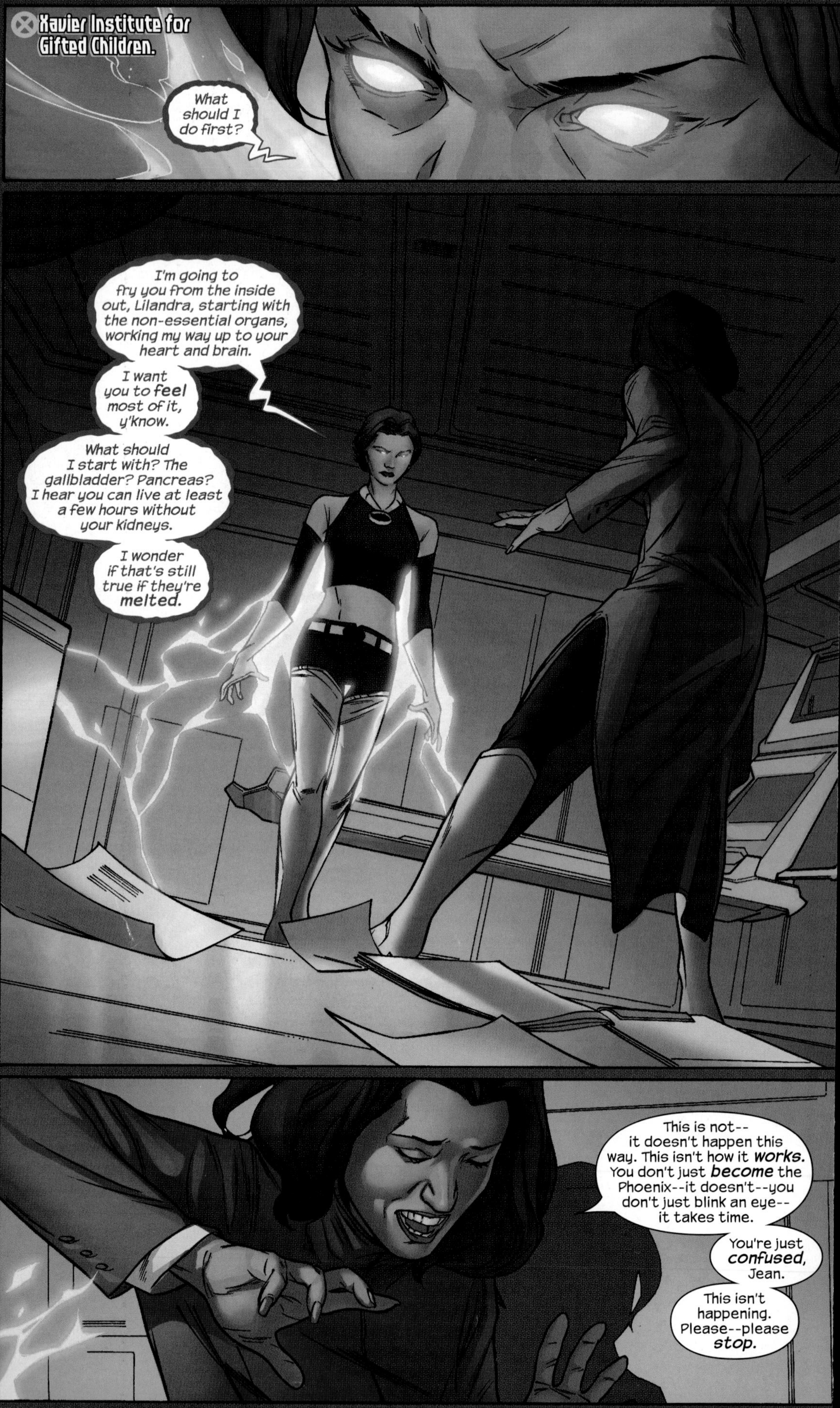
Xavier Institute for Gifted Children.
What should I do first?
I'm going to fry you from the inside out, Lilandra, starting with the non-essential organs, working my way up to your heart and brain.
I want you to feel most of it, y'know.
What should I start with? The gallbladder? Pancreas? I hear you can live at least a few hours without your kidneys.
I wonder if that's still true if they're melted.
This is not-- it doesn't happen this way. This isn't how it works. You don't just become the Phoenix--it doesn't--you don't just blink an eye-- it takes time.
You're just confused, Jean.
This isn't happening. Please--please stop.

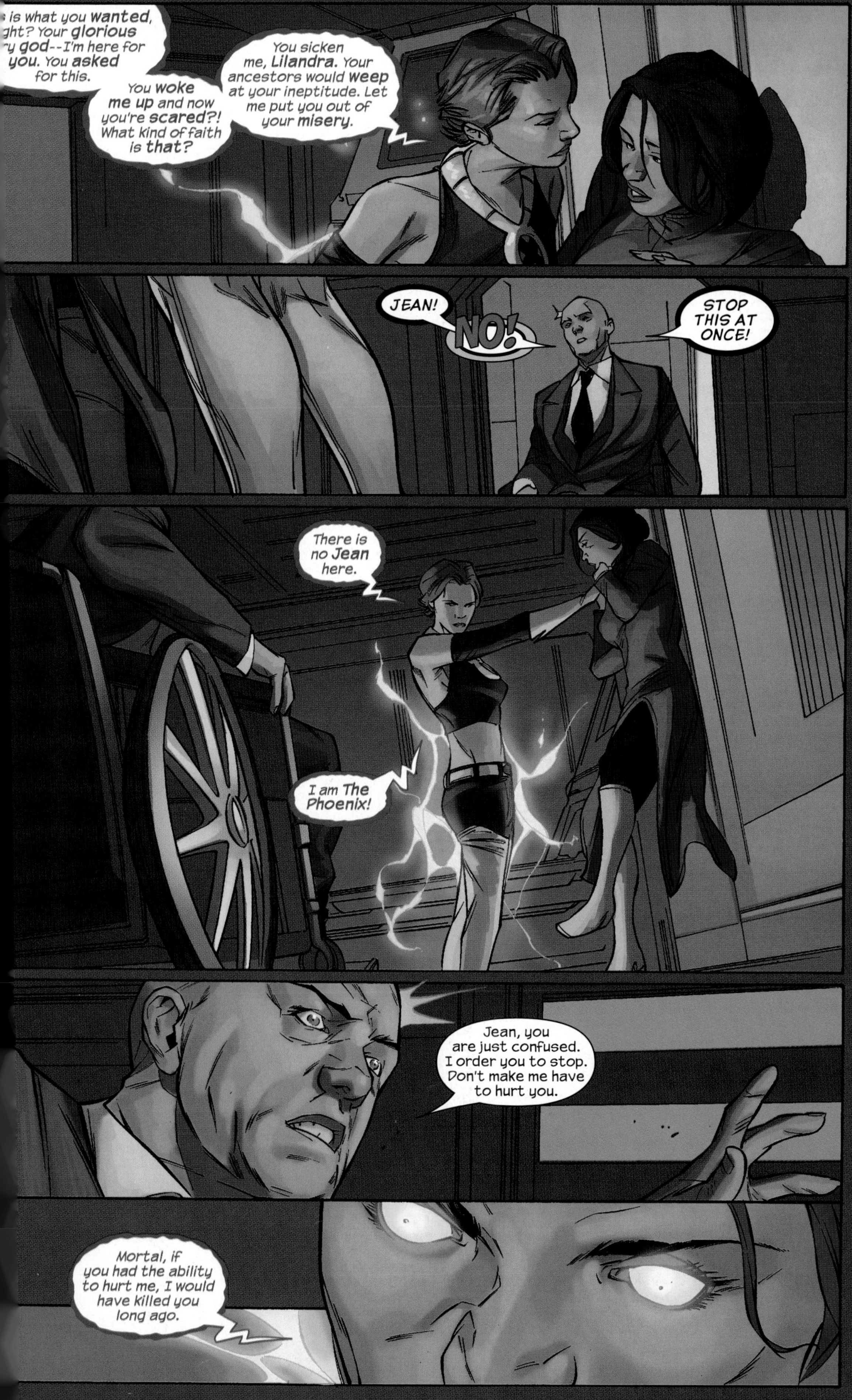
is what you wanted,
Your glorious
god--I'm here for
you. You asked
for this.
You woke me up and now you're scared?! What kind of faith is that?
You sicken me, Lilandra. Your ancestors would weep at your ineptitude. Let me put you out of your misery.
JEAN!
NO!
STOP THIS AT ONCE!
There is no Jean here.
I am The Phoenix!
Jean, you are just confused. I order you to stop. Don't make me have to hurt you.
Mortal, if you had the ability to hurt me, I would have killed you long ago.

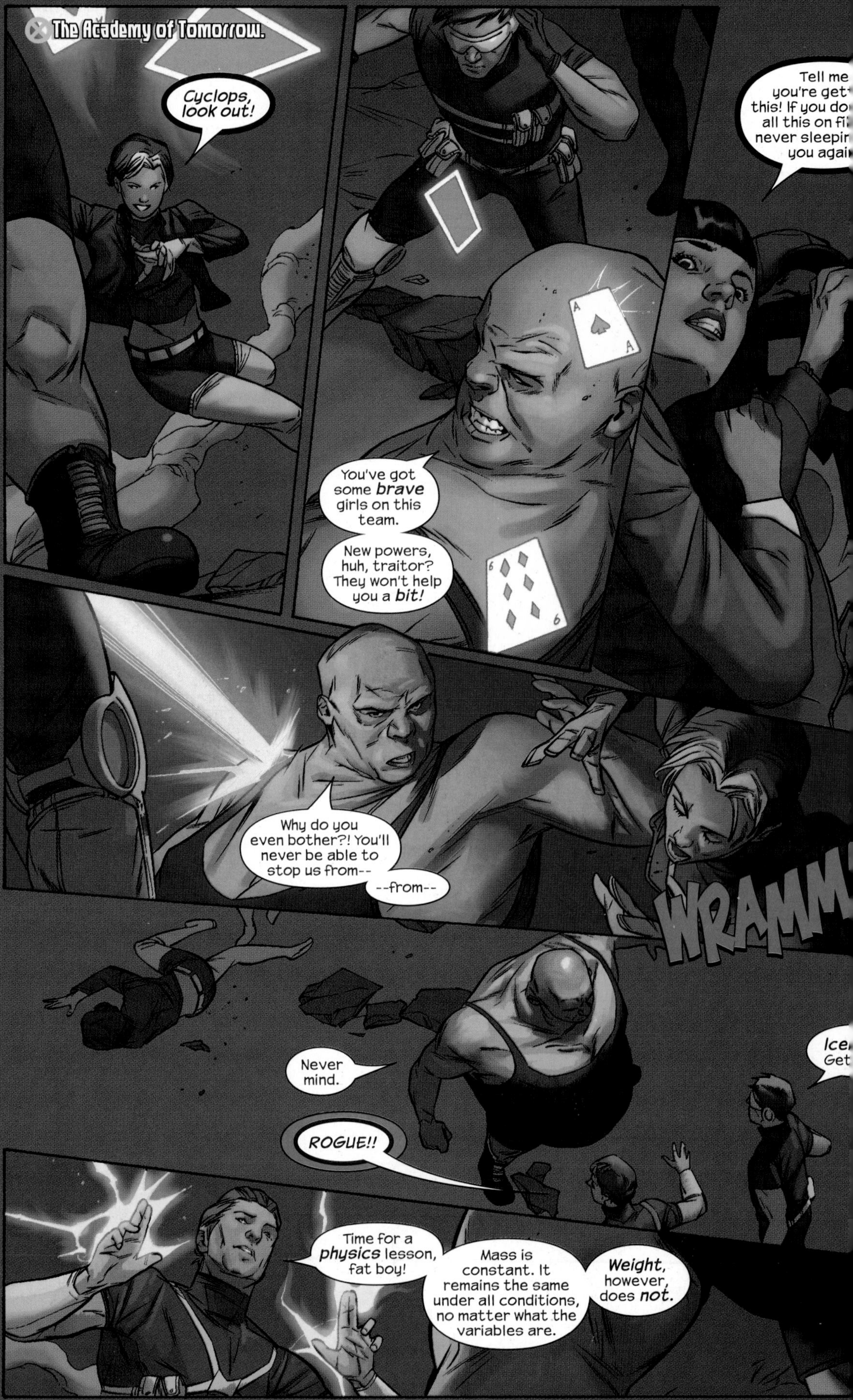

The Academy of Tomorrow.
Cyclops, look out!
Tell me you're get this! If you do all this on fi never sleepir you agai
You've got some *brave* girls on this team.
New powers, huh, traitor? They won't help you a *bit!*
Why do you even bother?! You'll never be able to stop us from--
--from--
WRAMM
Never mind.
Ice Get
ROGUE!!
Time for a *physics* lesson, fat boy!
Mass is constant. It remains the same under all conditions, no matter what the variables are.
Weight, however, does *not*.

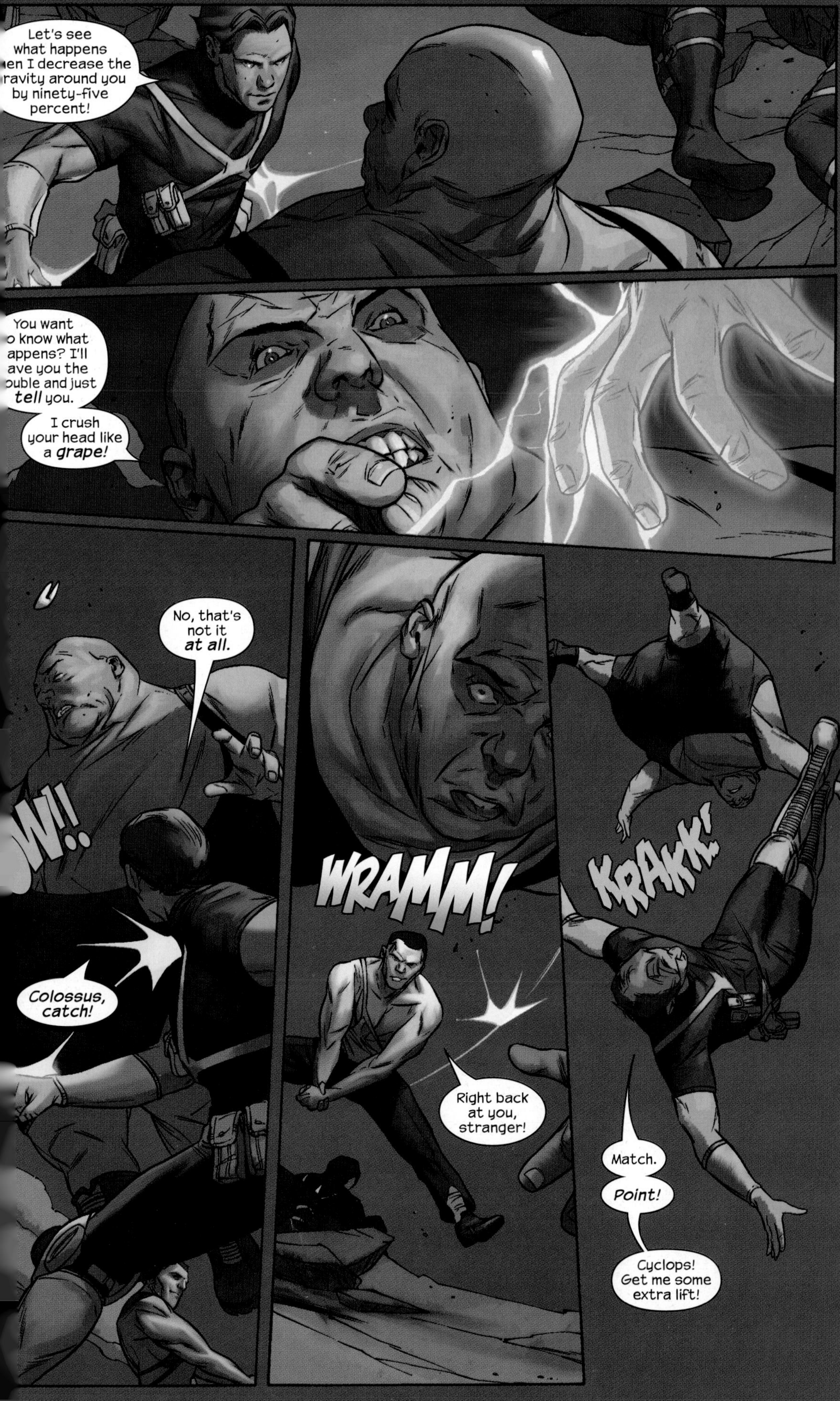
Let's see what happens en I decrease the ravity around you by ninety-five percent!
You want o know what appens? I'll ave you the ouble and just *tell* you.
I crush your head like a *grape!*
No, that's not it *at all.*
W!!
Colossus, catch!
WRAMM!
Right back at you, stranger!
KRAKK!
Match.
Point!
Cyclops! Get me some extra lift!

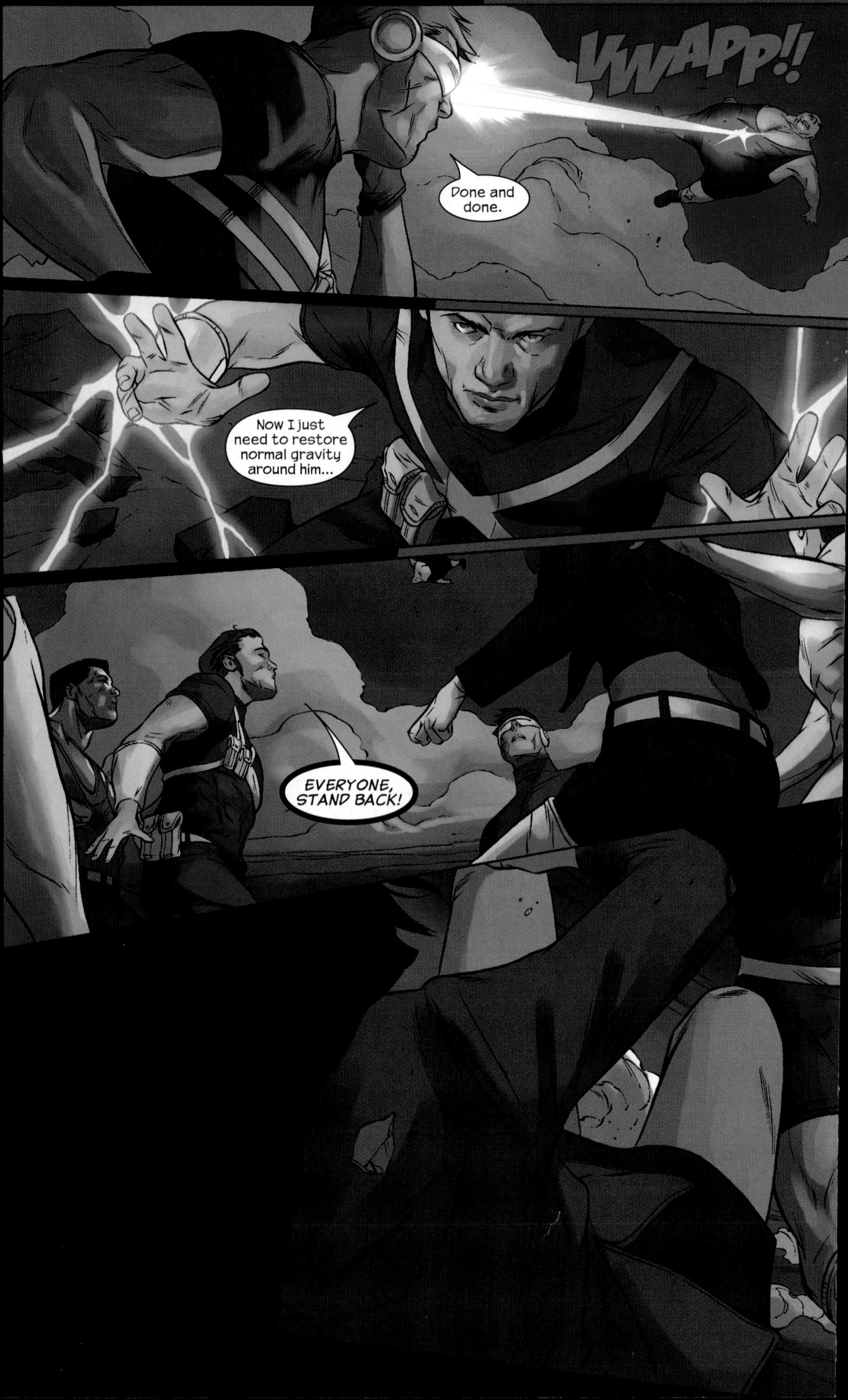
VWAPP!!
Done and done.
Now I just need to restore normal gravity around him...
EVERYONE, STAND BACK!

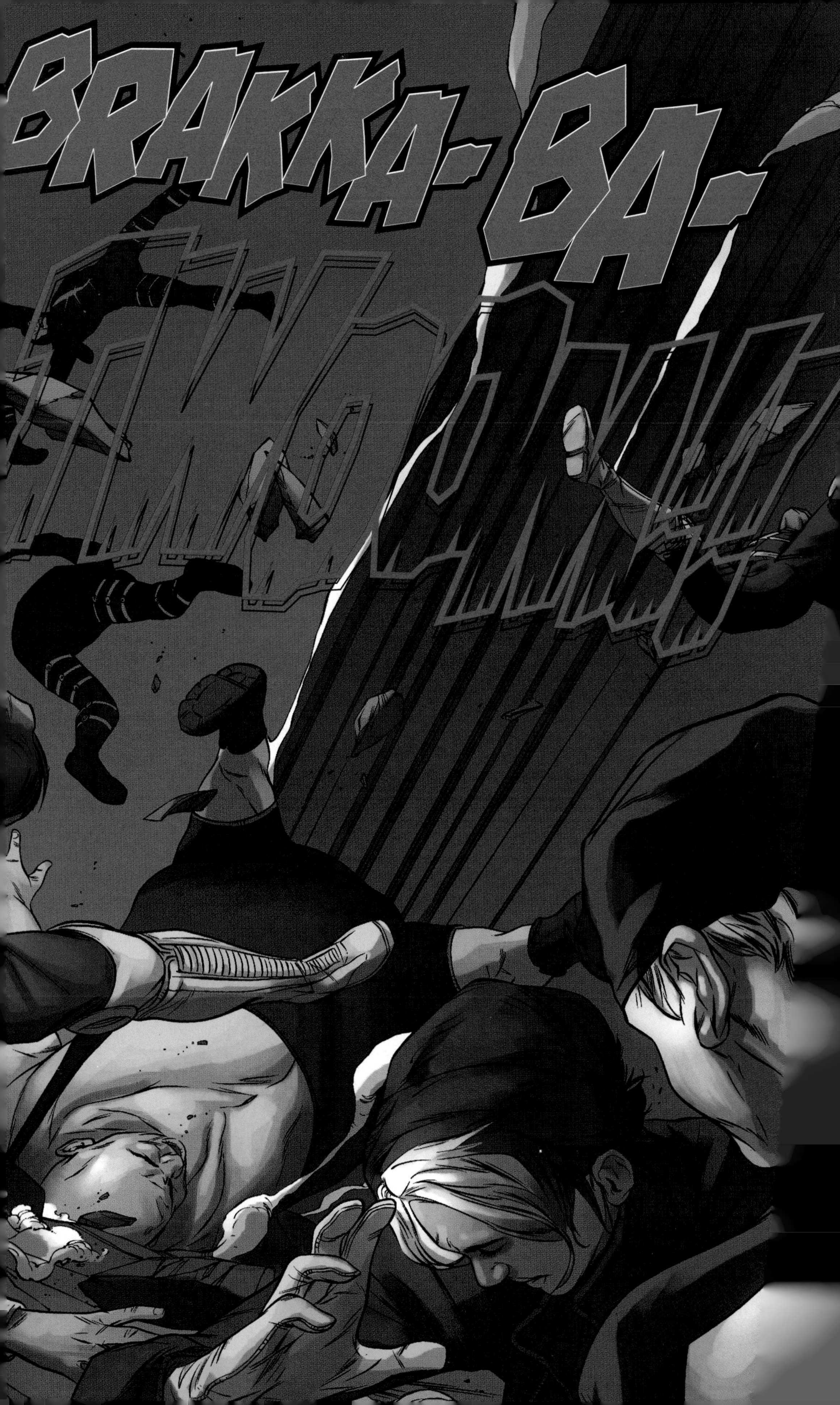
BRAKKA-BA-

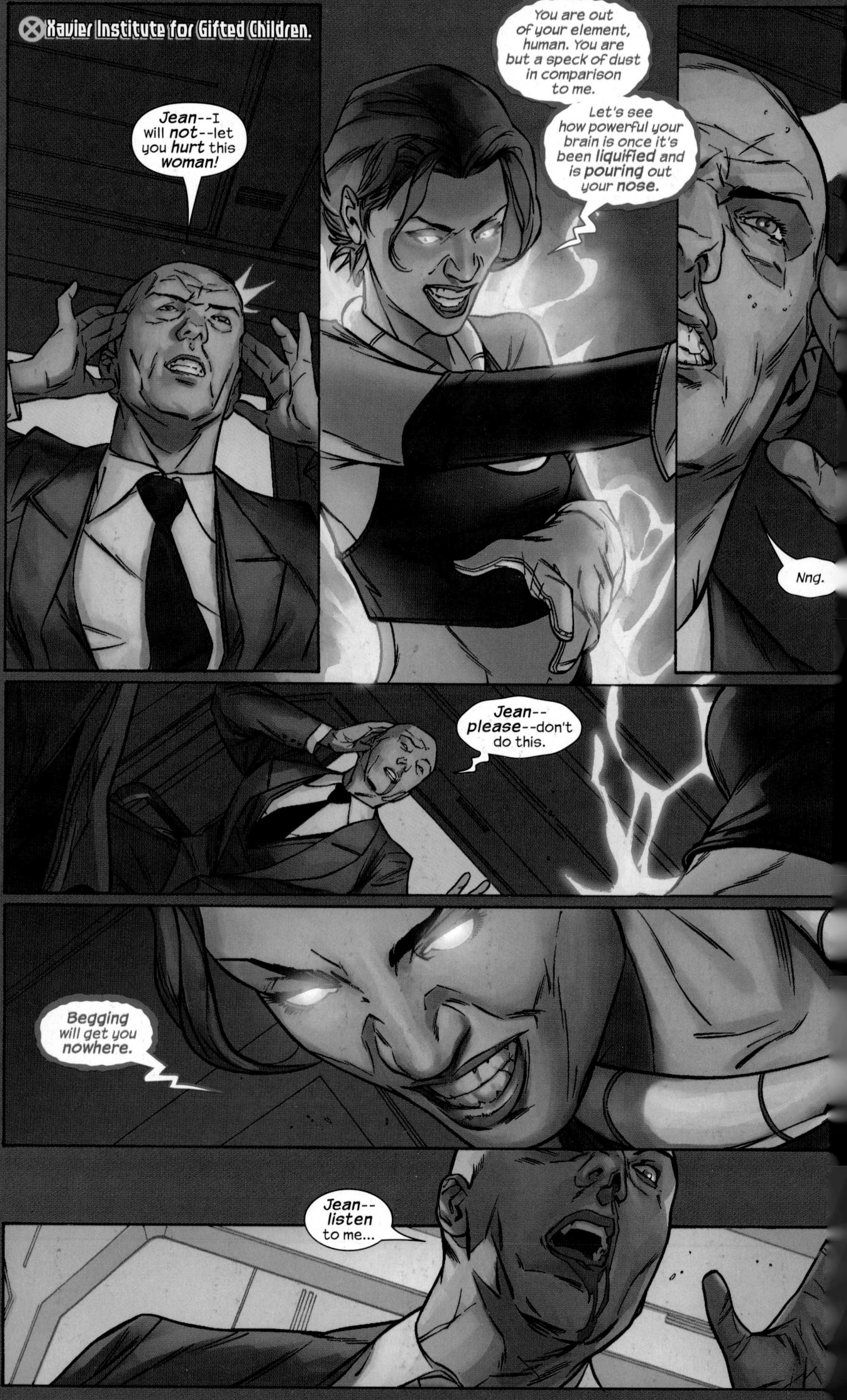
Xavier Institute for Gifted Children.
Jean--I will not--let you hurt this woman!
You are out of your element, human. You are but a speck of dust in comparison to me.
Let's see how powerful your brain is once it's been liquified and is pouring out your nose.
Nng.
Jean--please--don't do this.
Begging will get you nowhere.
Jean--listen to me...

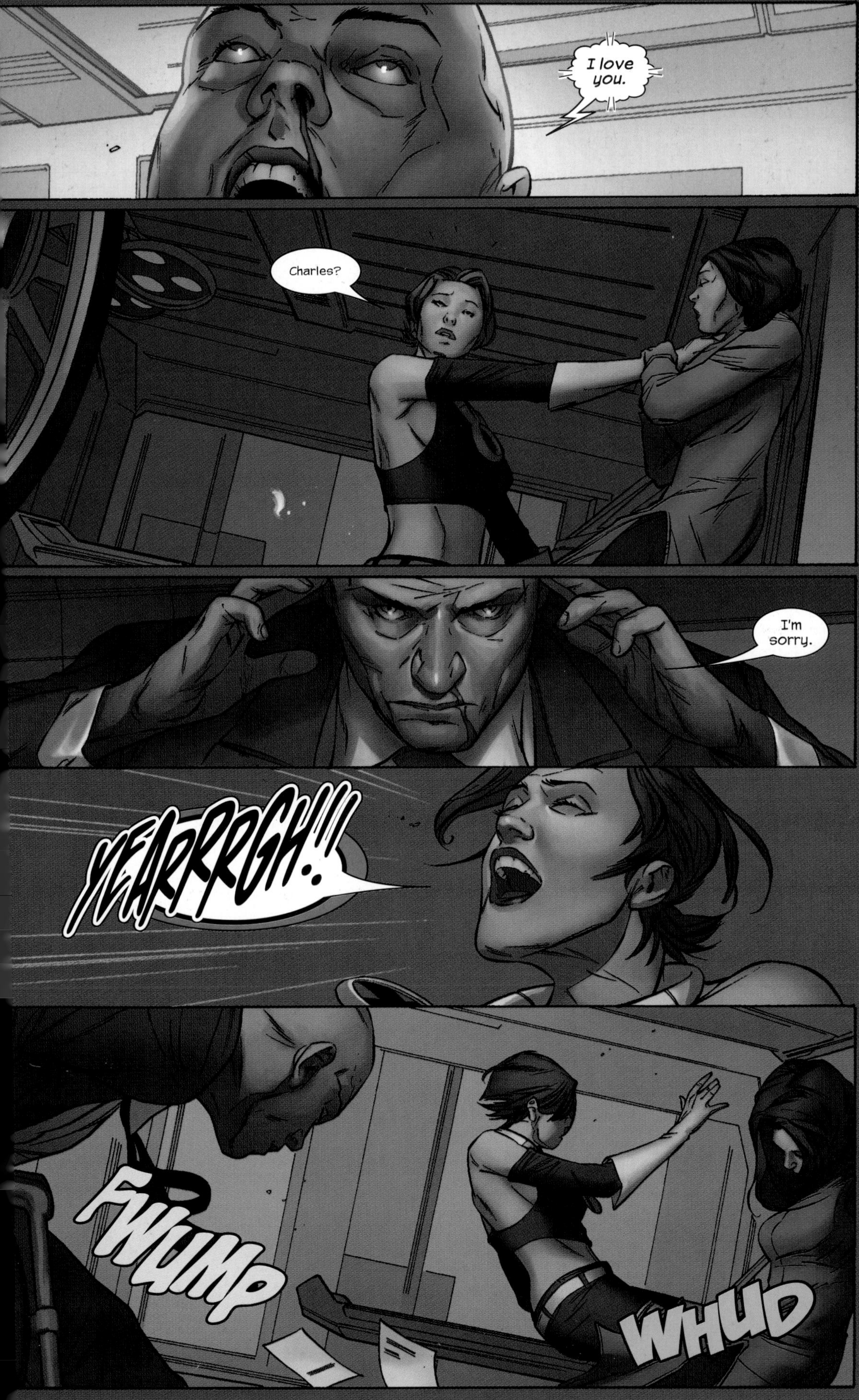
I love you.
Charles?
I'm sorry.
YEARRRGH!!!
FWUMP
WHUD

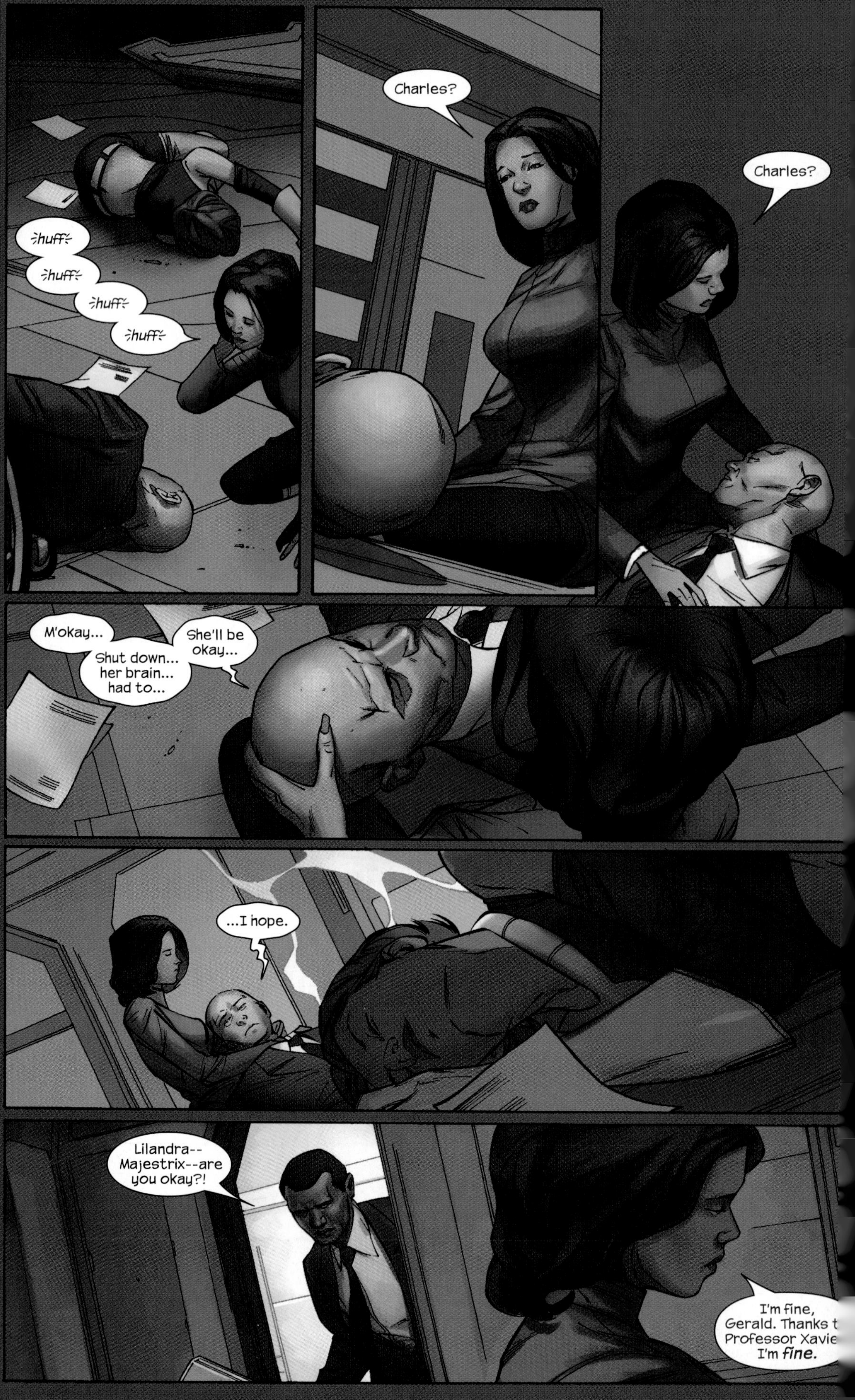

huff
huff
huff
huff
Charles?
Charles?
M'okay...
Shut down... her brain... had to...
She'll be okay...
...I hope.
Lilandra--Majestrix--are you okay?!
I'm fine, Gerald. Thanks t
Professor Xavie
I'm *fine.*

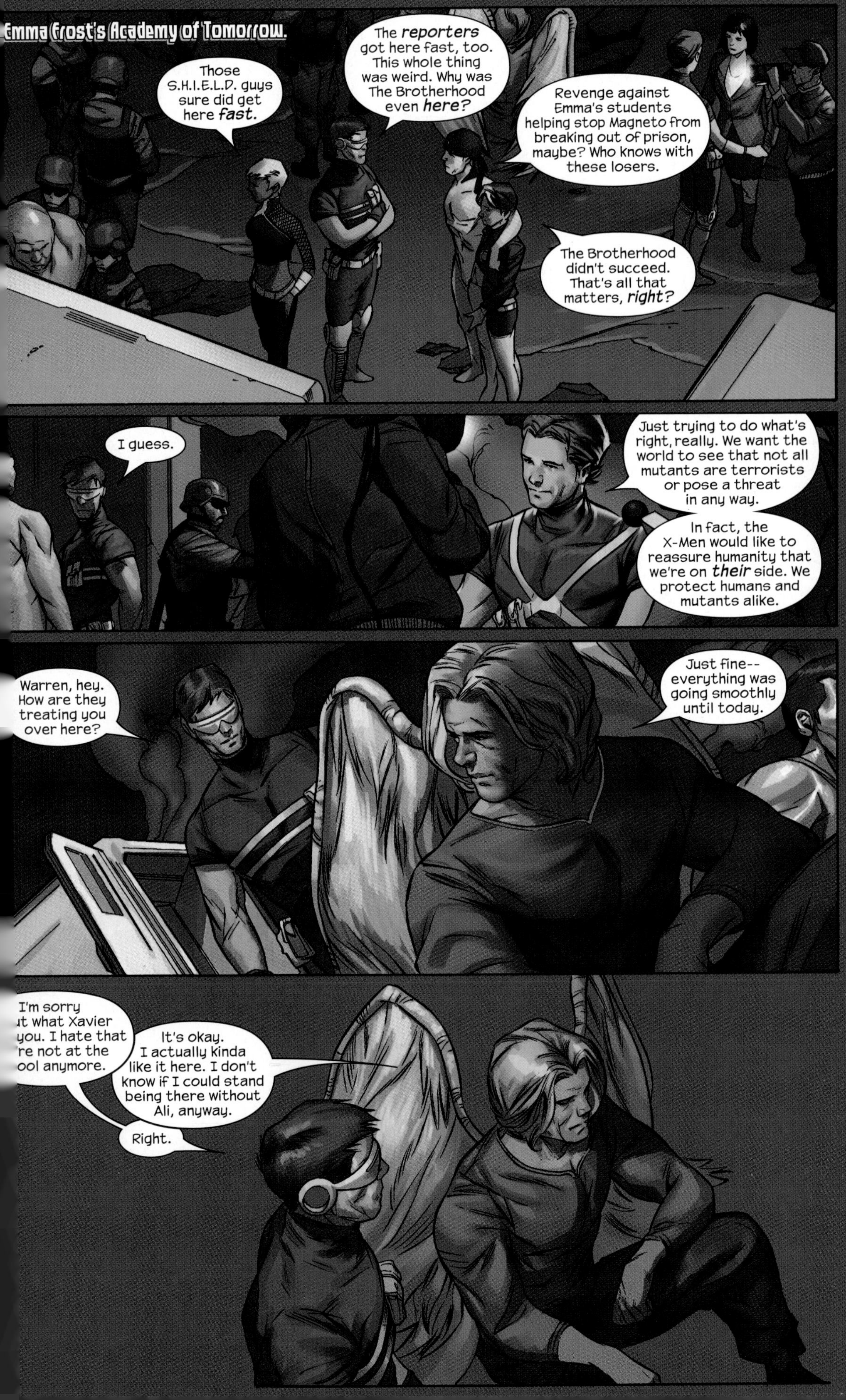
Emma Frost's Academy of Tomorrow.
Those S.H.I.E.L.D. guys sure did get here *fast*.
The *reporters* got here fast, too. This whole thing was weird. Why was The Brotherhood even *here*?
Revenge against Emma's students helping stop Magneto from breaking out of prison, maybe? Who knows with these losers.
The Brotherhood didn't succeed. That's all that matters, *right*?
I guess.
Just trying to do what's right, really. We want the world to see that not all mutants are terrorists or pose a threat in any way.
In fact, the X-Men would like to reassure humanity that we're on *their* side. We protect humans and mutants alike.
Warren, hey. How are they treating you over here?
Just fine-- everything was going smoothly until today.
I'm sorry
ut what Xavier
you. I hate that
're not at the
ool anymore.
It's okay. I actually kinda like it here. I don't know if I could stand being there without Ali, anyway.
Right.

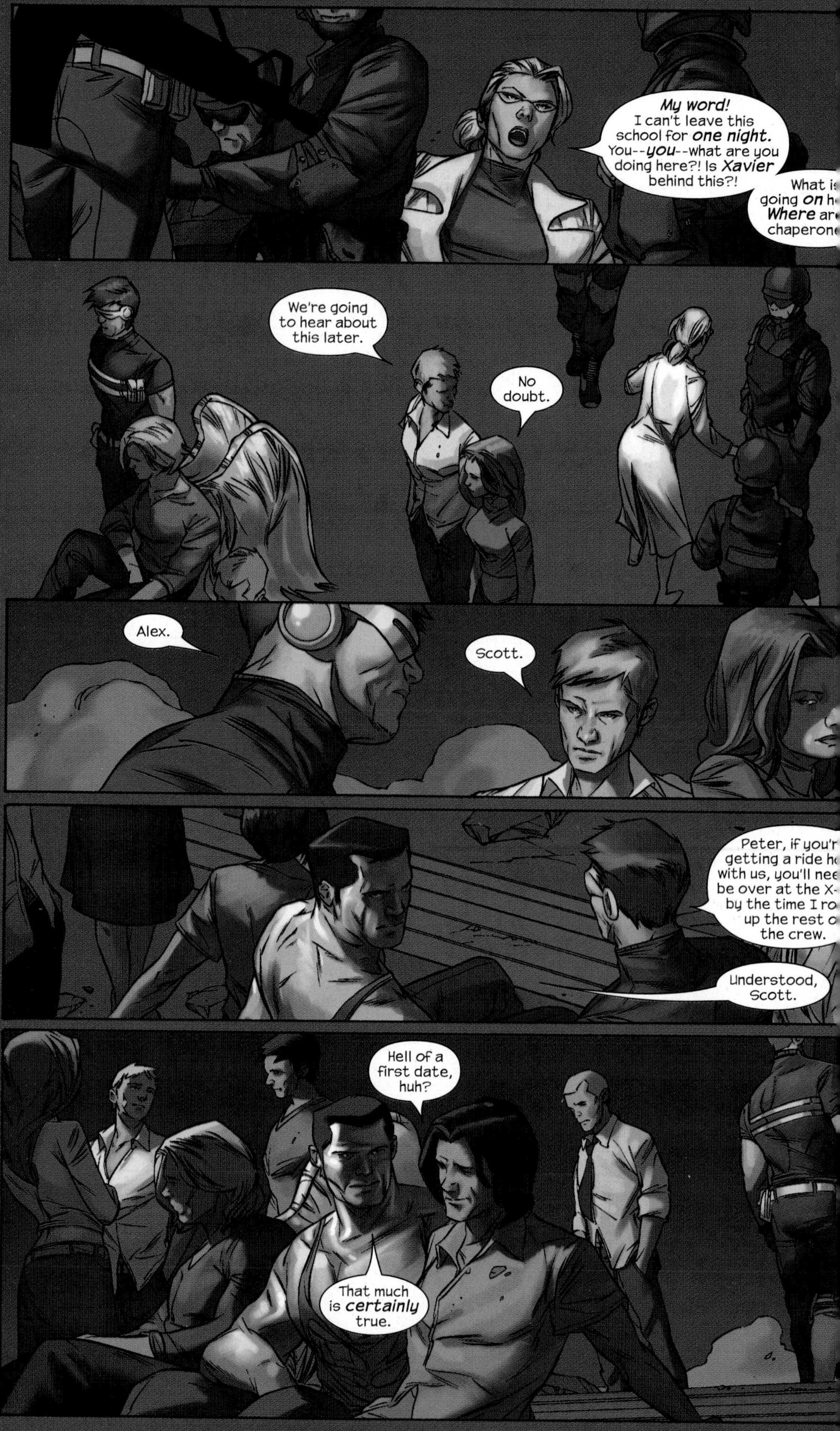

My word! I can't leave this school for one night. You--you--what are you doing here?! Is Xavier behind this?!
What is going on h
Where ar
chaperon
We're going to hear about this later.
No doubt.
Alex.
Scott.
Peter, if you' getting a ride h with us, you'll nee be over at the X- by the time I ro up the rest o the crew.
Understood, Scott.
Hell of a first date, huh?
That much is certainly true.

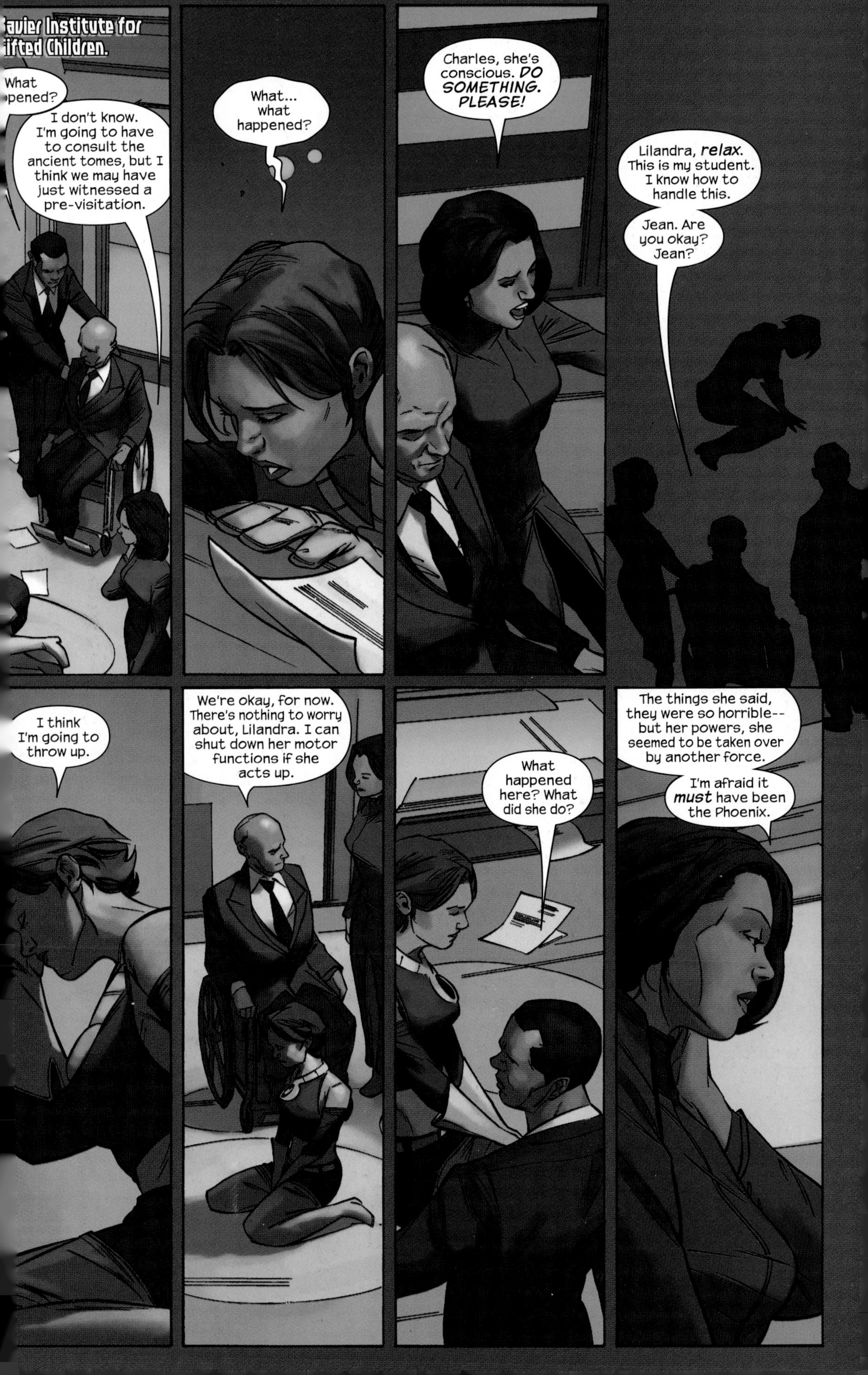

avier Institute for
ifted Children.
What
pened?
I don't know. I'm going to have to consult the ancient tomes, but I think we may have just witnessed a pre-visitation.
What... what happened?
Charles, she's conscious. DO SOMETHING. PLEASE!
Lilandra, relax. This is my student. I know how to handle this.
Jean. Are you okay? Jean?
I think I'm going to throw up.
We're okay, for now. There's nothing to worry about, Lilandra. I can shut down her motor functions if she acts up.
What happened here? What did she do?
The things she said, they were so horrible--but her powers, she seemed to be taken over by another force.
I'm afraid it must have been the Phoenix.

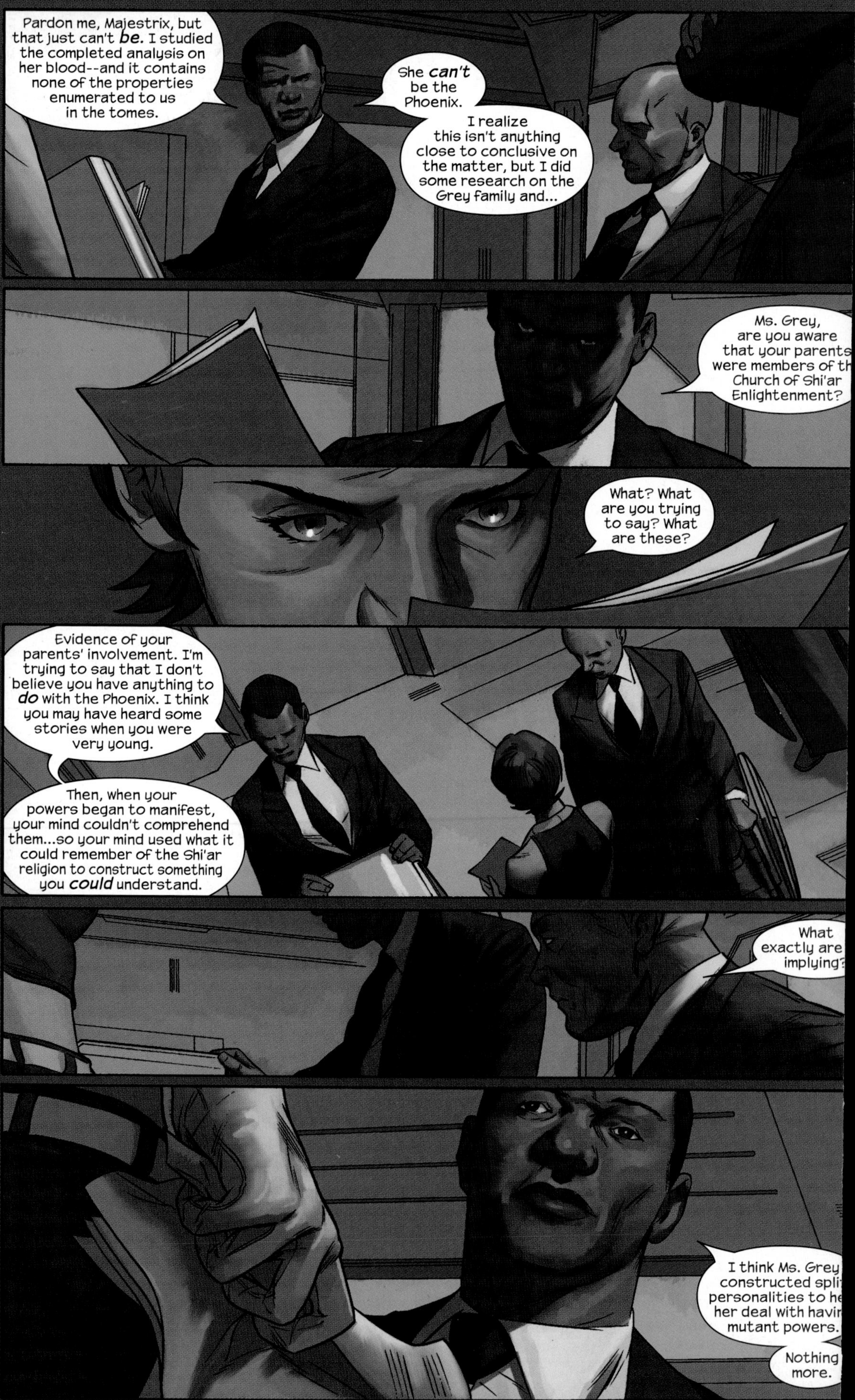
Pardon me, Majestrix, but that just can't be. I studied the completed analysis on her blood--and it contains none of the properties enumerated to us in the tomes.
She can't be the Phoenix.
I realize this isn't anything close to conclusive on the matter, but I did some research on the Grey family and...
Ms. Grey, are you aware that your parents were members of th Church of Shi'ar Enlightenment?
What? What are you trying to say? What are these?
Evidence of your parents' involvement. I'm trying to say that I don't believe you have anything to do with the Phoenix. I think you may have heard some stories when you were very young.
Then, when your powers began to manifest, your mind couldn't comprehend them...so your mind used what it could remember of the Shi'ar religion to construct something you could understand.
What exactly are implying?
I think Ms. Grey constructed spli personalities to he her deal with havi mutant powers.
Nothing more.

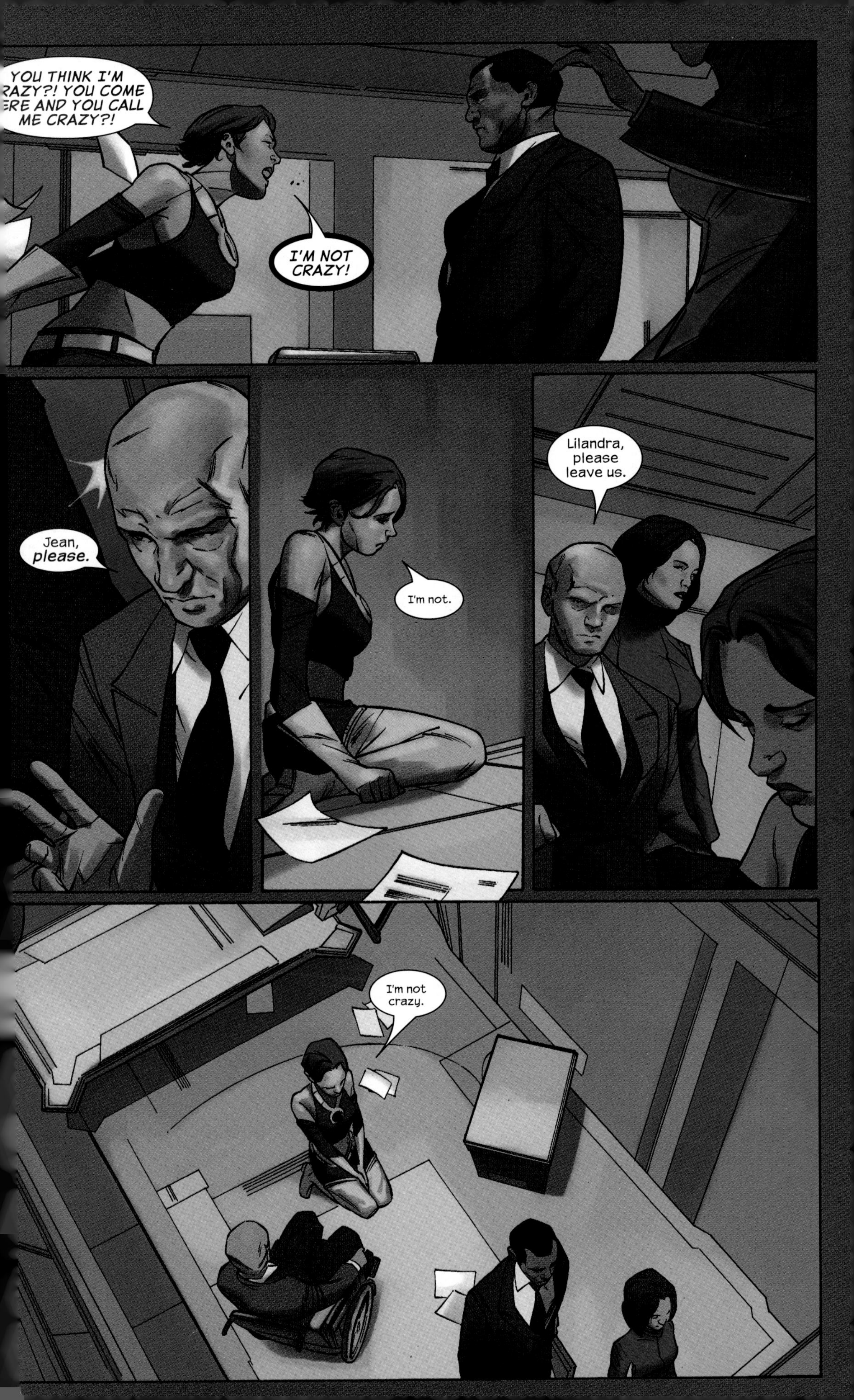
YOU THINK I'M RAZY?! YOU COME ERE AND YOU CALL ME CRAZY?!
I'M NOT CRAZY!
Jean, please.
I'm not.
Lilandra, please leave us.
I'm not crazy.

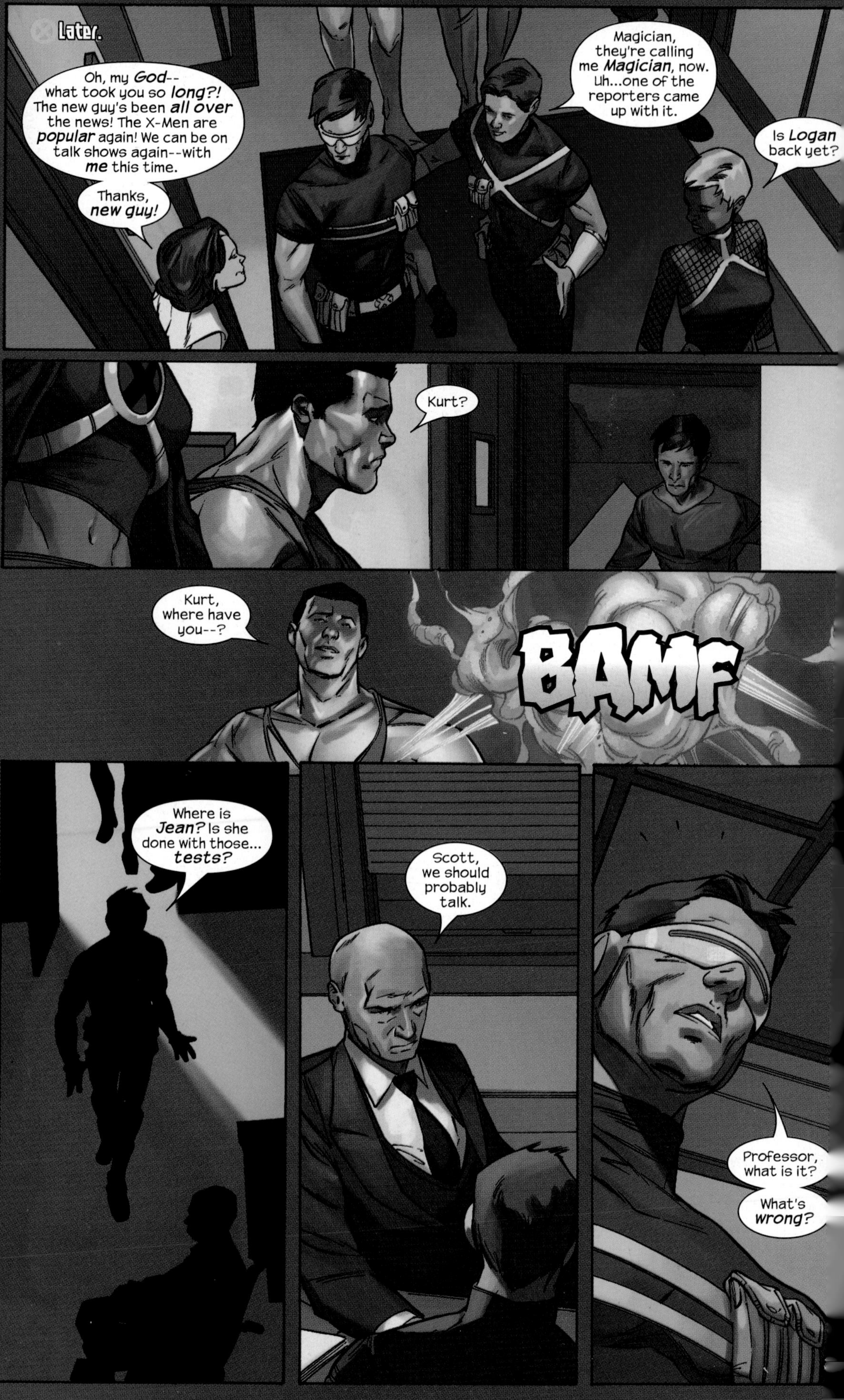
Later.
Oh, my God--what took you so long?! The new guy's been all over the news! The X-Men are popular again! We can be on talk shows again--with me this time.
Thanks, new guy!
Magician, they're calling me Magician, now. Uh...one of the reporters came up with it.
Is Logan back yet?
Kurt?
Kurt, where have you--?
BAMF
Where is Jean? Is she done with those... tests?
Scott, we should probably talk.
Professor, what is it?
What's wrong?

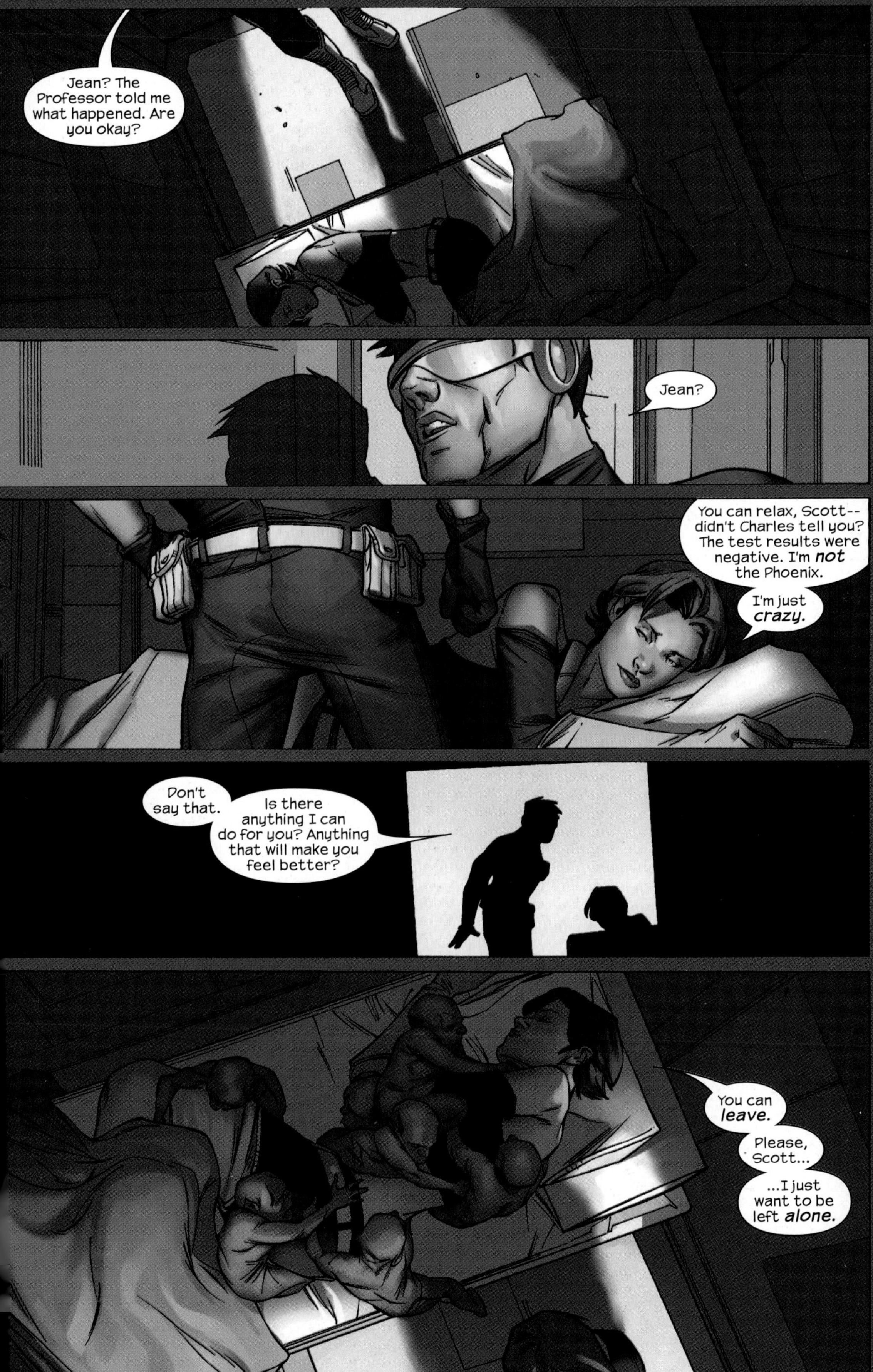
Jean? The Professor told me what happened. Are you okay?
Jean?
You can relax, Scott--didn't Charles tell you? The test results were negative. I'm **not** the Phoenix.
I'm just ***crazy.***
Don't say that.
Is there anything I can do for you? Anything that will make you feel better?
You can ***leave.***
Please, Scott...
...I just want to be left ***alone.***

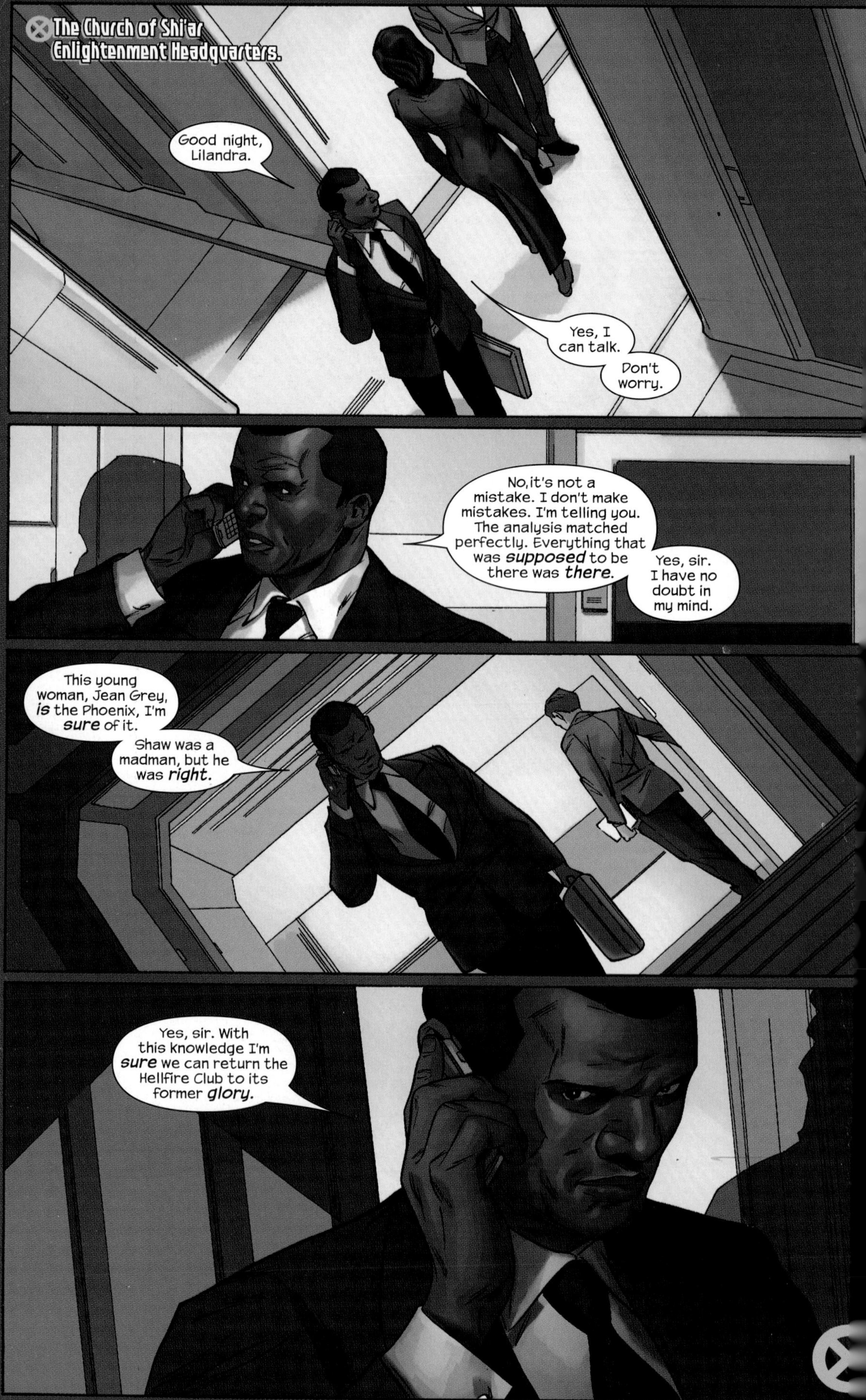
The Church of Shi'ar Enlightenment Headquarters.
Good night, Lilandra.
Yes, I can talk.
Don't worry.
No, it's not a mistake. I don't make mistakes. I'm telling you. The analysis matched perfectly. Everything that was supposed to be there was there.
Yes, sir. I have no doubt in my mind.
This young woman, Jean Grey, is the Phoenix, I'm sure of it.
Shaw was a madman, but he was right.
Yes, sir. With this knowledge I'm sure we can return the Hellfire Club to its former glory.